The Essential Nectar
Meditations on the Buddhist Path

Geshe Rabten

An explanation of the *Lam rim* text
of Yeshe Tsöndrü entitled
The Essential Nectar of the Holy Doctrine,
and the text itself

Editing and verse translation
by Martin Willson

Wisdom Publications • Boston

First published in 1984
Second printing 1992

Wisdom Publications
361 Newbury Street
Boston, Massachusetts 02115
United States of America

© Martin Willson 1984

ISBN 0 86171 013 4

Set in Bembo 10½ on 12½ point
and printed and bound
in Singapore by Eurasia Press (Offset) Pte. Ltd.

Indhira Lyman
April 2000

The Essential Nectar

Contents

PREFACE 7

INTRODUCTION by Geshe Rabten 15

THE PREPARATORY PRACTICES (1–96) 29

THE ACTUAL PRACTICE
Part One: Basics 55
1 Meditation 1: Guru Devotion (97–139) 57
2 Meditation 2: The Opportune, Fortunate Rebirth (140–176) 67

Part Two: Path of the Inferior Person 79
3 Meditation 3: Death (177–209) 82
4 Meditation 4: The Sufferings of the Realms of Woe (210–238) 91
5 Meditation 5: The Practice of Taking Refuge (239–252) 105
6 Meditation 6: How to Generate Confidence in the Laws of Actions and Results (253–264) 112

Part Three: Path of the Intermediate Person 119
7 Meditation 7: The Sufferings of the Happier Realms and the General Sufferings of Samsara (265–296) 121
8 Meditation 8: How to Think about the Process of Functioning of Samsara, and Practise the Path to Liberation (297–304) 132

Part Four: Path of the Superior Person 137

9 Meditation 9: The Development of Bodhicitta (305–366) 139
10 Meditation 10: How to Train in the Six Perfections (367–382) 152
11 Meditation 11: How to Train in the Four Means of Attraction (383–384) 158
12 Meditation 12: How to Meditate on Quietude (385–393) 160
13 Meditation 13: How to Meditate on Insight (394–423) 162
14 Meditation 14: How to Enter the Adamantine Vehicle (424–425) 171

THE TEXT by Yeshe Tsöndrü 173

APPENDICES

1 The Confession of Downfalls 247
2 A *Lam rim* Prayer by Je Tsongkhapa 251
3 Je Tsongkhapa on the Six Sufferings and the Three Sufferings 254
4 Je Tsongkhapa's Dedication Prayer 265
5 Structure of the Text 267

GLOSSARY 271

BIBLIOGRAPHY 283

NOTES 292

Preface

The root text by Yeshe Tsöndrü, used by Geshe Rabten in his explanation and published here, presents concisely and in their order of development all the meditations and practices involved in entering the Buddhist Path and proceeding along it towards Enlightenment, up to the point at which one is ready to practise Tantra. It is written entirely in verse, so that one can easily memorize it and use it in meditation.

Historically, it stands in a long tradition of Tibetan teachings on the *Lam rim*, the Stages of the Path to Enlightenment. The lineage goes back through the founder of the Gelukpa school, Je Tsongkhapa (1357–1419), to the Bengali pandit Atīsha (982–1054), who taught in Tibet for thirteen years. Atīsha himself combined into a harmonious whole two earlier Indian traditions, one concentrating mainly on Wisdom and the other emphasizing more the practice of Method, or Compassion, whose most prominent exponents were Nāgārjuna (second century AD) and Asaṅga (fourth century) respectively. Ultimately, of course, all these teachings derive from Shākyamuni Buddha.

The Buddhist scriptures being of immense bulk and chaotic arrangement, the need for condensed and systematic presentations of the Teachings is evident. Even while Sutras were still being written, Nāgārjuna compiled an anthology of scriptural quotations arranged under subject headings, his *Sūtra-samuccaya (Compendium of Sutra)*. Later, about the eighth century AD, Shāntideva composed a *Compendium on the Trainings (Sikṣā-samuccaya)*, again basically on anthology of quotations from the Sutras. Atīsha's text, the *Lamp on the Path to Enlightenment (Bodhipatha-pradīpa)* was a short verse outline of the Stages of the Path. His scholarly Tibetan successors expanded it into comprehensive textbooks such as Gampopa's (1079–1153) *Jewel Ornament of Liberation* and Tsongkhapa's *Great Stages of the Path (Lam rim chen mo)*, organized under an elaborate hierarchy of headings and establishing each point by reasoning and scriptural citation. Tsongkhapa's massive and complex work is more an exposition of the theoretical basis of the practice than an actual meditational guide. Therefore, many shorter and more practical texts have been written, presenting the material important to meditate on; the present text is one of these.

It begins with the preliminaries that any Buddhist practitioner should perform daily – taking Refuge in the Three Jewels, generating a proper motivation of *Bodhicitta* and the Four Immeasurables, offering a seven-limbed puja to the Objects of Refuge, and praying for success in the practice. Then the actual meditations on the Stages of the Path are described, from Guru Devotion up to Special Insight and entry into the Tantric Path.

First, the root of the Path, devotion to one's Guru or spiritual teacher, is to be cultivated. Then, one appraises one's present situation and its remarkable potentialities, the eighteen factors of opportunity and good fortune one has gained in this life although they are so rarely found. This makes it obvious that one must take advantage of this opportunity by practising the Dharma.

The rest of the *Lam rim* describes how one should take advantage of it. It is divided into three Paths according to the level of one's motivation. Inferior motivation, the lowest that still serves for Dharma practice, is concern for one's next life more than for happiness in this life. Intermediate motivation seeks one's complete Liberation from the round of rebirth, recognizing that even in the happiest states of samsara one is still bound to suffering. The superior motivation, that of the Bodhisattva, is not content with one's own Liberation but insists that one help all other sentient beings to become free of suffering also. If one wishes to be a Bodhisattva, one must meditate on all three Paths: each forms the basis for proceeding to the next.

This text was, of course, not written for Westerners. If it had been, it would have been necessary to preface the account of the Stages with a section on how to convince oneself of the reality of rebirth. For this simple fact of life, unquestioned by the Tibetans of a happier age, and on which most of the arguments presented depend, has been rigorously suppressed in our culture for some one-and-a-half millennia. First, the Christian church banned the teaching of rebirth (implicitly accepted by the early church fathers),[1] no doubt for fear that it would encourage laziness, while latterly the materialist orthodoxy of our own day pours ridicule on all reports of phenomena inconsistent with its dogmas, greeting their authors as liars and charlatans, or at best gullible fools.

Rebirth may be established by logical proof, appeal to authority, or observation. However, since the "proofs" take as their premises assumptions about the nature of mind that are just as difficult to establish and contradictory to Western orthodoxy as the fact of rebirth itself, and the sceptics have their own authorities, observation is by far the most convincing. Here, there are one's own observations, and those of others. One can acquire the power of recalling one's previous lives if, having realized Quietude (verses 385–393 below), one goes on to develop the four *dhyānas*. However, to reach this point one must already have traversed most of the Stages of the Path here described, so to start with, unless one resorts to methods not traditionally Buddhist, one must rely on the testimony of others. That available in print ranges from Dr. Ian Stevenson's investigations, with meticulous scientific method, of numerous cases where children have spontaneously recalled their preceding life, through life stories of Tibetan Rinpoches, to a flood of recent literature vividly describing recollections of past lives gained through hypnosis, Hindu yoga methods, or indeed yoga methods learned in past lives in Ancient Egypt.[2]

A related stumbling-block for the sceptical Westerner is the supposed existence of realms that we cannot detect – the hells and the realms of pretas and gods. On this matter, apart from numerous reports of ghosts, the Western evidence is comparatively scanty. In the literature just mentioned, I have so far found only one instance each of people remembering past lives as an animal, a preta, and what could be described as a special sort of hell being. However, this is not surprising. It is clear from the accounts that the past lives that people recall are those which exert a strong karmic influence on the present life. Since it is taught that when born in a realm of woe one has virtually no chance to create karma leading to a human rebirth, there is no reason to expect people to recall such births. And again, if high rebirth is as rare as is taught, one would not expect people to remember lives as gods.

On the other hand, it may be objected that the intervals between the past human lives recalled by one person are rarely more than a few centuries, and leave no room for intervening stays in hell or preta realms of the duration described in verses 225, 228 and 234. To this, one might point out that the large numbers found in Buddhist texts are often not to be taken literally but are there to give a certain impression in meditation, and who can doubt that subjectively even a second of the cataclysmic suffering of Avīci would indeed seem like years?

But if these durations are not meant literally, maybe the whole idea of realms of woe is really symbolic, a kind of stylization of sufferings one can actually encounter in the human realm? This interpretation is not impossible, although it is clearly not what the author intended. Deluged with information about the world we live in, we of the West at least cannot escape the dreadful truth – that virtually any form of torture which the human mind can imagine, humans actually do inflict on other humans. Moreover, considering that there are very likely more inhabited planets in this galaxy alone than there are human beings on Earth, it would not be reasonable to suppose that some are not a great deal more unpleasant than ours.

The physical tortures of the hells and other realms of woe are also a practical way to visualize mental tortures, which the mind inflicts on itself as a result of having harmed others. Thus whether or not they represent a literal, physical reality, they certainly represent a psychological reality. No justification can be found for dismissing these painful meditations as mere morbid fantasy, however comforting this might be.

The style of the text is exceptionally clear and straightforward, almost as if written for children – there is none of the convoluted grammar and excessive compression found in philosophical works, nor is the meaning concealed beneath heavy blankets of flowery metaphors. The author just states one idea plainly, then moves on to the next. His language includes a number of modern words not found in the Scriptures, so it would be inappropriate to translate it into an archaic, "biblical" style.

None of the material is the author's invention: all the details of the hells and so on come from standard texts, and the similes given here and there are likewise traditional, mostly originating in the Sutras. His contribution is to select what to put in, and give it harmonious expression in verse.

Three metres are employed in the body of the text. Most verses are in the commonest of Tibetan metres, nine-syllable lines with the odd syllables stressed. However, the sections on the opportune, fortunate rebirth and death (verses 140–209) are in an unusual metre of eight-syllable lines, stressed on the first and then the *even* syllables. This awkward rhythm, with its isolated first syllable, gives a restless, uneasy effect, appropriate to the sense of urgency that these meditations are designed to inculcate. I regret I found it too difficult to reproduce this in English. The sections on suffering are also distinguished by a special metre – fifteen-syllable lines, stressed on the odd syllables, as is normal, but divided into half-lines of eight plus seven syllables. The effective line length is thus shorter than elsewhere, producing a quickening of pace, suggestive of the ceaseless rain of sufferings that falls on us as long as we are in samsara.

In English one is not free to omit syllables virtually at will, as is done in Tibetan, so one must allow extra unstressed syllables. However, I have found it perfectly possible to maintain the same number of stressed syllables as in the original, without departing from a strictly literal rendering appreciably more than one would wish to do in a prose translation. There seems to be simply no need to resort to prose translation with a work of this nature.

Geshe Rabten delivered some thirty-one discourses on this text, at Tharpa Choeling on Friday afternoons spread over the period January 1981 to June 1982. Twelve discourses were translated by Ven. Stephen Schettini (Gelong Thubten Sangye), eighteen by Ven. Elio Guarisco (Gelong Jampa Lekshe), and one by Ven. Gonsar Rinpoche.

In adapting this course into book form I have freely re-arranged the material so as to bring out the underlying logical structure as clearly as possible; for example, when Geshe Rabten went over a topic again at the start of another discourse, this recapitulation has been merged with the original discussion. Unnecessary repetitions have been reduced, bearing in mind that a certain amount of repetition is intrinsic to the subject, but although the edited version has about forty percent as many words as the original oral translation, it is believed that nothing significant has been omitted. Translations of recognizable technical terms have been standardized, and headings superimposed, after the root text and *Lam rim chen mo*. The division into "Meditations" follows Yeshe Tsöndrü's marking of the end of a section with a request for inspiration or with a change of metre. Additions made for the sake of clarity are enclosed in square brackets, and should be in strict accord with the tradition within which Geshe Rabten was teaching – in fact, most additions longer than a few words are quoted directly from the *Lam rim chen mo*, as indicated in the notes. While I have once or twice allowed myself to comment from the viewpoint of a Western scientist, such remarks are confined to the notes. Where the notes cite authorities in apparent conflict with Geshe Rabten's explanation, this should not be construed as implying that the latter is in any way inferior, but merely that a range of legitimate opinions exists. Quotations could not always be identified with certainty from the oral translation, but those given are at least very similar and are authentic. Except in one instance, they are in my own translation from the Tibetan.

The root text has been printed as a consecutive whole, not broken up by commentary, for the convenience of those who wish to use the text for its intended purpose, namely meditation. The explanation is meant to be studied outside meditation sessions, while the root text is skilfully designed to give all the outlines one needs for the session itself.

The translation of the root text was made and released to students early in Geshe Rabten's course. This was possible thanks to the *Lam rim* teachings I had received from Geshe Thubten Lodan, Lama Zasep Tulku, Lama Thubten Zopa Rinpoche, Geshe Rabten and others. Comparison with the existing prose translation by Geshe Lobsang Tharchin and Benjamin and Deborah Alterman greatly facilitated checking and resulted in many improvements. Some further revisions were made subsequently in the light of Geshe Rabten's teachings. That these teachings could be given depended on the kindness of the benefactors and voluntary workers of Tharpa Choeling. I also thank Geshe Rabten and Gonsar Rinpoche for their assistance at various stages.

M.A.G.W.
Tharpa Choeling,
April 1981, revised June 1983.

Introduction
by Geshe Rabten

Introduction

WHAT IS LAM RIM?

Lam, the Path, is all the mental states and good qualities that take us from our present state to Enlightenment. The practice that leads to Enlightenment is not a mere tradition of certain countries, but something that benefits whoever engages in it.

This Path that leads to Enlightenment was taught by the Buddha Himself. Sometimes He taught different aspects of the Path, such as the Method and Wisdom aspects; at other times He taught the Path as a whole, all the various aspects together. Likewise, in such texts as *Abhisamayâlaṃkāra*, *Bodhisattvacaryâvatāra* and *Madhyamakâvatāra* we find all the Buddha's teachings, but arranged in different ways. This is not a mistake — each arrangement was chosen to suit the abilities of the particular disciples being taught.

The *Lam rim*, then, is a presentation of the Path (*lam*), conveying all the points arranged in a systematic, sequential order (*rim*): first do this, then do that. Thus if we wish to practise it, there is little danger of making mistakes.

GREATNESSES OF THIS TEACHING
1 *The Greatness of realizing that all the teachings are non-contradictory*

The intelligent can understand the many different teachings of the Buddha, and perceive that they are of the same nature. Some, however, may regard certain teachings as correct and others as incorrect, while others will see it just the other way round. For example, some have partial views of the Sutras and Tantras, saying the Sutras are genuine and the Tantras not, or vice versa; or within the Sutras, they may say the Mahāyāna is the real Path and the Hīnayāna is not, or vice versa. Through studying the *Lam rim*, one comes to understand that these different aspects of the Buddha's Teachings are not contradictory, but all form one Teaching, much as a skilful cook combines many foods into one delicious meal.

2 The Greatness of all the Buddha's Speech appearing as instructions

When one pushes the corner of a table, it is not just the corner that moves, but the whole table starts to turn. Similarly, when someone who really knows how to meditate on *Lam rim* contemplates one point, his understanding of all the points will be affected. For example, meditating properly on Devotion to the Guru, the opportune, fortunate rebirth, or the Path of the inferior person, will affect one's understanding of all the other points such as the Wisdom cognizing Emptiness, [so that one comes to realize that all of them are to be practised].[3]

3 The Greatness of easily discovering the Conqueror's Thought

The Thought or Intention (*dgongs pa*) of the Buddha is threefold: Renunciation, Bodhicitta, and Right View. If we wish to develop the practices leading to Renunciation, for example, it will be much easier and more straightforward to do so following the *Lam rim* teachings than following one of the great Indian or Tibetan texts such as Candrakīrti's *Madhyamakâvatāra* or Je Tsongkhapa's commentary on it, *dbU ma dgongs pa rab gsal*.

4 The Greatness of the automatic cessation of great misconduct

In our present, ordinary lives, we have many faults of body, speech and mind. Another virtue of the *Lam rim* is that when we practise it, these faults are automatically reduced. At each stage, everything adverse to that meditation diminishes – practising the Path of the inferior person reduces faulty conduct related to this life; practising that of the intermediate person reduces misconduct in relation to the next life, and so on.

While the *Lam rim* has these four qualities, we should note that the *Lam rim* is not the same as the person who is studying it or trying to practise it – he does not necessarily have these qualities too! He may be making mistakes and going in the wrong direction. It is always important for the practitioner to have the right attitude. We shall return to this point later.

SOURCE OF THE LAM RIM

While the actual root of the *Lam rim* is the Perfection of Wisdom (*Prajñā-pāramitā*) sutras taught by the Buddha, the effective root is the short text by Atīsha called *Lamp on the Path to Enlightenment* (*Bodhi-patha-pradīpa*),[4] because it is here that this particular presentation of the Path is made for the first time. There are two great "chariots" or traditions of Indian Mahāyāna Buddhism, the Wisdom Lineage of Nāgārjuna and the Method Lineage of Asaṅga. Atīsha received both these traditions, the former from Vidyā-kokila the elder, the latter from Dharmakīrti[5] of Suvarṇadvīpa (Sumatra), and combined the two ways of practice.

These traditions individually place much emphasis on the understanding of the texts; their approach, though effective, is rather difficult. Going directly to the *Lam rim*, one can develop the same kind of understanding with much greater ease.

Also, in the older Indian traditions, texts were rigidly divided into Sutra and Tantra, and the Sutra texts further into Hīnayāna and Mahāyāna, the different categories never being mixed. The *Lam rim*, however, brings together all these different aspects of the Path and shows how they inter-relate. We can see that although short, the *Lam rim* combines all these teachings without confusion or contradiction.

Besides the *Lam rim* texts that we study in the Gelukpa tradition, there are others such as Gampopa's *Jewel Ornament of Liberation*[6] in the Kagyü tradition, and the Nyingmapa text *Oral Precepts of Guru Samantabhadra*.[7] We can see for ourselves what an excellent text the *Jewel Ornament of Liberation* is. All these *Lam rim* texts, of every tradition, stem from the same root, the *Bodhi-patha-pradīpa* of Atīsha, and follow its outlines.

Based on this same root text of Atīsha, the great Tsongkhapa wrote his commentary *Lam rim chen mo*, the *Great* Lam rim, of over 500 pages; his *Middling* Lam rim, of some 200 pages, which omits the quotations to leave only his own composition; and his short *Condensed meaning of the* Lam rim,[8] which can easily be memorized and recited.

HOW THE LAM RIM IS TO BE TAUGHT

Three ways of teaching are enumerated:

(a) The teacher explains in great detail the meaning of each word and of each quotation and just how to practise the meditations. By practising as taught, the disciples increase their understanding.

(b) Besides his detailed explanations, the teacher speaks from the depth of his own experience. Each disciple, too, rather than just listening passively, tries to integrate the explanations into his own mind.

(c) The teacher explains from his own experience one point, such as the first, Devotion to the Guru, then the disciples go and meditate on it, the teacher helping them with any problems that arise. Then, once this point has become reasonably clear to them, the teacher goes on to the next point.

The third is really the best – this is the way Dharmakīrti taught Atīsha, and Marpa taught Milarepa – but it is rather difficult. We shall use method (b), where the teacher draws on his own experience and the pupils try to perceive it for themselves.

PROBLEMS IN LAM RIM MEDITATION

As we know, when we meditate on *Lam rim* there can arise nervous problems, or *lung*,[9] a certain lack of mental ease. It may help to explain the possible causes of this now:

(a) If in a previous life one has caused great fear in or harm to someone else, one may experience mental disturbance in this life.

(b) Certain external interferences such as various sorts of spirits can disturb the mind.
(c) Imbalance of the four physical elements making up the body can induce mental imbalance.
(d) Experiencing very great suffering can make the mind deeply disturbed.
(e) When one is working very hard at study or meditation, *sok-lung*[10] can arise with no apparent reason. This is the worst sort of *lung*.

Some Tibetans just used to play, without being made to do any sort of work, until they were twenty or more; they were quite relaxed. But in the West, children start to experience the pressures of education as young as two-and-a-half or three, or even earlier – they do not know certain things, their parents are anxious that they should know them, their teachers are trying to get them to learn them. These pressures can create very early in life the seed of the great nervousness called *sok-lung*. This disorder involves a gradual mixing of a malignant wind with the subtle life-wind entering the heart chakra. This increasingly disturbs the mind and obstructs whatever the person is trying to do.

Doctors cannot detect this problem with instruments and tests, but most of the patients in the mental hospitals of the West are suffering from this disturbance of the life-wind. The emanations from their state of disharmony can cause even the doctors caring for them to become similarly afflicted. Since doctors cannot help us if we get *sok-lung* disorder, and in general any sort of *lung* is difficult to cure, we should try to practise *Lam rim* in such a way as to avoid its arising.

A sign of the beginning of *sok-lung* is that the mind becomes disturbed very easily; great fear can arise for no apparent external cause. For example, if one is meditating on compassion, thinking about the sufferings of others, one becomes very upset and starts to cry.

If air tends to well up in the lungs so that one spontaneously takes deep breaths and exhales deeply, the *lung* is getting stronger. One should try to relax. If one is tired, it is good to sleep.

If the sternum starts moving backwards and forwards, this is

a sign that the *lung* is quite heavy. The mind becomes very weak. Next, one becomes unable to speak with any strength, and one's bodily movements are also weak and unstable.

In general, an unhappy state of mind makes the arising of *lung* likely. When meditating on *lam rim*, we should try to keep the mind quiet and happy with what we are doing, then there is little probability of *lung* arising and every chance of success. It is important to start off with the right attitude, as a mistake at the beginning can carry all the way through, just like an error at the start of adding up a column of figures.

The first four types of *lung* should also be countered in their respective ways:

(a) Disturbance due to the karma of causing fear in and harm to others is to be dispelled by purification of one's bad karma.

(b) Disturbance by spirits is to be countered by appeasing the spirits with special offering ceremonies (*pūjās*).

(c) If physical disease (imbalance of the four elements) affects the mind, one should consult a doctor and take the necessary medicines.

(d) When mental disharmony has been caused by intense suffering, one should overcome the power of the mental suffering through the practice of Dharma. If one finds one cannot do this, then at least one should identify the causes about which one has been thinking too much and distract the mind away from them by engaging in something else; "playing" can be helpful.

There also exists a direct technique for overcoming *lung* by meditating on the movement of the subtle wind itself, but this is very difficult. In general, if one finds one has *lung*, one should relax and try to make the mind easy and more open; but it is no use just doing nothing, one should try to identify the problem and see how to overcome it.

We should understand the five types of *lung* and their remedies, and when we have *lung*, recognize its cause so that we can work on it correctly. Even if we do not get *lung* ourselves, knowing about it may enable us to talk helpfully to others who do.

HOW TO STUDY THE TEACHINGS[11]
1 Benefits of listening to Dharma Teachings

Regardless of the qualities of the *Lam rim*, it can be of no use unless applied by the individual practitioner to his own mind. First of all, to know what to do, he must listen to teachings. Since one's subsequent practice depends on this, it is most important to have from the beginning the correct method of listening to Dharma Teachings.

Two faults in particular can create a serious obstacle. The first is the attitude of "collecting" teachings – just listening in order to acquire information, more pieces of knowledge, much as one reads a newspaper, without the proper intention of applying it to one's own practice. Having heard the teaching, one thinks "That's it, I've heard it," and does not want to hear it again but wants something new and "interesting". In fact, one should listen to teachings again and again, not forgetting them but bearing them in mind, trying to remain aware of every point. Then if one hears the same teaching repeated later, there is still much benefit to be gained, since one's way of looking at things may have changed a bit meanwhile. But the "collector" gains no immediate advantage from hearing a teaching again, merely a certain imprint on the mind.

The second fault is, though one intends to listen carefully to the Teachings, not understanding the benefits of doing so. Only with this understanding will one have the enthusiasm to overcome the difficulties; just as, for example, a man doing unpleasant work in a factory is kept going only by the thought of the money he is earning.

Therefore it is important to understand the benefits of listening to the Teachings. To explain them as in *Lam rim chen mo* would take a long time, but let us mention a few briefly.

(a) As any light overcomes darkness, so the function of listening is to gain the knowledge and wisdom that overcome the darkness of our mind. Hearing a teaching on any subject produces some understanding, which grows when one goes away and thinks about it, so that an area of one's ignorance is dispelled.

(b) All external possessions can be lost, stolen, or destroyed,

but once a Dharma realization, acquired through listening to Teachings, has been integrated with the mind, no-one can take it away.
(c) Such understanding of Dharma is our best possible friend. Unlike ordinary friends, it never deserts us, whatever the situation, but is always available to help us find the best solution to any problem.
(d) If we go into retreat to meditate, unless we have listened to the Dharma there will be no possibility of the wisdoms of hearing, thinking and meditating arising.
(e) If we wish to help others, our talking to them can be of some use provided we have experience of the relevant point developed from the understanding derived from listening to the Dharma. But if we merely repeat words we have heard, without experience, then even though they are the same words as of a person who has had the experience, it will be of no direct benefit at all.

2 Threefold analogy of correct listening

A Sutra says:

> Listen well, the best way, and hold it in your mind![12]

(a) "Listen well": just as an upside-down vessel will not receive whatever is poured on to it, so it is useless to sit in front of a Teacher if one is not listening well. Therefore instead of letting one's mind wander all over the place, one must be like a vessel the right way up, listening intently to receive the Teaching.
(b) "Listen the best way": a vessel that is dirty with refuse, filth, deposits of old food, or maybe even poison, is useless, as any water one pours into it will immediately become contaminated and unfit for drinking. Likewise, even if one listens hard to the Teaching, it will be no use if one has a wrong attitude such as trying to find faults with the other students, for the Teaching will be contaminated with one's unwholesome frame of mind. Like a vessel that is not only the right way up but also clean inside, one must listen with pure motivation, feeling "I am a Dharma

practitioner, listening to these teachings in order to help my practice."

(c) "Hold it in your mind": a vessel may be upright and clean, but it is still no use if it leaks at the bottom. Similarly, if the teachings just go in one ear and out the other we cannot benefit from them. It is important to hold them in one's mind, going over the points again and again until they are firmly integrated with it; in this way a very strong impression is left on the mind.

3 Further requirements of the student

Not only must the teacher of Dharma be unwaveringly truthful, the disciple also must be honest enough to recognise his own faults, so that he can use the teaching to eliminate them and develop good qualities. Otherwise, when shown by the teacher how to overcome some fault, he will simply react uselessly with anger. Often, looking into people's faces as I teach, I can see just this anger arising. In addition, the student needs intelligence, and a genuine longing to receive the Dharma.

A story of a previous life of the Buddha [from the *Jātakamālā* of Ārya Śūra[13]] illustrates these points.

Once the Bodhisattva was born as a prince called Sutasoma. [Now it happened that a certain king, Sudāsa, lost in the forest, had coupled with a lioness, who subsequently gave birth to a human child. This boy, though brought up by his father, inherited from his mother a taste for human flesh. Also, in exchange for their protection, he had promised to a group of *piśāca* demons, similarly inclined, a sacrifice of a hundred royal princes. So now he prowled the land in search of princes to eat or sacrifice.]

One day, this dreadful cannibal came to Sutasoma's palace. [As his army and attendants scattered in terror,] Sutasoma calmly called out, "Hullo, here I am. Take me by all means, [do not bother those poor people]!" So the son of Sudāsa carried him back to his lair to cook and eat him.

But then, astonished at the Bodhisattva's demeanour, his fearlessness in the face of death thanks to his complete lack of self-cherishing, the son of Sudāsa accepted his request to return home for last farewells, after which the Bodhisattva promised to return. So Sutasoma went home, explained the situation to his father, and in fulfilment of his promise came back to the cannibal's lair, saying "Now I am back. You can eat me if you wish." The son of Sudāsa, amazed to see him return just to keep his word, questioned him. [The Bodhisattva explained the virtues of truthfulness, and how he had no reason to fear death, since all his life he had practised Generosity and avoided evil actions.] Greatly moved, the son of Sudāsa begged the Bodhisattva to teach him the Dharma, in these words:

> Seeing the form of my evil conduct
> In your righteousness' clear mirror,
> Great longing is born within my mind,
> And I turn towards the Dharma.[14]

[Thus the Bodhisattva saw that the son of Sudāsa was open-minded enough to admit his own faults and had the necessary desire for teachings.] But still he would not teach the Dharma straight away, but insisted on certain preparations:

> Sitting on a lower seat
> In token of your humbled pride,
> Gaze with joyful eyes, as if
> Drinking the nectar of the Words!

> Devoutly and one-pointedly
> Incline your mind, serene and pure,
> And listen in reverence to the Dharma
> As a sick man to his doctor's words![15]

So the son of Sudāsa made a pile of wood to serve as a throne, and covered it with his upper garment as he had nothing else for a cushion. Then, seated on the throne with the son of Sudāsa at his feet, Sutasoma taught the Dharma and persuaded the cannibal to abandon killing and harming sentient beings [and the eating of human flesh, and also to release the other royal princes he was holding captive for sacrifice].

THE MANNER OF TEACHING

Just as those who listen to Dharma Teachings should consider the benefits of doing so, the teacher in turn should reflect on the benefits of teaching the Dharma, so that he can teach tirelessly. A Sutra quoted in *Lam rim chen mo* lists twenty such benefits.[16] Explaining the Dharma involves actions of mind, speech and body, all of which bring benefits.

The intention with which one teaches is very important. One must not teach wishing for people to admire one's virtue and learning, or give one money, but with the thought of Great Compassion, wishing that all beings may be free of suffering.

Finally, the teaching itself must be unmistaken and presented intelligibly, with plenty of illustrations and analogies taken from everyday life. Never thinking that teaching the Dharma is hard work, the teacher smiles and delights in it untiringly, but takes care to teach only what is useful in leading towards Enlightenment.

AFTER THE TEACHING

If one receives a teaching and then meditates only on something else, little is gained. Definitely one should meditate on the new teachings one receives, but rather than drop one's existing meditational practices, one should combine them with the new teachings.

To get to wherever one wants to go, one must keep to the path without being diverted: this applies to the Path of Dharma practice just as to ordinary paths.

The Preparatory Practices

The Preparatory Practices

Many people in the West wish to meditate; but in order to do so effectively, one needs an abundant store of merit so that one can easily surmount the obstacles that arise. *Lam rim* texts mention six preparatory practices[17] that one should perform at the start of each session of meditation so as to accumulate merit:

[1 Clean the room well and set up representations of the Body, Speech and Mind [of the Buddhas].
2 Seek offerings, without dissembling, and set them out in a beautiful arrangement.
3 Seated in a comfortable place, in cross-legged or half-cross-legged posture, with the body straight, take Refuge and generate *Bodhicitta*, successively and together.
4 Visualize clearly the field for the accumulation of merit.
5 Train the mind with the seven limbs that combine the points of accumulating merits and purifying obscurations.
6 Offer a mandala, and pray many times with strong desire for inspiration quickly to stop all perverse states of mind, produce all non-perverse states of mind, and quell all external and internal hindrances.[18]]

[The first part of the text (verses 1 to 96) is designed to be recited with the last four of these practices.]

1 CLEAN THE ROOM WELL AND SET UP REPRESENTATIONS OF THE BODY, SPEECH AND MIND OF THE BUDDHAS

If one is going to meditate, or study a Dharma teaching, in one's own room, cleaning the room with the thought that it is a place of Dharma practice creates powerful merit. If one is going to meditate or receive teachings in a temple, even just visualizing it as a very clean place accumulates merit. Five advantages are given for this kind of practice:

(a) One's own mind becomes pure and lucid.
(b) The minds of others entering the room become pure and lucid.
(c) In the future, one's complexion will be bright.
(d) Beneficial spirits (belonging to the deva realm) will be attracted to the clean room and help to keep hindrances away.
(e) The seed is created for birth in a Pure Land, such as Tushita or Sukhāvatī.

The story is often told of a notoriously stupid disciple of the Buddha who attained Arhantship through this practice, but it must be remembered that the attitude with which it is carried out is all-important – cleaning simply as a chore will be of little benefit.

It is also very helpful to have in the meditation room representations of the Body, Speech and Mind of the Buddhas, in the form of pictures and statues, books of scriptures, and either a *stūpa* or a vajra and bell.

2 SET OUT OFFERINGS

It is good to put attractive offerings such as food, flowers, [lights and incense] in front of the images, with the motivation of gaining merit for the advancement of our practice. Various mistaken ways of offering should be avoided. It is pointless to set out offerings just to impress visitors and win praise, and of no value to offer unwanted things such as food that is going off; but it will be positively harmful to obtain things to offer by theft or deception, or to sacrifice animals. As

Shāntideva points out:

> Someone whose body is being burned by fire
> Will find no mental pleasure in sense-objects.
> Just so, if one also harms sentient beings,
> There is no way to please the Greatly
>   Compassionate.[19]

The essential meaning of offering is to please the object of offering, in this case the Buddhas, thus nothing that harms sentient beings can ever be an offering to the Buddhas.
Conversely,

> Also, what else can repay
> The non-dissembling Friends, [the Buddhas,]
> Who have helped immeasurably,
> Apart from pleasing sentient beings?[20]

We should therefore understand that offerings are not restricted to material things that we put on the altar, but include the "offering of practice", all our practice of the Dharma, which benefits sentient beings and so pleases the Buddhas.

3 SEATED IN THE MEDITATION POSTURE, TAKE REFUGE AND GENERATE *BODHICITTA*

Some practices, such as meditating on the breath, are common to both Buddhists and non-Buddhists, but taking Refuge in the peculiarly Buddhist Objects of Refuge transforms one's meditation into an exclusively Buddhist practice. Its purpose is to prevent one from falling away from the Path. Generating the wish of *Bodhicitta* serves to maintain one in the highest Path, that of a Bodhisattva, so that one does not fall into the lower Paths of the Hearers and *Pratyekas*.

3a TAKING REFUGE
3a.1 *Visualizing the Objects of Refuge*

Sitting in meditation, we should build up the visualization of the Objects of Refuge. If we can, it is best to do this as described in the text (verses 1 to 8); however, as this demands considerable skill in visualization, an easier alternative will also be given.
  [1] First we visualize many offerings around us, such as

flowers fit for gods. In the centre of them, we visualize eight lions supporting a four-sided throne, two on each side, with their front paws. The lions symbolize eight powers of the Buddha,[21] and the four sides of the throne the four Means of Attraction – Buddhas and Bodhisattvas attract disciples and lead them along the Path by giving, pleasant speech, helping them with beneficial explanations of the Dharma, and becoming living examples of their own teaching.

On the throne, which is of precious materials, are a large white lotus, a sun disc, and a moon disc, representing in turn the Buddha's renunciation, understanding of Emptiness, and *Bodhicitta*.

[2] On these we visualize Shākyamuni Buddha, indivisible from our own root Guru, his body shining and endowed with the thirty-two major Marks and eighty minor Signs of a Great Being.[22] [3] There are many postures in which the Buddha can sit, each with its particular significance, but here he is sitting with his legs crossed in the vajra position, his right hand touching the earth, and his left in his lap holding a begging-bowl full of *amṛita*, or nectar. The gesture of touching the earth (*bhūmi-sparśa-mudrā*) symbolizes that he has overcome the four *Māras* – Death, defilements, the aggregates, and the Son-of-gods *Māra* (*Deva-putra-māra*) – which obstruct the practice of Dharma, in both their coarse and their subtle aspects. It is this last detail that distinguishes him from the Hearer and *Pratyeka* Arhants, who have overcome only the coarse aspects of the four *Māras*. One explanation of the Buddha's title, *Bhagavan*, relates it to this overcoming of the *Māras*.[23] The left hand in the gesture of contemplation (*dhyāna-mudrā*) indicates that he is always absorbed in direct meditation on Emptiness, while the bowl, full of four different types of *amṛita*, indicates his action of explaining the Dharma to sentient beings. Their juxtaposition means that the Buddha engages in both these things at once, unlike any non-Buddha, who may be able to do them separately, but never together. The four types of *amṛita*, coloured white, red, yellow and blue, are associated with the four classes of Buddha-activity – pacifying, increasing, subjugating and fierce activities.

From the Buddha's body there radiates light, which looks

like a web. [4] He is called "matchless" since no non-Buddha can match him, although of course other Buddhas have the same qualities and powers.

Now we visualize light coming from Shākyamuni's heart and going off to his right. On it appear the Buddha Maitreya and a group of Gurus of the lineage stemming from him, who taught especially the Method side of the practice. More light emanates from Shākyamuni's heart and goes off to his left, and on it appear Mañjushrī and the Gurus of the Wisdom lineage. A third mass of light from Shākyamuni's heart goes behind him (upwards in a two-dimensional picture), producing the Gurus of the lineage that combines the teachings of Method and Wisdom. The Buddha dominates this assembly as the moon dominates the star-filled sky on a clear night.

[5] Again light comes from Buddha Shākyamuni's heart, and spreads out downwards. On it appear many tiers of beings who help other Dharma practitioners – the *Yidams*, the Buddhas and Bodhisattvas, the Hearer and *Pratyeka* Arhants, the Heroes (*śūra*) and Ḍākinīs, and the Dharma-protectors. While the text describes these as "surrounding" (*mtha' skor*) Shākyamuni and the three groups of Gurus, actually it seems to mean simply spread out below them.

Visualizing the Gurus and other beings as arising in this way, from light produced from Shākyamuni's heart, helps us to remember that they are not a crowd of quite separate people, but are all of the same nature as Buddha Shākyamuni, whom we are already visualizing as of one nature with our own root Guru. Thus all the beings in this visualization are of the nature of our own Guru. However, if we find the generation from light too difficult, we can omit it and just visualize the secondary figures directly in their final position.

[6] Beside each of the Gurus we now visualize books, expressing what they taught – texts on *Bodhicitta* for the Method lineage, on the Wisdom realizing Emptiness for the Wisdom lineage, plus of course whatever texts each Guru actually wrote.

[7] These Gurus are not just idly sitting there, but are constantly active in helping sentient beings. They do this by sending out to every realm in which sentient beings exist rays of

very brilliant light, which emit emanations of themselves.

[8] We should also visualize each of these beings in whom we are taking Refuge as looking at us with much love and compassion, very happy and pleased to help us. This helps to establish an auspicious condition which will enable us actually to please our own Guru.

3a.2 Simplified visualization

Many Western students are likely to find the complete visualization as described above too complicated. In this case, it is sufficient simply to visualize the central figure, Shākyamuni Buddha, who is of the same nature as one's root Guru. This image is then called the Comprehensive Body (*saṃgrahakāya*), since it includes the attributes of all the various Gurus, Buddhas, Bodhisattvas and so on.

3a.3 Producing the thought seeking Refuge

[9] It is good if we can visualize around ourselves countless suffering sentient beings of all sorts, either in their actual forms as animals, hell-beings, etc., or all in human shape. This is because it is better to take Refuge on behalf of all sentient beings rather than just for ourselves. However, we are the main person seeking Refuge.

[10] When we go to a lawyer for help, we have to explain to him all the details of our problem. In the same way, now that we are seeking the aid of the Buddhas, we explain our problem to them, that for an inconceivably long time we have been experiencing every possible sort of suffering over and over again and have never found a chance to escape.

[11] Next we think to ourselves that now at last, for the first time, we have this chance to leave suffering behind – the opportune, fortunate rebirth. We have found the perfect Refuge, the Buddha and his excellent Teaching, which can release all sentient beings from their sufferings. We must look within our minds to confirm that this is so, that we really have made contact with the Buddha's Teaching – this is not something we can check by looking outwardly, like whether or not we have come into contact with dirt.

We should also think that since beginningless time, defilements (*kleśa*) such as greed, hate and delusion have occupied a stronghold in our mind, causing us endless hardship, and we still have not managed to overcome them. But our present situation gives us the chance to do so. We can look in our minds and see whether we now have the hope of freeing ourselves of defilements.

[12] Now we should concentrate on the fact that we have no idea at all when we are going to die. It might be in a few years, or in a few weeks, or even today. I am older than any of the students listening to this teaching, but it is not certain that I shall be the first to die – unfortunately, it is quite possible for people to die young, without having had time to study or develop their practice of the Dharma.

Having recognised strongly this uncertainty, we should consider how little control we shall have over our destiny when we do come to die. Even now, we do not get everything we want, and if we die without having accumulated strong roots of virtue in this life, it will be no use at all saying we would rather take a happy rebirth. If we spend this human life mainly in accumulating more negative actions, we are sure to be reborn in one of the realms of woe – in hell, the preta realm, or the animal realm. If this happens, it is no trivial matter. The sufferings of these states are so great that they are hard to bear even for a short time. We know of many examples of cruel punishments, torture and brutality that people inflict on other human beings, and of horrifying accidents. If these things happen just in the human realm, whatever will it be like in hell? Now we find it unpleasant just to go for one day without food or heating – how much worse will it be to take birth as a preta? Even as human beings we can find it very difficult to understand one page of a Dharma book, but if we become animals, we shall have no chance of understanding anything.

Such a rebirth depends on how we live now. Are we using this life to prepare to go to the realms of woe? If we do not want to go there, we must start right away preparing to go the other way.

With this motivation, we take Refuge in the Objects of Refuge we have visualized. But we should continue the contemplation, thinking [13] that although we are at present in one of the happier states of birth, as human beings, we know from our own experience that we still have to endure many sufferings, both the sufferings of birth, aging, sickness and death, common to everyone, and many other sufferings, great and small, which we have to go through again and again. Besides, if we are using this opportunity as human beings to accumulate as many good actions as we can, that is all very well, but far more likely we engage sometimes in actions which can result in happy rebirth, and sometimes in the opposite sort. In this case, we see that our human state is unstable, like a boat that can carry a non-swimmer across water but can also leave him helpless if it should be overturned by some monstrous creature on the way. It allows the possibility of progress, but no guarantee.

[14] While recognizing the instability of our present situation, we must also recognize its value as a basis for practising the Dharma. We should see how this value is enhanced by the availability of teachers who can guide our practice and point out what to do at each step – especially if we have found one. Then we should try to recognize the defects of samsaric existence and the advantages of liberation from it. As we learn to discriminate the real nature of samsara, we see that virtually every samsaric situation is one of great suffering. Since any situation that can cause us suffering tends to arouse fear, there will grow in us a genuine fear of samsara, impelling us to seek Liberation.

[15] This contemplation has further developed our thought seeking Refuge, but still we have not reached the supreme thought of Refuge, that of the Mahāyāna. We must go on to consider that seeking Liberation just for ourself, without thinking of the welfare of others, will only increase our self-centredness. Instead, we should seek Refuge for the sake of all sentient beings.

The text suggests we should develop compassion towards other sentient beings through thinking that there is no being who has not at some time been one's father, and at some other time one's mother, then developing the wish to repay the kindness they gave us on those occasions. But for Westerners, though some can use it, this method often seems to be more of a hindrance than a help. It is best simply to consider our own situation and see that our state of self-centredness is counter-productive and actually harms us; then to develop joy in the happiness of other sentient beings, wishing to help them in any way we can.

[16] Who is there really able to accomplish this task of releasing ourself and all sentient beings from samsaric existence, and leading us towards complete Awakening? However hard we look, we shall find no effective Refuge other than the Buddha, Dharma and Sangha.

At this point, firm faith in the efficacy of the Buddha is of great value. For those who have such faith, reciting this verse will help to develop their minds and increase their wish for Liberation. Those who do not, who are doubtful whether or not the Buddha can help, may see in it no more than a narrow-minded, sectarian assertion of the superiority of Buddhism over other religions, and it will only increase their confusion and doubt.

If we are interested in developing a genuine practice of the Dharma, we must study widely, so that when any sort of confusion or doubt arises, we can identify the precise nature of the problem and apply the specific remedy. In the present case, it is important to study the many reasons why the Buddha, Dharma and Sangha are considered to be the only final Refuge. The better we understand these reasons, the stronger will be our faith, and the more effective this verse.

3a.4 *Actual taking of Refuge*

[17] Now we should think with great determination and fervour that we are going to go for Refuge to the Three Jewels for the present life and always until we have accomplished Perfect Buddhahood. As we recite the lines, we develop the attitude taking Refuge in the Gurus, the root of all virtue, the Buddhas who teach, the holy Dharma, and the Sangha of *Ārya* beings. To diminish our self-centredness, we should visualize all sentient beings around us also taking Refuge, in the same words. If we find it awkward to imagine human speech coming from cows and sheep, for example, then as stated above we can visualize all the sentient beings in human form. Even taking

Refuge for oneself alone accumulates vast merit; if one takes Refuge for the sake of all sentient beings then the merit is multiplied accordingly.

The verse is written only once, but it is good to repeat it many times, improving one's visualization and intensifying the thought of Refuge each time.

[18] When we recite the Refuge formula, we should visualize coming from the bodies of all the Gurus, Buddhas and other Objects of Refuge before us a rain of white light and amṛita, which enters equally the bodies of ourself and all the sentient beings surrounding us, and also their minds, purifying all faults of body and mind. First all physical sickness disappears, then all external and internal hindrances, then all interferences to a long life.

[19] The rain of light and amṛita also purifies the many negativities we have accumulated through thoughts, speech and physical actions that were disrespectful to the Three Jewels of Refuge, especially during previous lives when we had not yet understood their qualities. In addition, we visualize that it increases our life and merits and our qualities of [understanding of] scripture and realizations, and purifies all manner of obstacles. We should feel now that the Objects of Refuge have accepted us, ourselves and all sentient beings, and taken us under their protection.

Taking Refuge in the way described above is an exceedingly powerful practice. If we can do it with real strength of mind, we can accumulate even more merit than by the practice of "Giving away and Taking over" (*gTong len*) (see verses 347–348). This is because not only are we considering the welfare of all sentient beings and visualizing them around us, but we are visualizing the Objects of Refuge, the Buddhas, Gurus, Bodhisattvas and other high beings in front of us. The power depends on the state of mind and the visualization – it does not matter whether we recite the Refuge formula of verse seventeen or a different one such as *Namo gurubhyaḥ...* [or *Buddhaṃ śaranaṃ gacchāmi ...*].

As already pointed out, to perform this practice requires faith. For those who lack firm conviction about the existence of past and future lives and the supreme ability of the Buddha,

Dharma and Sangha to help, this teaching is not much use. But if we do have such conviction, then in accordance with its strength, the benefit is immense. It is said that were the merit accruing from the practice of taking Refuge to have form, the whole world would not be big enough to contain it.

To have a large store of merit is very important for effective practice. Someone of great merit will experience little suffering and much happiness, and his wishes will be easily fulfilled; he will readily overcome whatever difficulties he meets, whether in Dharma practice or in worldly tasks. But with an inadequate accumulation of merit, even if one develops faith in the Three Jewels and takes Refuge, one may later fall away from this Refuge; or one may find one's practice obstructed by sickness, premature death, and other problems.

Therefore Tibetans, when they face obstacles of any kind, seek to increase their merit by such practices as prostrations and reciting mantras.

The visualization of light and *amṛita*, which also plays an important role in Tantric *sādhanas*, is of great significance. *Amṛita* is a Sanskrit word composed of the negative prefix *a-* and *mṛita*, "death", thus it means "overcoming death". Its Tibetan equivalent *bdud rtsi* is likewise in two parts, *bdud* meaning "*Māra*" and *rtsi* indicating a medicine for overcoming them. Thus the main function of *amṛita* is overcoming the obstructions that are personified as the four *Māras*, including Death. In combination with light, *amṛita* represents the Method aspect of the Path, while the light concerns the Wisdom aspect. In the higher Tantras, further levels of significance are taught.

3b GENERATING BODHICITTA

[20] This section begins with the contemplation of one's own situation, bound in the prison of samsara by the bonds of karma and defilements, and suffering continually. We can see from our own experience that defilements are present in our mind, that we keep creating new actions, and that we are suffering.

Now we apply our experience of our own condition to others. As at verse fifteen, the text mentions all sentient beings as having been one's mother; but again, it is probably easier simply to look at one's own suffering and realize that just as one helps oneself, one should be trying to help others. The mother-child relationship is singled out because this is the closest relationship between people in worldly life. Until the child is able to look after itself, the mother is completely responsible for every aspect of its existence. Not only human mothers but mother birds, monkeys and other animals take great care of their young. And it is not just a matter of one lifetime, but every time we have taken birth as a human being, a monkey, a little bird, or one of countless other sorts of animals, our mother in that existence looked after us carefully until we were independent.

[21] When we were completely helpless, we depended totally on our mother to do everything for us. Now we must see that the situation is reversed: the sentient beings who have been our mother are in trouble and need help, so just as they gave us help when we needed it, so it is our responsibility to give them help now. Of course, if we do not understand the existence of previous lives, it is hard for this contemplation to have much effect on the mind.

But at present, we are hardly in a position to lead all mother sentient beings out of the problems of samsaric existence, when we cannot yet lead ourselves out or even see where we are going to go when we die. We have no way of predicting our future destiny, and to liberate oneself from suffering is extremely difficult.

[22] Even Hearer and *Pratyeka* Arhants, who have accomplished part of the Path, still have obscurations, which must be abandoned before they can attain full Enlightenment. Therefore, the best thing we can do to help all sentient beings is to attain Buddhahood ourselves. [23] In that state, one has both eliminated all one's own faults and obscurations, and developed all the qualities that enable one to benefit others. In our present state, we can accomplish a very limited amount, and that with great difficulty. But a Buddha's actions are both effortless and of maximum effectiveness.

[24] We therefore develop the resolve to attain perfect Buddhahood for the sake of all sentient beings; and not content with this thought, we prepare actually to engage in the conduct that leads to the accomplishment of Buddhahood, namely the

six Perfections of Giving, Morality, Patience, Energy, Concentration and Wisdom. It is no use thinking "That is very difficult, I can't really do it": we should develop strong self-confidence and become determined to act in this way.

Bodhicitta is a state of mind that firstly is concerned to accomplish the welfare of all sentient beings, and secondly, seeing that this is possible only on the attainment of Buddhahood, is determined to attain Buddhahood. This promise to attain Buddhahood we now make to the Gurus, Buddhas and other Objects of Refuge whom we are still visualizing in front of us.

[25] When we make this promise, we visualize that Buddha Shākyamuni in the centre of the visualization is extremely pleased, and sends out an exact duplicate of himself. This emanation, of the nature of light like all the rest of the visualization, comes to the top of our head and merges into our own body. [26] At that very moment, all our obscurations are dispelled, and our body also becomes a body of Buddha Shākyamuni, identical to the one in front of us, of the nature of light, and emitting countless rays of light. We should visualize that these light-rays go out and touch all the places where sentient beings live, transforming them into Pure Lands of deities. They also touch all sentient beings, whom we are still visualizing around us, instantly purifying their obscurations, and transforming their bodies into the form of Shākyamuni, still of the nature of light.

Thus visualizing ourself and all sentient beings around us as being Shākyamuni, we should contemplate all this work we have accomplished, and rejoice in it, thinking it is excellent. At this point we should remain in meditation, maintaining this thought for as long as possible.

This is an extremely powerful method, called "developing *Bodhicitta* by taking the result", because we visualize the result, our own Buddhahood and that of all sentient beings, in order to develop the state of mind.

3c THE FOUR IMMEASURABLES

When we come out of this concentration, we should realize that it was only a visualization, and in fact all sentient beings have not yet been liberated from suffering. So we go on to increase the power of the *Bodhicitta* we have just generated by developing the four Immeasurable thoughts.

[27] First[24] is the measureless thought of Equanimity. Every sentient being has experienced every possible relationship – father and son, brother and sister, etc. – many times with every other. But not recognizing this fact, they feel attachment towards some and aversion towards others. Out of this arise all sorts of fighting and disputes, and an incredible amount of suffering. We do not see the past relationships, but we do see the attachment and hatred and the suffering.

[28] Considering this, we develop Immeasurable Equanimity in a sequence of four thoughts.[25]

(a) Desiring: "How wonderful it would be if I and all sentient beings could abandon all attachment and aversion towards each other, all thought of some being close and others distant, and see everyone equally!"
(b) Wishing: "May we all indeed come to see everyone equally!"
(c) Superior intention: taking the responsibility upon oneself, "I shall bring it about that we do all come to see everyone equally."
(d) Requesting: realizing that we do not yet have the power to carry out this resolve, we ask the Gurus and Buddhas visualized before us to inspire us with that power.

[29] We develop Immeasurable Loving-kindness through thinking that the best way sentient beings could exist would be in a state of happiness, and reflecting as the verse indicates. It is plain to see that many people continually accumulate more and more negative actions, unaware that to attain happiness they must avoid non-virtue; and that there are some who still engage in non-virtue even though they do know this. [30] The four thoughts of desiring, wishing, superior intention and requesting are developed, as with Equanimity.

[31–34] Then Immeasurable Compassion, and finally Immeasurable Joy are developed, again with the same series of four thoughts. The text is clear enough.

Many of us perform daily practices which begin with the three items just explained, taking Refuge, generating *Bodhicitta*, and the four Immeasurables. If we think about them every day and go through the contemplations described, the benefits are extremely great. If we just recite the words without thinking, the benefits will be far less.

3d SPECIAL GENERATION OF BODHICITTA

[35] Considering the suffering of sentient beings, and their kindness, we develop the strong determination to attain Buddhahood as quickly as possible, in order to be able to help them immediately. It is the emphasis on speed that distinguishes this from the generation of *Bodhicitta* [in 3b]. "Quickly, quickly" implies in this very lifetime, and even in the shortest possible period of three years and three months.

Like a machine that can do a great deal of work in a short time, the power of *Bodhicitta* enables one to accumulate in a short time the immense merits necessary to attain Buddhahood.

4 VISUALIZE CLEARLY THE FIELD FOR THE ACCUMULATION OF MERIT

The present text suggests that we maintain the same visualization of the field of Gurus, Buddhas etc. that we used for taking Refuge and generating *Bodhicitta*.[26] [This heading has therefore already been dealt with under 3a.] We should imagine that it includes all Buddhas, Bodhisattvas, Hearer and *Pratyeka* Arhants, and other *Arya* beings who help us in our practice of Dharma.

5 TRAIN THE MIND WITH THE SEVEN LIMBS
5a BATH OFFERING

Here the text inserts an additional practice, the offering of a bath, which is not essential but is something we can do in order to accumulate more merit.

[36–37] We address all the Objects of Accumulating Merit, saying, "Please listen to me! I wish to attain *Bodhicitta* and Enlightenment, but for this I need much merit. So please come here so that I can accumulate great merit by bathing your bodies!" And by their magical powers, they descend before us.

[38] Now we visualize a large bath, not like an ordinary swimming-pool with ordinary water, but very beautiful and built of precious materials, as detailed in the text, and full of amṛita water. [39] When Shākyamuni Buddha was born from the right side of his Mother, the gods Shakra and Brahma appeared and offered him a bath like this.

[40] Since the bodies of Buddhas and Arhants are already completely pure and cannot become dirty, it is clear that the purpose of offering them this bath is not to clean them. Rather, we are going through the actions of washing them for the sake of our own accumulation of merit, so that we can attain the state where we are able to purify the body, speech and mind of all sentient beings of their defilements and other obscurations. It is the same as when we set out food and the like on the altar as offerings to say, Tārā – we do not do this because Tārā is hungry and needs something to eat, but in order to accumulate merit for ourselves.

[41] We visualize going out from our hearts innumerable goddesses, who are to perform all the actions of washing and so forth. They are of many different sorts and colours – red, yellow, blue, green, white and multi-coloured. Some hold precious vases of special water for washing, some towels of heavenly cloth for drying the bodies, some perfume for anointing the bodies, some beautiful clothes to be offered afterwards, and so on. They go out from our heart and perform their tasks, then come back and reabsorb into our heart.

While some goddesses bathe the Buddhas with excellent water from their vases, [others] sing and play beautiful music, all of which is part of our offering.

We may find certain problems with the visualization at this stage, since the Objects of Offering include all the Tantric deities, in particular the fierce deities such as Yamāntaka, who have flames streaming from their bodies – one may wonder what happens when one tries washing them. However, we should not think that the flames are real fire. Actually they are intense light, depicted as fire so as to symbolize the Wisdom-knowledge of the Buddhas, which consumes all the obscurations previously existing in the mind-stream as fire consumes wood. All deities should be visualized as having light coming from their bodies, but in the case of fierce deities it is usually shown as flames to enhance their fierce aspect.

It may also seem very tricky to wash deities who have many arms and legs, and even heads. If so, we should remember that each deity appears in different aspects, according to the situation. Yamāntaka, for example, is said to have forty-nine different aspects – he does not always have nine heads, thirty-four arms and sixteen legs. In fact, he is not even always fierce, for he is the same person as Mañjushrī. Je Tsongkhapa also is another aspect in which Mañjushrī-Yamāntaka has appeared. Avalokiteshvara, again, appears sometimes, for specific reasons, with eleven heads and a thousand arms; but at other times he appears differently. The commonly-depicted aspect of Tārā is only one of many ways in which she has revealed herself to meditators, and has particular meanings – the right hand extended in the gesture of granting boons invites all who wish for happiness to come to her, the left hand in the gesture of the Three Jewels means "Do not be frightened, you can find complete Refuge here!", and the flowers whose stems she is holding symbolize that one should not be attached to samsaric happiness, but seek Liberation.[27] Thus if we find it hard to visualize the washing of the deities in complicated aspects, we can and should visualize them in simpler aspects, so that we can do this practice well.

We should also be aware that the bodies of the Objects of Offering are not of flesh and blood, but made entirely of light.

[42] Bathing the Buddhas etc. with the best possible materials, we ask them to inspire us to accomplish whatever we need to accomplish, and to grant us all the merits we require.

[43] After washing the bodies, we have to dry them. We should visualize that all the water collects into five spots – on the head, on each shoulder, at the heart, and at the navel – leaving the rest of the body completely dry. All that the goddesses with the towels have to do, therefore, is press the towel on each of these spots in turn. They do this to the accompaniment of the five mantric syllables, OṂ HŪṂ TRĀṂ HRĪḤ ĀḤ.

[44] Now we visualize more goddesses coming forward

and offering clothes – not ordinary, gross clothing such as we wear, but of a very light, rainbow nature. To the beings who manifest in the form of monks they offer monks' robes, to those in the form of gods, clothes of gods, and so on.

[45] Since it is not fitting for monks to wear ornaments, the offering of ornaments is made only to the beings not manifesting as monks. Buddha Shākyamuni's only ornament is his begging bowl! To those in the aspect of gods and lay people, the offering goddesses from our heart present all suitable kinds of ornaments, such as diadems, necklaces and bracelets. We say that although the Buddhas are already completely adorned with the thirty-two Marks and eighty Signs of a Great Being, and so need no external ornament, we are offering ornaments to them in order to gain the merit to become Buddhas ourselves.

[46] [47] Finally, [having reabsorbed all the offering goddesses into our heart,] we ask the beings to take their places again and remain there while we offer them the seven-limb puja.

5b THE SEVEN LIMBS
5b.1 *Prostration*

There is prostration of body, of speech, and of mind. Prostration of speech includes praising and speaking respectfully of the Object of prostration, that of mind is a respectful attitude of mind, and that of the body is deferential physical actions, not necessarily standing and making a formal prostration, but perhaps putting the hands together at the heart.

For prostration to be complete, it should be done with awareness of the true nature of the object being prostrated to, the person prostrating, and the action of prostrating.

Those who wish to do prostrations as a special practice, such as the hundred thousand prostrations, should obtain clear teachings on how it is to be done, so that they understand all the details.

[48] Here we prostrate first to the King of Sages, Shākyamuni Buddha, and next [49] to the Gurus, who teach the miserable beings in samsara the way to Liberation.

[50] Thirdly, we prostrate to the *Yidams*, the tutelary deities who, if followed in pure Tantric practice, can grant all realiz-

ations. A *Yidam* is not necessarily fierce. For example, the *Yidams* of the Kadampa tradition were Ārya-Tārā and Avalokiteshvara; it depends on one's personal inclination.

It is essential that we see clearly that Guru, Buddha and *Yidam* are of one nature. In illustration of this, an incident from the life of Marpa[28] is frequently recounted. Once, when travelling in search of his Guru, Naropa, Marpa had seen in the sky the *Yidam* Hevajra with his attendant goddesses; on this occasion he recognized them instantly as a manifestation of his Guru.[29] But later, when he had found Naropa and was living with him and receiving teachings, Naropa woke him up from sleep one day, showed him again the mandala of Hevajra in the sky, and asked, "Will you prostrate first to me or to the *Yidam*?" This time, Marpa thought it was a much rarer thing to see the *Yidam* than his Guru, so chose the *Yidam*. Naropa told him, "Without the Guru, the *Yidam* does not exist for a moment. All the countless Buddhas arise only in dependence on the Guru." And the mandala dissolved into Naropa's heart.[30] In consequence of this blunder of Marpa's, Naropa prophesied that his family line would soon become extinct, which came about when his only son died young.

Therefore we must bear in mind in *yidam*-practice that Guru, *Yidam* and Buddha are inseparable. Otherwise, we shall be unable to accumulate merit as we should. This does not mean that anyone who is a guru is necessarily a Buddha – he may be a Bodhisattva, an Arhant, or an ordinary being – but to practise Guru-yoga and *Lam rim* properly we have to learn to see him in this way.

Having prostrated [51] to the Buddhas, we prostrate [52] to the Dharma Refuge, visualized in the form of books, of the nature of light, as described in verse six. Then, moving down the tiers of figures, we prostrate to [53] the Bodhisattvas, [54] the *Pratyeka* and Hearer Arhants, and [55] the Heroes and *Ḍākinīs*. The latter are male and female emanations of the Buddhas, who take birth in different situations all over the world and help those who wish to practise Dharma. Then [56] come the Dharma Protectors, who are always available to prevent the arising of obstacles and hindrances to Dharma practice and to destroy those which do arise. Finally [57] we prostrate to the entire assembly of beings with good qualities.

If we find it hard to visualize so many different aspects of the Buddhas and make prostrations to them, then as before, with Refuge, we can simply visualize the figure of Buddha Shākyamuni, feeling that he has the nature of all of them – the Comprehensive Body.

Prostration serves to purify negativities of the body, speech and mind. In particular, it is the direct opponent of pride. Clearly, pride tends to make one avoid any sort of deference to others. It is important to overcome pride as it directly prevents the accumulation of merits.

5b.2 *Offering*

The offerings we make begin [58–61] with eight standard types of offering, in order: water for rinsing the mouth, water for washing the feet, flowers, incense, lights, perfumed water for anointing the body, food, and music. Then [62] we make offerings to the five senses.

Detailed commentary is unnecessary. We should visualize very beautiful offerings, as described in the verses. Ideally they should be of the nature of things from the realms of the gods, but since we do not really know what those are like, we should just make them as pure and as wonderful as we can imagine.

The general purpose of offering is to accumulate merit. Its particular function is to be the direct opponent to avarice.

5b.3 *Confession of sins*

[66] We should think that all the suffering we have experienced in the past, are experiencing now, and are to experience in the future, is caused by the negativities in our own continuum. We have not accumulated these negativities in this life alone, but in many previous lives.

Then from the depths of our heart we should generate the feeling of regret towards this, and ask the beings in the Field of Merit before us, "We confess all this – please help us to purify it!"

Evidently the main purpose of confession is to purify our accumulated negativities of body, speech and mind. In particular, it acts as a direct antidote to all defilements, such as greed and hatred.

5b.4 *Rejoicing*

[67] We think of all the good works of all beings – Buddhas, Bodhisattvas, [*Āryas,*] and ordinary beings of all sorts – and rejoice in them from our heart, trying to share in this virtue.

This practice is the best way to accumulate great stores of merit with very little effort. In particular, it is the direct opponent of jealousy, one of the worst negative emotions. Jealousy is the state of mind that feels unhappy on seeing the good qualities and happiness of others, while rejoicing is precisely the opposite, feeling happy about others' happiness and virtues.

5b.5 *Requesting the turning of the Wheel of Dharma*

[68] We ask the Buddhas [and their emanations] to continue spreading the teachings of Method and Wisdom.

Through this, we acquire much merit. In particular, it acts as a direct opponent to the negativities that we have accumulated with regard to the Dharma, as for example by criticizing it in previous lives.

5b.6 *Asking the Gurus to remain*

[69] We ask the Gurus and Buddhas to remain in this world, not passing into Nirvana but continuing to help sentient beings overcome suffering as long as there are any left.

This is the best way to increase the life of one's Guru, and one's own life. In particular, it is the direct opponent to negativities accumulated with regard to our Gurus, in this and previous lives.

5b.7 *Dedication*

[70] Finally, we imagine collected together all the virtues we

have accumulated, and also those of all sentient beings, and dedicate them to [our Enlightenment for] the benefit of all sentient beings.

This protects the power of our virtue from destruction by anger. In particular, it is a direct opponent to the mental karma of wrong views, such as denial of rebirth and the laws of karma. Even if we do not hold such wrong views now, we have indulged in them in previous lives.

The seven limbs are extremely important. They include all the causes and conditions needed to accomplish the two essential aspects of Dharma practice, purifying faults and accumulating merits and positive qualities. The limbs of Prostration and Confession are ways of purifying negativities, and the other limbs, except Dedication, are ways of developing the positive. Dedication increases and stabilizes this merit.

6 OFFER A MANDALA, AND PRAY FOR INSPIRATION
6a THE MANDALA OFFERING

The Sanskrit word *maṇḍala* has been translated into Tibetan as *snying po len pa*, "taking the essence",[31] implying that it is a good way to make this human life very meaningful, by eliminating the causes of suffering and accumulating the causes of happiness.

When offering the mandala, one first of all takes in the left hand the plate one is using as a base and rubs it three times clockwise with the right forearm. One thinks of the arm as being of the nature of the three principal points of the Path – Renunciation, *Bodhicitta*, and the understanding of Emptiness – and of the plate as being one's own mind. Rubbing it three times signifies purifying the mind of all the negative impressions accumulated from actions of the mind, speech and body, and all obscurations and stains.

Then one puts a little rice on the mandala base and goes round three times anticlockwise with the right arm. This symbolizes receiving blessings of body, speech and mind from the Field of Merit visualized in front of one.

Next one makes the visualization, while reciting and putting on the rice. If one can, it is good to recite the list of offerings –

the world-system of Mount Meru with the four continents and eight sub-continents, the seven precious things and so forth. If not, it is sufficient simply to visualize many marvellous offerings, thinking of them in the fourfold manner to be described below.

At the end, the rice can be tipped off the base either away from or towards oneself. The first means that one is making offering externally in order to accumulate virtue within oneself, the second that one is receiving the pleasure of the beings in the Field of Merit produced by one's offering to them.

The physical objects that we use in the mandala offering, such as the plate and the rice, are not really the mandala. They are only a support for visualization, on the basis of which we should offer mentally four kinds of mandala simultaneously – the outer, inner, secret and Suchness mandalas.

(a) Offering the outer mandala means offering a pleasing external environment, [i.e. a visualization of the universe, filled with all manner of precious things.]
(b) One offers the inner mandala by thinking that that visualization is of the nature of one's virtues of the past, present and future.
(c) Offering the secret mandala involves thinking that this virtue one is offering has the nature of all happiness and bliss.
(d) To offer the Suchness mandala, one must understand the ultimate nature of this offering, its Emptiness of true existence.

There is also a manner of offering the mandala related to the practice of the six Perfections.

This explanation is not sufficient for doing the practice of a hundred thousand mandala offerings. Those who wish to do this should request a special teaching. Some details are best taught by practical demonstration.

6b PRAYERS FOR INSPIRATION

[First [71–78] we call upon our Root Guru and the Gurus of the various lineages in turn, then [79–96] we make specific requests for their inspiration in the successive stages of practice. In effect, the rest of the text serves as commentary on this section.]

CONCLUDING REMARKS

We are exceedingly fortunate in our present situation, so rich in opportunity. We must realize how fortunate we are, and put this opportunity to good use by accumulating a great deal of merit. If we lack merit, there are many obstructions that can arise. Hindrances to the body, such as sickness, prevent us from taking advantage of the human state; hindrances to the lifespan cut short our life. But worse than these are hindrances affecting the mind, which can lead us astray from the Dharma Path with the result that for extremely long periods we do not meet it again. Therefore we should increase our stock of merit to help us overcome all such hindrances and make the going easier on the Path. The best method to accumulate merit is through the practices described above – Refuge, *Bodhicitta*, the Four Immeasurables, the Seven Limbs, the Mandala Offering and the rest.

However, it is difficult for these methods to give rise to a proper accumulation of merit if our mind is filled with anxiety. I, for example, am sixty-two years of age, which is quite old for a Tibetan, and sometimes experience anxiety about this, but much of this anxiety is quite useless. So we should try to keep our minds relaxed and happy, and further our practice by study and meditation in this state.

The Actual Practice

Part One
Basics

Meditation 1
Guru Devotion

1a THE ADVANTAGES OF DEVOTION AND DISADVANTAGES OF NON-DEVOTION
1a.1 *The advantages of devotion to one's Spiritual Friend*

If we understand well the advantages of devotion to the Guru, we can develop the right attitude and practise it properly; if we do not, the practice will not be very fruitful. The same applies in worldly activities such as working in a factory or farming – to do the job properly one needs to know what sort of return one can expect from it.

[97] If one has a Master, or Spiritual Friend, who is able to teach correctly the entire Path to full Enlightenment, and devotes oneself to him properly, the advantages are too numerous to mention.

[98] The benefit of engaging in difficult ascetic practices for vast periods of time is less than that of reliance on the Spiritual Friend for a short time, because of the great kindness of the Spiritual Friend.

[99] If a mother sees her child is intelligent and assiduous and doing well in his studies, she is pleased because she predicts that he will be successful later on. In the same way, when the Buddhas see someone devoting himself correctly to his Spiritual Friend, they are very glad, because they know this person will be able to make much progress on the spiritual Path.

[100] If one has the correct attitude towards the Spiritual Friend, then even though one is not deliberately inviting the Buddhas before one, they enter the Teacher so that one receives their inspiration or blessing through him. Offering him even one apple will then accumulate as much merit as offering it to all the Buddhas.

[101] Much as a gutter collects all the rain that falls on a roof, faith in one's Spiritual Friend serves to collect all the rain of blessings or inspiration. Through proper devotion, all hindrances, external and internal, to the practice are overcome, and all the successive realizations are easily accomplished. For example, Sakya Pandita and Milarepa were so successful in their practice because of their intense devotion to their Gurus, as will be described later (verse 137), and Atīsha's cook also achieved exceptional realizations similarly.

[102] If one maintains the right attitude of respect and devotion towards one's Guru, then out of the wish to please him one will feel strongly that one should not think bad thoughts or engage in wrong actions, and automatically one's mental defilements and wrong actions will diminish. Also one can observe that if one is close to one's Guru, it is much easier to engage in virtue, thus one's practice progresses and one's positive qualities increase; but if one goes off on one's own the whole practice is much more difficult. If one follows his instructions exactly then one's qualities increase very quickly. This falling-away of faults and increase of virtues leads one to experience much happiness straight away, in this life, while the practice will also bear the fruit of more happiness in future lives.

[103] The karmic results of proper reliance on the Spiritual Friend include the ripening in a fortunate rebirth and the result similar to the cause. The latter is that in future lives one continues to relate correctly to one's Spiritual Friend and to receive unmistaken teachings from him, and thus one will continue to practise and progress.

[104] Thus to sum up the advantages of devotion to the Spiritual Friend, in the short term one is born as a human being or a god, not falling into the realms of woe, and in the end one attains Liberation or complete Enlightenment.

1a.2 The disadvantages of not being devoted

[105] These then are the benefits of devoting oneself correctly to the Spiritual Friend. What problems arise if one does not do so?

[106] The essence of devotion to one's Guru is to see in him the nature of all the enlightened activity of the Buddhas. If then one acts badly towards him, one is in effect acting badly towards all the Buddhas, and nothing could be more negative than that.

When we look at our Teacher he seems to be flesh and blood just like ourselves, so the thought that he is of the nature of all the Enlightened activities of the Buddhas is hard to develop. Certain arguments are given (section 1b.1) to help convince oneself of this.

[107] A single moment of anger towards one's Guru is extremely negative – it will destroy the virtues accumulated through him over a very long period and result in an extremely long hell existence, as is taught in the *Kālacakra-Tantra*.

[108] The five immediate sins [see Glossary] are extremely serious and hard to purify, but even so they can be purified completely by certain tantric practices. Anger and contempt towards one's Guru, however, is much more difficult to purify. At best, with great effort one can perhaps achieve a temporary amelioration.

[109] If one engages in very powerful, advanced practices, even practising continuously without sleeping, but at the same time feels aversion and contempt in one's heart towards one's Guru, all the arduous, ascetic practice will be in vain.

[110] If one loses one's faith and respect towards one's Teacher, not only will one be unable to make any further spiritual progress but even the qualities one has already developed in dependence on him will be lost. In this lifetime all sorts of internal and external hindrances will arise, and in many future lives one will be reborn in ill destinies.

[111] Even after that, when one is again reborn as a human being, the result similar to the cause of despising one's Guru will be that one continues to lack faith and respect towards

Gurus. One will be separated from the Spiritual Friend and from the teaching. Thus one will lack the opportune, fortunate rebirth (see Meditation 2).

[112] Thus if one lacks devotion to one's Spiritual Friend, or worse, having had it one turns away from it, then in this life and in future lives nothing but suffering and problems will result.

[113] So we can weigh up the advantages of proper adherence to a Spiritual Friend and the disadvantages of the contrary course, and come to understand how we should behave. Just as in business one thinks first of the possible profits and losses that will ensue from the various courses of action, so here, wanting to make a profit and avoid loss, one thinks of the advantages and disadvantages and resolves strongly to devote oneself properly to the Guru, who is the root of all good qualities, and not to misbehave towards him. Then besides the happiness one attains in this life, one will meet this Guru again and again in the future.

1b HOW TO DEVOTE ONESELF TO THE SPIRITUAL FRIEND IN THOUGHT

1b.1 *The development of faith*

The essence of proper devotion to the Spiritual Friend is to have faith in him. If one has faith, then the actual practice of devotion follows naturally; if not, there will be no real devotion. To develop faith in the Guru, we practise an analytical meditation using certain reasonings, which make us aware of his good qualities. If we are not aware of these, faith cannot arise.

[114–5] The central point is to consider that our Teacher is of the nature of the Wisdom-knowledge of all the Buddhas, which they have manifested as him in order to lead us. The sole purpose for the existence of the Buddhas is to benefit sentient beings, and they manifest to whatever extent they can help sentient beings by doing so. To some beings, whom they can help by manifesting in the Enjoyment Body, they will manifest in that way; to others, whom they can benefit by manifesting in an Emanation Body, they manifest in that way. To others again they manifest as ordinary Spiritual Friends, or even as deer and other animals, if this can help. Thus they must also be appearing to me in the way that is best for me, which since I am interested in the practice of Dharma must be in the form of the Spiritual Friend — this being a particularly effective way to benefit a disciple. The Buddha himself has said in a Sutra that Buddhas manifest for the sake of all sentient beings like this.

[116] In the Tantras too, it is taught that at the end of the eon, in the period of destruction, Vajradhara himself will manifest as a Guru to teach the Dharma. So there is no doubt that he will manifest now to someone like me who is interested in Dharma.

[117] Sometimes the Guru may treat us roughly and speak harshly to us, but we should bear in mind that he is an emanation of Vajradhara and try to avoid seeing faults in him.

[118] If we met a completely perfect and faultless person, we would still perceive faults in him. When Buddha Shākyamuni was in India, He was fully enlightened and completely free of faults, yet still Devadatta and many non-Buddhist teachers saw his actions as mistaken, though in fact these actions were devoid of any imperfection. [119] We project faults onto what is actually faultless because our mind is obscured by negative karmic tendencies. Our perceptions are distorted, just as in severe jaundice the eyesight can become affected so that even a white conch-shell appears yellow, or with other diseases a white, snow-covered mountain can appear blue, or one may hallucinate things that are not there at all. Grasping our distorted perceptions of the Guru as true, we react negatively towards him and thus accumulate further negative tendencies. We must therefore remind ourselves whenever we start seeing faults in our Guru's behaviour, that this way of seeing is conditioned by our own karmic obscurations, and actually he is the manifestation of the Wisdom-knowledge of the Buddhas.

We may think that [at present we are free of diseases like jaundice and] what appears to our sight is true. But this is far from the case. Things appear to us as separate from us and existing truly and independently, but in fact they do not exist in the way in which they appear — they have no true existence. Similarly, that our Spiritual Friend appears to us to have faults does not necessarily imply that he really does.

In the main temple of Lhasa is a famous statue of the Buddha, called the Jowo, to which Tibetans have for centuries gone on pilgrimage – now that the temple has been reopened by the Chinese authorities they go again. But it is said that some people's minds are so heavily obscured that despite all the butter lamps in front of this image they are unable to see it, they perceive only a dark space. When these people undertake special practices to purify their negativities, then gradually they become able to see something of this statue.

Similarly, the same Guru is seen quite differently by different people. Some will feel spontaneous devotion as soon as they meet him, some will see him as just an ordinary person like themselves, and others will just feel anger towards him. If he has ten disciples, they will each perceive him in different ways, depending on their own karmic obscurations.

[120] Again, it is known that for special purposes the Buddhas sometimes manifest themselves in apparently faulty forms, even as *māras* or demons.[32] Sometimes, for example to help animals who cannot speak or understand speech, they manifest as animals or birds. Sometimes, when necessary, they even manifest as material things such as water. For human beings, they manifest principally as Spiritual Friends and teach the Dharma through them. Thus if our Guru appears less than perfect, we can think that it is simply through skilful means that the Buddhas are manifesting in this way, to ripen us and other sentient beings according to our dispositions.

[121] In fact, when our perception is so restricted by the power of our karmic obscurations and defilements, this is really the best the Buddhas can do for us. For if they were all to stand in front of us in their perfect forms endowed with all the thirty-two Marks of a Great Being, saying "We are the Buddhas," we would be unable to see them.

[122] So when we see faults in our Spiritual Friend, either they are simply our own mental projection, due to negative karmic impressions, or [the Buddhas] are manifesting in this apparently faulty way in order to guide us. Either way, it is as inappropriate to attribute the faults to him as to blame a mirror for the blemishes it reveals in one's make-up. In reality, he is completely perfect.

[123] For these reasons, when we relate to a Spiritual

Friend, we must not only abandon negative behaviour towards him but must develop the firm recognition that he is the manifestation of the Compassion, Wisdom and Power of all the Buddhas. On the basis of recollecting his qualities in this way and abandoning our wrong projections about him, we develop faith in him. When we have this faith, we can devote ourselves properly to him and benefit from his teaching, but without it, our relationship will be incorrect and will not bring much benefit.

1b.2 *Becoming respectful, by remembering the Guru's kindness*

Besides this faith in the Spiritual Friend, we need a certain attitude of respect, so that we wish to put into practice all the teachings he gives us. This respect is developed by recollecting his kindness.

[124] We must think that not only is our Guru the manifestation of all the Buddhas, free of any fault and endowed with every good quality, but he has the greatest kindness to us, benefiting us incredibly. [125] On a worldly level, if someone gets a person released from prison and provides him with a pleasant house, good food and so on, the ex-prisoner will remember his kindness constantly. [126] But our Spiritual Friend's kindness is much greater than this. Not concerned only with this life, he shows us how to eliminate the mental defilements and impressions that would otherwise lead us to extremely uncomfortable future existences in the realms of woe. Thus he brings us to be reborn as gods or human beings. [127] In addition, he shows us how to see that any kind of samsaric existence is unsatisfactory and how to attain Liberation, in which the faults of samsara are abandoned. Then he leads us into the Mahāyāna Path and through all the Bodhisattva Stages to the attainment of the Three *Kāyas* of a Buddha. Since all these attainments depend on the kindness of the Spiritual Friend, how can this kindness not be great?

[128] To repay the kindness of teaching even one sentence of Dharma would take a very long time, but the Spiritual Friend does not teach just one sentence – he teaches us the complete Dharma. How could such kindness be repaid?

[129] The lay life, completely involved in worldly activities,

work, worry and frustration, is like burning in a pit of fire. That one leaves this [and enters the religious life] is due to the kindness of the Spiritual Friend.

[130] Meeting pure Dharma teachings that are able to help us and developing confidence in them is the result of the Guru's kindness.

[131] So our Spiritual Friends are our rescuers saving us from the three realms of woe; ... guides who lead us to high rebirth as human beings or gods, and to the ultimate bliss of Liberation and Buddhahood; [132] the greatest doctors, able to cure our most deeply-rooted disease, the mental defilements; ... [133] those who free us from the bonds of defilements and karmic impressions that keep us bound in samsara; and the other things [listed in the root text]. If we remember these verses, we can recollect our Gurus' kindness towards us and so develop respect and adhere to them properly.

If we have not developed faith in the Spiritual Friend by recollecting his qualities, we shall regard him as just an ordinary person, and through pride consider ourself to have better qualities. If we have not developed respect by contemplating his kindness, then although we have faith in him and see him as a great being, we see no particular relationship between him and ourself. Only if we develop respect can great benefit come to us through this relationship so that our mind is effectively transformed.

1c HOW TO DEVOTE ONESELF TO THE SPIRITUAL FRIEND IN ACTION

[134] To sum up the previous section, every benefit and happiness we receive is the result of the kindness of our Spiritual Friend – both when we are ordinary beings, and when we have attained the Path of Insight and become *Ārya* beings. It is natural to wish to repay this kindness. While it is extremely hard to repay it all, we should engage in practices by way of respect to him.

[135] From his side, the Guru has no desire to receive our offerings, service and respect, any more than the ground in which seed is sown desires the fruit of its growth. But as the farmer who sows the seed reaps the benefit by harvesting the

crop, so the disciple who serves his Guru in action as best he can will gather limitless merit within himself.

[136] How can giving offerings to the Spiritual Friend bring more merit than offering to all the Buddhas? One may feel doubtful about this, but to understand it, one must receive certain special teachings from the *Lam rim*.

[137] Many examples are given of the great benefits that come from devoting oneself in action to one's Spiritual Friend.

Naropa was treated extremely harshly by his Guru, Tilopa, for some twelve years, but through it all he kept one-pointed confidence in his teacher and did everything he said, in any situation, however difficult. For this reason he attained Buddhahood in that very life. If you are interested, you can read his biography.[33]

Milarepa too carried out every instruction of his Guru, Marpa, building several houses for him, carrying stones on his back even when his back became one great sore, and undergoing many other hardships. But because of this strong devotion to his Spiritual Friend, he also won Enlightenment in that life and became famous among Buddhist yogins. All this you can read about in Milarepa's biography.[34]

Then there is Drom-tön-pa, who before meeting his main Guru had a teacher who owned many sheep and cattle. Drom-tön-pa never slept but spent the whole night watching in case somebody came to steal these animals, while during the day he was doing every job needed on the farm. Because of serving his Guru day and night like this he became Drom-tön-pa the Wise, the central support of the Kadampa lineage.

Sakya Pandita, when his master became chronically sick and bed-ridden, nursed him day and night until he died. Through this intense devotion he became renowned as outstandingly wise.

Cha-yül-pa also nursed his Guru with extreme devotion when he was sick, reverently carrying his excreta down three flights of stairs with his own hands. While he was doing this he received powers of clairvoyance, such as the divine ear which enables one to hear the sounds of people and even insects at a great distance.

The text quotes just these few examples, but in fact all the great meditators of India and Tibet gained their realizations because of powerful devotion to their Gurus, regardless of their own body, life and wealth.

[138] Therefore we who want to attain similar realizations must devote ourselves to the Spiritual Friend as these Masters of the Path did – making offerings to him and serving him in every way, prostrating to him, standing when he enters the room, massaging his body when he is sick, and anointing him with perfume. With our speech too we should honour him with praises, not necessarily reciting texts but informally.

[139] We should do everything that can make our Spiritual Friend happy, because to displease him is an obstacle in our practice. The best way of all to please him, the best means of devotion to him, is to practise all his instructions meticulously, doing exactly as he says and not doing anything he says is bad. For example, although Marpa had many other disciples, he was most pleased with Milarepa because it was Milarepa who practised the Dharma teachings he gave.

We should examine our own manner of devotion to the Spiritual Friend. If we find it is good we should rejoice and set our mind continually that way. If on the other hand we lack confidence in our Guru and regard him lightly, we must contemplate the meaning of these teachings so as to correct our attitude.

Meditation 2
The Opportune, Fortunate Rebirth

2a RECOGNITION OF THE OPPORTUNE, FORTUNATE REBIRTH

[140–146] We must understand that our present existence did not come from nothing, but we have had other lives before. After death also, this life will not be consumed without residue, like a candle, but we shall take other types of existence. Our situation is samsara, a continual round of rebirths – from a human existence we go to a god existence, then become an animal, and so on, always dying and taking rebirth in one or other of the three samsaric realms, the Realm of Desire, the Realm of Form, and the Formless Realm. We have no power to decide where we shall go, but are driven helplessly to our next destiny by the defilements and karmic imprints in our mind.

It is our actions (*karma*) that govern the type of rebirth we take. Bad actions lead us, although we do not desire it, to rebirth in the realms of woe; practising the Dharma will lead us to fortunate destinies. It depends solely on our actions, good or bad – we are not free to choose. Since most of us have a large accumulation of negative karmic imprints, the chances are that after this life we shall enter an ill destiny. While we are here in this very special human existence, we must be fully conscious of its value.

There are periods when no Buddha comes to the Earth to give teachings; but at present the teachings of the Buddha are available in this world. We should rejoice in this opportunity.

Then, there are many human existences even on this Earth where the teachings of the Buddha are present, which allow no possibility of meeting these teachings. Such an existence, however well-off one is, is of no great use. But we are actually able to receive the teachings.

The possibility of access to the teachings does not in itself make one's existence valuable, for there are people who live in a Buddhist country and may even sleep next to the Sutras but have no interest in the Buddha's teachings. If one has a whole library full of Buddhist texts, but does not want to put them into practice, one is no better than a library mouse. But we have a certain interest in the teachings and wish to practise them for ourself.

Another favourable condition we have is that we are not lacking any of the senses – we can see our teacher, and hear what he says.

All this, though good, is not sufficient. If we did not have a teacher with personal experience of the Dharma who could explain it to us, it would be like having a field with nothing to plant in it. However, not only are we human beings, in a place where the Buddha's teachings exist, but we have found a teacher who can explain the teachings.

In addition, we are not all alone, but have the support of others practising similarly. We are not on the point of dying for lack of food and shelter, but have the material necessities of life, so we are free to practise the Dharma.

This is just a brief explanation of the meaning of the text[35] so that you can contemplate on it. It is important to analyse this teaching in direct relation to oneself, otherwise it can be of no real benefit. We have to recognize that our present state of existence is quite extraordinary in that so many conditions favourable to the practice of Dharma have come together all at once.

If we go into town we can see many other human beings, but we should ask ourself how many of them have the special circumstances described here, such as meeting the teachings of the Buddha and having a Spiritual Friend. Most of them are not in a position to come into contact with the Dharma, because of their mental attitude: they do not accept it. We should try to be conscious in this way of the preciousness of these special circumstances, wherever we are.

Our remarkable present situation has not come about accidentally, without cause. The principal cause is that we have practised Dharma before this life and so received the inspiration of the Three Jewels. It is good that we have attained this rare opportunity, but it does not last long and we cannot see where we are going to go afterwards. We must therefore be careful not to waste it while we have it, but use it well by engaging in the practice of Dharma, setting our mind firmly in a positive direction right now. To spend such an existence in trivial actions, motivated by greed and hatred, pursuing good food and a pleasant situation, getting attached to some people and fighting with others, so accumulating only causes for bad rebirths in the future, is really not worthy of it.

2b THINKING ABOUT THE GREAT VALUE OF THE OPPORTUNE, FORTUNATE REBIRTH

[147] This opportune, fortunate rebirth that we have now is not merely rare – many combinations of conditions are rare but of no particular significance – but it is extremely useful. If we could choose between an entire universe full of jewels and an opportune, fortunate rebirth, we would have to select the opportune, fortunate rebirth, for it is far more valuable than any external wealth. If we had all the wealth in the world then of course we could have good food every day, fine clothing, and comfortable accommodation, but that wealth could not free us from even the smallest suffering in future lives.

There are many purposes for which the opportune, fortunate rebirth is useful. Most immediately, it enables one to live a wholesome life and thus experience happiness in this very life. [148] It is also very valuable in terms of the next life, since it provides the basis for practising the method for avoiding rebirth in the realms of woe, where the worst of experiences are encountered. Rebirth in a realm of woe is caused by the imprints of negative actions which are present in our mind. By getting rid of these imprints we can close the door which would otherwise lead us to unfortunate rebirths. We can get rid of them only by ourself performing practices of purification – no-one else can do it for us. The practices of purification involve [the four forces]:

(a) becoming strongly aware of the negative nature of the unvirtuous action;
(b) determining not to commit such an action again;
[(c) taking Refuge in the Three Jewels and generating *Bodhicitta* for the benefit of all sentient beings, since any negative action is against the Three Jewels and sentient beings;³⁶] and
(d) remedial practices such as reciting mantras.

Using the opportune, fortunate basis that we have now, we can become human beings again in the next life, or gods, by practising morality and creating the specific causes. But with millions of American dollars, one could not buy a human or divine existence, thus from the point of view of the Dharma, this opportune, fortunate basis is far more precious than any external wealth.

[149] With this human basis, we can not only attain high estate within samsara, but if we desire to free ourself from samsaric existence altogether, we can obtain, based on this opportune, fortunate rebirth, an existence with eight special qualities that is ideal for achieving Liberation.³⁷

[150] The most deep-seated purpose of human existence is the aim of benefiting oneself and all others, not just superficially and temporarily, but perfectly and forever. To do this we must attain the state of Enlightenment. This can be done on the basis of this existence, but although this is our innermost desire, there are many obstacles and it is not easy to accomplish. It is often said that one can attain Enlightenment in this very life-time by the practice of Tantra; this is so, but to practise Tantra one needs certain qualifications. If we have not already ripened our mind through training in the Sutra teachings, we can see for ourself that we cannot achieve anything through Tantra.

Therefore we must be skilful in the way we try to practise. There are, for example, practices available to us which enable us to be reborn in Pure Lands such as Sukhāvatī, Yiga Chödzin, Shambhala, or the Pure Land of Tārā. In these places it is very easy to practise the Dharma. On the one hand, unfavourable conditions are absent: there is no suffering of sickness or old age, or of heat or cold; and the defilements such as greed, hate and delusion are suppressed and cannot interfere with the practice. On the other hand, every favourable condition is present: one can meet Buddhas, Bodhisattvas and deities and receive teachings from them, and with one's mind unobstructed by the arising of defilements one has clear wisdom and faith and all the internal requirements for Dharma practice.

To make an analogy, suppose one wishes to travel from Switzerland to India. Some people hitch-hike, but this is very difficult and uncertain; you may eventually get to India but the journey is very long. It is much easier and quicker to work hard in Switzerland for a few months, earning money, and then take the plane.[38]

The practices for rebirth in Pure Lands are quite easy and very effective. First one must learn about the fine qualities of these places, from study or from teachings such as the present one. Then the desire to be reborn in such a place naturally arises; much as when people keep telling us that such-and-such a beach is very beautiful and pleasant, we start wanting to go there.

Then we must establish a special connection with the lord of the Pure Land we have chosen. For example, if we wish to be born in Sukhāvatī, we must try to set up a link with Amitābha Buddha; or if in Yiga Chödzin, with Maitreya. We must also dedicate the virtue of whatever positive activities we do, such as prostrating, reciting mantras and meditating, to be reborn in that Pure Land so that we can train our mind there and become able to help others.

We cannot get to such a Pure Land by going around with a lot of money trying to buy a ticket, but we can do these practices. Therefore this opportune, fortunate rebirth, which enables us to do these practices, is of far greater value than any material acquisition.

We human beings are like bees in a room, who although there are doors open, just keep hitting themselves against a closed window. There are doors leading to positive states of existence, but we are so involved in mundane affairs and worry that we cannot see the right door.

[151] With this existence we can practise the means to attain Liberation, free of all the sufferings and dissatisfactions of samsaric existence.

[152] On this opportune, fortunate basis, this human body, we can go still further and attain perfect Enlightenment, and benefit others with Buddha-activities. While we are not actually putting all our effort into trying to do this, still the possibility is there, and many beings such as Milarepa and Tsongkhapa serve as examples.

[153] If we ripen our mind by training on the common Path taught in Sutra teachings, we can then enter the door of Tantra and undertake practices that can lead to Enlightenment in this life, even in a few years.

In fact, countless human beings have attained Liberation and Enlightenment in one life, and our situation is no different from theirs: we can do it too. We have the same opportunity that Milarepa had, perhaps better, since we are in good material circumstances, well-fed and strong. Of course, he and the others had to follow completely and without mistake the Path shown by their Spiritual Friends, but we are not doing this; we just waste our life in worldly involvements, so we are still here.

[154] Through this opportune, fortunate human existence, then, we can avoid being born in realms of woe, and we can attain Liberation or Enlightenment. Thus it has very great value, superior even to that of a wish-granting jewel. [155] If, having met such an existence, we are still attached to fruitless work, confused with trivial matters, and not practising the Dharma, then really we must be crazy.

[156-7] If we sit just a few minutes contemplating the defects of samsaric existence, thinking that we must train so that we can benefit all sentient beings, and perhaps reciting a mantra such as OṂ MAṆI-PADME HŪṂ, this is of great benefit. Even one minute, even a single second of this human life has great value if used in the right way. Here in Switzerland

there are factories with very expensive machinery that is run day and night so as not to leave it unproductive for even five minutes. But actually if such machinery is left idle it is not important, for even if you run it all the time it produces only lifeless objects. It cannot produce anything of the slightest value for future lives. The really great waste is that of not using our opportune, fortunate existence to accomplish the benefit of ourself and all other beings.

We must be aware that whether we practise Dharma or not, this existence is going to end. When he arrives at the point of death, the Dharma practitioner can look back on his life and see that he made as much effort as he could to make it meaningful, so now it is all right if he dies. But one who has not practised the Dharma will see that although he attained such a wonderful opportunity, he just let it go to waste. We tend to think that we are very stable and will last for a long time, whereas a rosary, for example, may break at any moment. But in fact, if the rosary is just left, it will last for centuries, unless some mouse eats it – we are not as durable as that. Many people have quite fragile objects that belonged to an ancestor of theirs perhaps two centuries ago, such as a pair of glasses, still in good condition, [although the original owner has long since passed away].

This contemplation should make us conscious that our present opportunity is very precious and must not be wasted. The reasons given are very hard to refute. We must therefore develop the attitude of striving to make the best possible use of this existence.

2c THINKING ABOUT THE RARITY OF THE OPPORTUNE, FORTUNATE REBIRTH

To further induce us to make proper use of this opportune, fortunate rebirth, we contemplate a third point, its rarity, or the difficulty of obtaining it.

[158] To illustrate the rarity, the Kadampa geshes frequently quoted this story about a man crippled in both legs, who fell from the upper story of a house and landed on the back of a wild ass who happened to be underneath. The ass bolted, with the man hanging on for dear life. When they eventually came to

a settlement, a spectator observed that the man was singing, and asked him why. The cripple replied that it was the first time he had ever ridden on the back of a wild ass, and there was no chance of its happening again. When could he sing for joy if not now?

Clearly it is very unlikely that a cripple would not only fall on the back of a wild ass but manage to stay on; our falling into this special human situation is similarly unlikely. What else should we do but take this unique opportunity to practise Dharma to the best of our ability?

Some may think the example inapt, since we can see human beings all around us but never see cripples falling on the backs of wild asses. But [as explained in 2a above,] we are not discussing just the obtaining of a human form, but the very special human existence with the [eighteen] factors of opportunity and good fortune.

[159–160] By looking at the causes of the opportune rebirth, we can see how difficult it is to obtain the result. The main cause is the practice of the morality of abandoning the ten unvirtuous actions. The co-operative causes are the practices of Giving, other types of Morality, Patience, and so forth. So that these causes ripen properly, one must also pray in a pure manner, unmarred by the eight worldly concerns.[39] These causes do not arise spontaneously but are established with difficulty.

Seeing in this way the difficulty of obtaining this opportunity, we should realize that since it is so rare we must make effort to use it well. After each point in the meditation, we should make this strong decision.

[161] We should also realize that it is extremely hard for us to obtain another such opportunity in the future – we have to make effort to create the causes. If we think we have already created sufficient causes, this will weaken our practice. We may think that five years ago we did this, last year we did that, and last month we did something else, all of which was creating the causes for an opportune, fortunate rebirth. This may be true, but still it happens that great anger arises in one's mind – if this is directed towards certain objects, it can destroy all the virtue one has created. Wrong views too can destroy one's roots of

virtue. Thus no matter what we have done in the past, there is no certainty in the future, and we must continue to strive.

[162] Perhaps we think that in the past we made great effort in accumulating the causes, and in the meantime we have had no great anger or wrong views, so we are probably all right. This again may be true, and it is excellent that we have accumulated such virtue and not allowed it to be destroyed. Still we should examine our mind to see which is stronger, virtue or negativity. If we are honest with ourself, we shall probably have to admit that negativity is stronger, for defilements such as attachment, pride and jealousy arise easily and spontaneously, whereas to do anything virtuous requires conscious effort and care. We see people who lose control of themselves, taken over by strong defilements; but to see the strong arising of positive states of mind is very rare. Thus now and in the future, non-virtuous attitudes are likely to be more prevalent in our mind than virtuous ones. We should therefore continue to make effort in our practice of Dharma.

[163] We can also see that the opportune, fortunate rebirth is rare since one of its factors, the presence of the Buddha's Teaching, only occurs rarely and does not last long. This too should motivate us to make the most of this opportunity.

[164] The Buddha himself taught the rarity of human existence by picking up a little dust on his fingernail, and explaining to the monks that while they were then in a happy state of existence, it was very easy to fall into the realms of woe. The number of beings in happy destinies was like the dust on his nail, while the number in ill destinies was like the dust of the whole Earth. [165] He also taught that of the five destinies of samsaric beings, the greatest number of beings were in hell states, the next greatest number were pretas, and next animals. Although we cannot ourselves see the hell beings and pretas, they are spoken of in the Sutras. The Buddha explained the states of rebirth as dependent on the degree of negativity of the action which throws a being into them: extremely negative actions throw one into the hell realms, less extreme ones into preta rebirth, and ones of comparatively slight negativity into rebirth as an animal.

[166] We can also make direct comparison from our own

experience to see that there are vastly more non-human than human beings. In Switzerland, for example, there are about six million human beings in the whole country; but in just one Swiss field, in summer, there are far more insects and small creatures than that. The text compares the number of such tiny creatures in a small area to the number of people in a city or country. The author who said there were not more than a few hundred thousand people in a city or country was writing in a sparsely-populated region of Tibet; even if we carp and say there are cities of ten million and countries such as America of over two hundred million, the force of the comparison is unchanged. Obviously there are far more animals than human beings in the world.

[167] Going one step further, let us divide human beings into those who are interested in spiritual practice and those who are not. The former are a small minority, and even among them it is hard to find any who have the complete opportune, fortunate rebirth and are genuinely engaging in practice that will be fruitful.

[168–9] The text quotes several examples from the Sutras[40] that illustrate the extreme rarity of the opportune, fortunate rebirth.

[170] So we should use these three approaches to realize that the opportune, fortunate rebirth is very rare:

(a) "Cause": since the causes are hard to create, the result must be rare.
(b) "Effect": considering the numbers of beings in the various destinies, [which are the effect of their actions,] the fraction with the opportune, fortunate rebirth is tiny.
(c) "Examples", as given in verses 168–9, develop our understanding of the rarity.

Having recognized the rarity of the opportune, fortunate rebirth, we must make the strong decision to use it well.

[171] What are we doing with this rare and precious opportunity? A Kadampa Geshe said we should feel about it like a certain Tibetan who was visiting one of the few places in Tibet where one could get fish to eat. Having had a large meal of this rare delicacy, so tasty and difficult to obtain, he was so worried

that he might vomit it up and waste it that he tied a cord tightly round his neck to keep it down. Likewise, if we just die without having used our opportune, fortunate rebirth, it is a complete waste.

If we do not make an effort to accomplish the benefit of ourself and others, then one year goes by after another until we arrive at the point of death, and looking back we see this marvellous opportunity has just run to waste. A certain lama said, "The first twenty years of my life I did not practise Dharma because I did not know anything about it. The second twenty years I decided I was going to practise but I did not have time just at that moment. Then the next twenty years I spent saying I was not able to practise any more. That is my life."

[172] There are supposed to be some lakes where a great many jewels naturally occur. If we come to such a place and do not fill our pockets and our bags with these jewels, it is an opportunity wasted. Similarly now, if we do not recognize the value of our life and use it in Dharma practice, there could be no greater loss.

[173] We have a lot of conditions conducive to Dharma practice, each one rare. [See root text.] [174] Wisdom that can discriminate clearly between right and wrong or between the various aspects of things is rare. Since negativity arises much more easily than virtue, periods when the mind is positive and fit to engage in Dharma are rare. In addition, we need friends to help us, people who will strengthen our practice. [175] If each condition is rare in its own right, for them all to come about at the same time is prodigious. Recognizing strongly how very special this opportunity is will enable us to put great effort into making it really meaningful.

[176] Whatever we have done up to now is past. If we have accomplished something worthwhile, good; if we have let our life go to waste in distraction, just drifting without control, that cannot be changed. But from now on, we should do our best to use our life meaningfully and not waste it. We must resolve strongly to do this.

To return to the example of the expensive factory machinery, given in the last section: we can easily recognize the waste involved in leaving the machinery idle, because we can see directly what it can produce and what value this has. The value of the opportune, fortunate rebirth, on the other hand, is not something we can see immediately. Though we may say we believe it is valuable, very likely we do not have real conviction about this as we do about the machinery. If we did, we could not bear to waste even a moment.

A certain lama had stuffed his meditation cushion with chips of wood, for want of anything better. As he was sitting in meditation, a sharp splinter stuck in his leg and a trickle of blood ran down and across the floor. Just then, someone came in and asked him why he did not pull the splinter out so that he could meditate better. The lama replied that if he died while he was taking the splinter out he would have wasted a very precious opportunity. This is the kind of conviction required.

Like most meditations of the *Lam rim*, this is an analytical meditation, using many reasons to overcome the many possible doubts and to incite one to use the present opportunity to the utmost of one's ability.

The Actual
Practice

Part Two
Path of
the Inferior Person

Note

[The first two meditations are concerned with laying the foundation for the practice and inciting oneself to practise. The rest are the actual practice of the Path, divided into three grades according to the motivation involved, as described in the Preface (pp. 8–9) and in the section on Taking Refuge (verses 12–15). The "inferior" religious person, whose practice is aimed at avoiding rebirth in the realms of woe (see commentary to verse 12), must practise Meditations 1 to 6. The "intermediate" religious person, aiming at Liberation from samsara (verses 13–14), must practise Meditations 1 to 8. The "superior" religious person, or Bodhisattva, aiming to free all beings from suffering forever (verse 15), must practise all the meditations.]

Meditation 3
Death

The main obstacle one tries to overcome on the Path of the inferior religious person is the eight worldly concerns.[41] These are elements of our own mind, not something physical that could be cut out by surgery. The most effective way to overcome them is by meditating on one's mortality.

The eight worldly concerns are concern with getting four pleasant things in this life – pleasures such as good food, praise, [gain, and good reputation] – and avoiding their four opposites. Whenever our mind is contaminated by any of these concerns, whatever we are doing becomes a mere worldly practice, even if it is an ostensibly Dharma practice such as reciting prayers.

Some people think that meditating on their mortality is useless and only makes one depressed. Others think that they need not meditate on death because this is a practice for inferior people, those [spiritually] weak and immature. Both these attitudes are quite mistaken.

The Buddha himself taught many times the importance of meditating on impermanence and mortality. He mentioned it in his first sermon near Varanasi, and almost his last words as he passed into parinirvāṇa at Kuśinagarī were, "Everything, whether stationary or movable, is bound to perish in the end."[42]

He also illustrated its importance with many examples. In the [*Mahāparinirvāṇa-*]*Sūtra*, he said:

> Of all ploughings of a field, the autumn one is the best. Of all footprints, the elephant's footprint is the best. And of all recognitions, the recognitions of impermanence and mortality are the best. They eliminate all attachments of the three realms, ignorance, and pride.[43]

In addition,

> It is also praised as being the hammer that destroys all defilements and misconduct at once, and the great gateway leading to the accomplishment of all virtues at once.[44]

Mindfulness of impermanence and death is important at the beginning of the Path, to impel one to engage in the practice; it is important in the middle, to maintain one's energy; and it is important at the end, to induce one to complete the practice [and receive Enlightenment].

Still, while in general this meditation is an excellent method, it can be harmful if one is in a state of great nervous tension. In that case one should relax and contemplate more pleasant aspects of the Dharma, then meditate on death again once one has got rid of the nervous tension.

3a THINKING ABOUT THE CERTAINTY OF DEATH

[177] This opportune, fortunate basis that we have is, [as we have seen,] very rare and valuable. Now we are to contemplate how fragile and short-lived it is. The text compares this body to the dew on the grass in the morning, which lasts only a short time before either the wind blows it off or the sun dries it up.

[3a.1 *Death will certainly come, and is not to be turned back by any circumstance*][45]

[178] This is not a feature peculiar to our own present situation. Every samsaric body one can possibly take, whether that of a human being, an animal, a hell being, a preta, or a god, is

extremely impermanent and will quickly pass away.

[179] Wherever we go, death is inevitable: whether we live on the moon, in the sky, on the sea-floor, or hidden away in mountains, there is no way to avoid it.

[180] Nor is there a time in which one can avoid death. Of beings who have lived in the past, even very long ago, not one has escaped death. We cannot find anyone escaping it now, and we can be sure no-one will be able to do so in the future either.

[181–2] Not even the strongest samsaric beings, even Brahma, Shiva or Vishnu, have the power to overcome death, any more than a small insect has. There is nothing we can do about it: we cannot bribe our way out of dying, there is no special diet that will let us avoid death; it is impossible to stop death by raising a great army and making war on it. Also, although usually if we are sick we can receive some help from a doctor, when it is time for us to die, all the doctors in the world cannot save us.

[3a.2 *My life is diminishing without interruption, and nothing can be added to it*]

This human life is the result of actions we have done in the past. Now we have obtained it, there is no way to make it any longer. The same applies in all samsaric destinies. The various Tantric practices for long life can clear away certain hindrances that have arisen since we were born and would otherwise have shortened our life, but they cannot add anything to our karmically-determined span.[46]

So far from increasing, this life is all the time being used up. Whatever we are doing – working, playing or sleeping – it is gradually ebbing away. Second by second, hour by hour, day by day, we are approaching the end.

[183] We can read historical accounts of people who lived in the past, describing just what they did so that they seem to be alive; but usually when we check we find they have already passed away. And we can see there are many millions of people in the world today, but in a hundred years' time, only one or two of them will still be alive. This is easy to understand.

[184] Our life is like a butter lamp: from the moment it is lit, its fuel is exhausted without pause and it inexorably ap-

proaches the end. [185] In the same way, from the moment of conception onwards, our life is being exhausted and we are heading towards the end.

When a cow is walking towards the slaughterhouse, each step brings it one step closer to death. With our own life, too, each day that passes brings us one day closer to our death. Between now and one week ago, a week has passed, therefore I am now a week nearer death than I was then. With analytical meditations of this pattern we can induce the feeling of impermanence.

Perhaps at present we have a good situation – good food, adequate clothes, pleasant surroundings – but even so we are preoccupied with trying to get more, so that we can be even happier. The reason for such dissatisfaction is a lack of recognition of the fact of impermanence and mortality. If one really has this recognition, then the constant desire for even more pleasures, though not abandoned completely, dwindles into insignificance.

[186] If, while a man, led by soldiers, is walking the last mile to his place of execution, people offer him all sorts of things such as flowers and good bread which normally make one happy, it will not cheer him up in the least, since he will be completely absorbed in the thought of his coming death. [187] But I too, from the moment of conception on, have been racing towards my death like a galloping cowboy in a movie, and still am. Do I have any occasion for being happy and indulging in negative actions?[47]

[188] At present, we have somewhere to live, friends and relatives, possessions, and our body to which we are very attached – if someone injures our body we feel we ourselves have been hurt. Yet all these things are ours only for a while: soon we shall separate from them. We think "my house, my relatives, my body," but this state in which they are ours is just like a dream, which will soon pass away, so why should we be attached to it?

[189] Continually the years, the months, the days and nights are going by. Our life is like a heap of grass from which a white mouse and a black mouse take one blade after another, in turn – the white mouse being the days and the black the nights.

Since the heap is finite, eventually it must all be used up.

[3a.3 *Even while I live, I have no time to practise Dharma*]

[190] Much of our life has already gone; we do not know how much we have left, but a lot of it we shall certainly spend in sleeping and necessary tasks, and probably a lot in arguing and insignificant actions, so that the time left to practise Dharma seriously will be very small. [191] If we examine our day carefully, we find that much of it is consumed in trivial tasks and activities, and very little in genuine spiritual practice. Seeing how little time we actually have for practice, we should develop the urge to use it as well as we can.

[192] Thus we must realize that our life is very limited, but since at present we have conditions suitable for the practice of Dharma, we must use what time we have in the most positive way possible.

We go through life like a cow trying to eat a patch of grass on the edge of a cliff, involving ourself in one worldly situation after another and trying to get something out of it. Eventually we fall over the cliff, still unsatisfied; or maybe we do get what we were after, but then immediately fall over the cliff anyway.

Around the world we can see many palaces that belonged to the kings and queens of different countries; but in most cases the kings and queens have gone. We must see that everyone is mortal, including ourself, and ask ourself if we are really succeeding in eliminating negativity and practising virtue, so that we shall be able to die without regret.

3b THINKING ABOUT HOW THERE IS NO CERTAINTY WHEN I SHALL DIE

[193] We contemplate the uncertainty of the time of death to see that we must engage in the practice of Dharma immediately, without procrastinating. At present we have life in our body, but it may well happen today that these two will separate and this body become a corpse, ripe for burial or cremation.

[3b.1 *The lifespan of people of Earth is uncertain*]

[194] [While elsewhere there are human beings whose life-

span is fixed,] here the lifespan is very variable. Once upon a time people lived for countless years; one day they will again, but first the typical human lifespan will decrease so much that it will be considered remarkable if someone lives to be as old as ten years. Besides, we cannot predict on the basis of his present age how much longer any particular person will live. We can see for ourselves that many young people die while there are old people who go on living for years and years.

It is easy to see this uncertainty in the case of other people, but we have to apply it to ourself and realize that the time of our own death is completely uncertain, and therefore we must practise Dharma straight away.

[195] Some people get up in the morning but are dead by the afternoon. Some go to sleep expecting to wake up, but never do. Some are alive in one moment and dead the next. Take for example President Sadat,[48] who one moment was watching a parade and the next moment was dead. Just seeing that others can die suddenly is not necessarily going to change our attitude, but if we apply their example to ourself and see that our own life is equally uncertain, it is very beneficial.

[3b.2 *Very many sets of circumstances lead to death, and few to staying alive*]

[196–7] Circumstances that can shorten our life or end it suddenly are extremely common. Apart from all kinds of accidents that induce sudden death, there are other external conditions such as harm by human and other enemies, [and internal conditions such as diseases.]

[198] The circumstances conducive to maintaining life, however, are very limited. [199] Even these can turn into conditions for ending the life. Food, for example, normally helps us to continue, but sometimes it can become harmful and poisonous, and kill us. Medicines likewise are designed to help us live, but sometimes they work in the opposite way. We therefore cannot assume that these things will automatically help us stay alive.

[200] Our life is like [the flame of a lamp or] a leaf on a tree, blown violently by the strong gale of these conditions causing death. At any moment [the flame can blow out or] the

leaf can be torn off the tree. Yet though it is unquestionable that our life can disappear very easily, we feel that it is stable and will continue indefinitely, like the ground on which the world is built. This unrealistic thought is a manifestation of the mental demon of grasping ourself as permanent.

[3b.3 *The body is very weak*]

[201] Our life is as fragile as a bubble that appears on fast-moving water and is gone in a few moments. Any idea that we shall be here for a long time is completely mistaken.

[202] The rocks, mountains and so forth of the world are extremely durable, yet even they are eventually broken down into dust. But our life is more like a clay vessel, which breaks very easily when at any moment the conditions arise, such as being dropped a little way.

[203] What if I am healthy just now? Conditions that cause sudden death can appear any moment and envelop us, like clouds on a mountain. One minute we look out of the window and see it is a beautiful, sunny day; the next, the clouds have rolled in and it is dark and gloomy. Thus if we do not look after our mind but are simply concerned with petty things such as our work, last year, or next year, then some time or other, death will suddenly be upon us.

[204] Usually we make plans for what we shall do tomorrow morning: I have this work to do and I shall get up at such and such a time. But in reality, we cannot say which will come first, that awakening and work, or the experience of the intermediate state between death and birth. Quite possibly we shall not wake up. Therefore we must resolve to practise the Dharma now.

Reflecting again and again, over a long period, on these reasons why the length of one's life is uncertain and one could very well die soon, one develops an increasingly strong awareness of the imminence and unpredictability of death. In proportion to this increase of awareness, one's interest in trivial activities will diminish, until one is concerned only with the practice of Dharma and nothing else matters. Such mindfulness of one's mortality is the gateway to genuine spiritual practice.

3c THINKING ABOUT HOW NOTHING EXCEPT THE DHARMA CAN HELP AT THE TIME OF DEATH

If we may die at any moment, then what is there of any value that will not be negated by our death? The next point in the meditation makes us realize that only the Dharma is of any value.

[3c.1   *Friends and relatives [cannot accompany me]*]

[205] When Death seizes me, then even if all the sentient beings throughout the three realms of samsara have great love for me and wish to help me, none can be of the slightest use. However much they want to save me from death, it is impossible.

[3c.2   *Possessions [cannot accompany me]*]

[206] Material wealth also cannot help when one is dying. Even if one owns all the riches of an entire country, not a single atom can he take with him, although he has strong attachment and cannot bear to part with anything usable.

[3c.3   *My body [cannot accompany me]*]

[207] Even this body, which we have cherished so much, is no use at the time of death. It is left behind, while the component of consciousness that goes on is propelled unpredictably by the force of karma to any of the six destinies, just as a leaf blown off a tree by an autumn wind may end up anywhere.

[208] When we die, our body, possessions and friends and loved ones are of no use to us at all. But there is something that can help at that time, namely our own spiritual practice.

[209] Since at the time of death only our practice of Dharma is useful, all the work and involvements of this life will fade away like a dream. In the light of our death, they are quite worthless, since they are then left completely behind. If we

dream of being very wealthy or of eating or drinking very well, the objects we dream about cannot help us: when we wake up, the dream food has not filled our stomach at all. Equally, when we die, all our worldly activities will fade uselessly away. So we must now put all these insignificant activities aside and engage wholeheartedly in the practice of the *Lam rim*, the Path to Buddhahood.

Many people are obsessed with the idea that ordinary work and involvement in worldly responsibilities have some benefit. Some wear out their hands with toil, making them so hard and callused that when one shakes hands with them it is like holding a piece of wood. They keep working until the very day they die, when they no longer have a body to work with. Such people are completely confused: they are simply running around in circles, achieving nothing at all. Not only is such work useless: a great deal of physical and mental evil accompanies it, so that the longer one lives in that way, the more evil one accumulates.

The force of attachment completely blocks one's advancement on a spiritual Path. One is a prisoner, bound by ropes of greed. Consider a wealthy entrepreneur, who owns many factories: he knows that he must die and that he will be able to take nothing with him, yet he continues to live a completely pointless life, just following his greed.

For meditating on death to induce the wish to practise, we have of course to accept the existence of future lives. Anyone we ask will agree that he or she is going to die, but how they feel about this will vary widely, because of their different ideas about the future life.

A Tibetan lama asked his disciples: "The future lives are much longer than this one – do you have provisions for this journey? They are much harsher – do you have a suitable companion?" The provisions and companion we need are our own practice of the Dharma. A whole mountain of gold cannot help us in our future lives; but the imprint of one mantra can.

It is best if we can devote our daily life completely to the Dharma. If we still have many other tasks and cannot do this, we must strive to increase the influence of Dharma in our life.[49]

Meditation 4
The Sufferings of the Realms of Woe

4a HOW TO MEDITATE ON THE SUFFERINGS OF THE HELLS

If we do not prepare for our death by practising Dharma, then most probably we shall be reborn in a hell. For Westerners, certain explanations are necessary at this point. If one teaches about the sufferings of the various hells to Tibetans, they accept it without question; in Christians of the more traditional type also, such teachings would not arouse doubt. But people with little trust in the Dharma and with a strongly sceptical attitude will probably believe little of them.

They disbelieve because they cannot see hells in this world. If one tells them the hot hells are like the hottest deserts in Africa and the cold hells are like the Arctic, they would still doubt their existence until they could locate them exactly.

[But we may understand the existence of hells by considering their causes.] Our actions of mind, which determine our actions of speech and body, can cause us to experience either physical and mental suffering, or physical and mental happiness. On the positive side, if we develop our mind through the practice of the Dharma, it can get better and better; one can attain the destiny of a human being or a god; one can become completely free of samsara and attain Arhantship; and ultimately, developing the mind to total perfection one can realize complete Buddhahood. These positive states of mind are described in many texts. But it is also possible for the mind to become more and more habituated to negativity, in which case one's state of being becomes increasingly degenerate. This degeneration can continue virtually without limit.

We know that developing the mind needs a lot of effort; but degeneration just comes naturally. Looking into our mind, we can see that we have many thoughts coming up all the time, and most of them are negative rather than pure. These thoughts leave behind their own type of trace or imprint on the mind. Subsequently, these imprints lie latent until one meets conditions that activate them; then they can ripen as a new state of existence, type of body and so on, or they can create one's environment, or cause an unpleasant or pleasant experience. Every suffering one experiences is the result of the ripening of a negative karmic imprint carried on one's own mind. The worlds we find ourselves in are not separate from us but arise from our own mental imprints.

Shāntideva asks:

> By whom were they zealously
> Forged, the weapons of the hells?
> Who made the burning iron ground?
> Whence did those conflagrations come?[50]

Another reading [in accord with the extant Sanskrit text] has "women" instead of "conflagrations", meaning the temptresses of the Shālmalī Forest (see commentary to verses 222–3 below). And he answers himself:

> The Sage has taught that everything
> Like that is from evil mind.
> There is nothing to be feared
> In the three realms, apart from mind.[51]

When we are born in a hell, our aggregates – body and mind – as a hell being are the karmic fruition (*vipāka-phala*) of an evil action we have done in the past, whose imprint ripened [as we died from the previous life in such a way as to throw us into this new existence]. The various frightful appearances around us, such as the red-hot iron ground, the surrounding mountains, the fire we are in, the guardians, and their weapons and machines of torture, are the "dominant result" (*adhipati-phala*) of further evil actions, whose imprints on our mind are also ripening.

Explanations differ, but I think that all these appearances and the experiences we undergo in hell are illusory.[52] It is not like our present world, where if we commit a crime we are arrested by real police and put in a real, externally existing prison. It only appears to be real, and we experience suffering created by our karma.

The different types of mental imprints can not only generate the appearance of corresponding surroundings, but block the perception of incompatible ones. For example, if one is born as a preta who must experience great thirst, then even if one was just by the Lake of Geneva, one's active set of imprints would prevent one from seeing even a small drop of water. Or if a hell-being were in this room, he would be unable to see it, since his mind would be completely taken up by his own experience of suffering.

On our own mind there are a great many imprints of evil thoughts and actions. If we do not purify them by confession, they will certainly ripen in some future existence, and go on producing suffering until their power is exhausted. But by sincere confession we can render them powerless to bring about a suffering result. To avoid meeting a hell existence, we must practise confession at once, and be careful not to add yet more negative imprints to our store.

4a.1 *How to meditate on the sufferings of the hot hells*

[210] "Alas!" (*kye ma!*) is an exclamation of sorrow and suffering at the thought that this rare opportunity we have gained, with a human body, will soon perish. Certainly we shall die; and after that, our future destiny is governed by our karma, we have no choice where to be reborn. Moreover, negative attitudes and behaviour are very strong in us, while the positive is very weak; if this accumulated negative karma

throws us into the realms of woe, shall we be able to bear the suffering?

[211] "Underground, many leagues from here":[53] it does not matter whether the hells are really at *x* kilometres below the earth's surface. It is a natural way of thinking about "higher and lower" realms to imagine the "higher" realms [of the gods] up in the sky and the "lower" realms down below.

The ground is of red-hot, burning iron and the whole place is full of flames. The beings born there experience the suffering of being burned alive, like animals caught in a forest fire, with nothing but fire on all sides and no way out, but their karma is such that it hurts them even more than being burned in an ordinary fire hurts us.

In the present life, people engage in very heavy negative actions such as killing others, and even laugh while they are doing so, but in the future they may well be experiencing the result of this karma and crying and crying. There are eight types of hot hell,[54] with different degrees and kinds of suffering, where one is reborn according to the strength [and type] of one's negative imprints.

[212] Some people in this world harm other sentient beings with various kinds of weapons. This has its special result. You are born in this hell, caught in the fire as described, and find weapons in your hand. Around you are other beings, also armed. In a distressed state of mind, you become very angry with them and fight them, "killing" them and also being wounded and "killed" yourself by their weapons.

If we cut a finger off and fry it in a pan, the frying does not add anything to the pain of having the finger cut off. But in this hell it is different – if a drop of your blood falls on the red-hot iron ground and boils, although it is already separate from your body you experience the pain of its boiling.

All these appearances and sufferings are not separate from you, but entirely the result of your own negative karma.

Having "died" or fallen unconscious in this hell, you come back to life and start fighting again, and the cycle of suffering continues. There is no way to use your mind in Dharma practice such as confessing your past actions: you have to go on experiencing this suffering result until the karma that produced

Meditation 4: The Sufferings of the Realms of Woe 95

it is exhausted. After that you will be reborn in a different existence, possibly even worse.

[213] Next is the hell of the Black Lines, so called because hell guardians with terrifying faces like lions, bulls and so forth seize you and measure your body and mark it out at suitable point with black lines burnt into the flesh. Then they cut you in pieces along these lines. These guardians are not separate individuals, but illusory appearances created by your karma.

If we are put in a fire [or cut up] then after a while we die, but in hell it is different; you may lose consciousness occasionally but then you revive again, you cannot die. The mind cannot depart somewhere else, but must stay there and endure the pain.

When we walk with bare limbs through thick brambles, the thorns tear our flesh and hurt us very much, but this is nothing compared to the suffering in this hell. The causes for such an experience lie within us now, and if we cannot get rid of them in this life, as soon as possible, then in the future they will give rise to their result.

While many actions can lead to this type of existence, the most usual is killing other people or destroying a country with weapons.[55]

[214] In the Crushing Hell, you are again standing on a burning iron ground. Sometimes you are crushed between huge iron mountains, squeezed until all your blood flows out. Sometimes, instead, great rocks or pieces of iron fall from the sky and crush you similarly. Sometimes you are squeezed in a huge machine like a sugarcane press or a printing press. Although you come out as flat as a piece of paper, you remain alive and conscious, and even the squashing and boiling of the blood that has run out produces suffering. Your body is much bigger than a human body, and more sensitive to pain. You cannot die but must undergo the same cycle of suffering again.

This experience too is most likely the result of killing other people. There are a great many ways of doing this, with knives, bombs and so forth – each one leaves an imprint on the mind, which will produce a result of similar nature to the cause. The mountains, rocks and machines are not really there, separate from us, like stones on the road that we see in this life. Some texts say the mountains resemble the faces of the people or animals you have killed. Obviously, the people are not actually there in the shape of mountains and crushing you. All the appearance comes from your karmic imprints; only the suffering it produces is true.[56]

Just as a barley seed can give rise, after it is planted, to a barley sprout and after some months to an ear of barley with many other grains, so the imprints left on our mind by evil actions can throw us into a hell existence and give rise to many sufferings. If we do not purify them by confession, their power will remain and in due course they will produce their fruit.

[215] Now there are the Howling Hells. Still on the burning iron ground, you are surrounded by frightful armed guards, on horseback, who lead you away to an iron building. As soon as you go in, the door shuts automatically and the whole place starts to burn. With no way out, there is nothing to do but howl and cry.

In some places fish are cooked alive, and one can see them suffering unbearably, jumping about in the boiling oil. In this hell the suffering is even worse. It is again the result of killing sentient beings. Whether you kill animals with elaborate machinery as in the West, or by less refined methods such as crushing lice between your fingers, you are just preparing to experience the same suffering yourself in the future.

[216] In the Heating Hell also, you experience the suffering of heat, being cooked like noodles in an enormous cauldron, which instead of water is full of molten iron. While this is like the suffering of a fish fried alive, the fish does die after a while, but in this hell you cannot. Then you are impaled on a big iron rod which they use for stirring the pot; it is stuck right through your body so as to come out at the top of your head.

[217] In the next hell, the guardians impale you on a trident and hold you against the burning iron, turning you over and over as when one roasts a sausage. Your skin is burnt and the blood flows out, and your whole body falls apart. Then the guardians throw the bits on the ground and they all grow together again so that you have the same body as before, and the cycle recommences.

[218] The Avīci Hell is the most fearful of all, completely

filled with fire, which burns your body totally. Someone looking at you from outside could see nothing but fire, and would only recognize there was a being there because of your shrieks of agony.

[219] While you are burning, hell guardians come and inflict other types of suffering. They may pull your tongue out of your mouth, stretch it enormously, and plough it up like a field. Several of them may stand around you and open your mouth with pincers and other tools, pull it so that it is very big, then put in red-hot iron balls, or boiling molten metal, which burns your stomach and all your entrails.[57]

The sufferings described in the text are only a few examples of the possibilities. In fact, there are countless varieties of evil actions, and countless forms of suffering result from their imprints.

Our life is very short, but we spend most of it just amusing ourselves or sometimes fighting with others. In this way we accumulate the causes for rebirths like these. We have to engage in Dharma practices to confess and purify these negative actions, using meditation, mantras and so forth. Contemplating the sufferings of the realms of woe will, if we have faith in their existence, impel us to practise confession very strongly, so that we really can eliminate even the smallest negative imprints from our mind. There will then be no basis for experiencing such terrible sufferings in the future. If we do not believe in the sufferings described here, then although we can still engage in the confession of evil, the practice will not be as powerful.

4a.2 *How to meditate on the sufferings of the Supplementary Hells*

[220] In the [four kinds of] supplementary hells, [which are found outside each gate of the eight hot hells,] the suffering is slightly less.

(a) Reborn in the Pit of Hot Coals, you see a large field full of fire and burning embers, which you have to walk on. Each time you put your foot down it sinks into the burning embers and the skin and flesh are burnt away, giving you much pain. Each time you raise it it is restored, ready to experience the same suffering again.

(b) [221] In another place is a big swamp of stinking excrement. You are made to enter it and have to remain there as long as your karma dictates. Sometimes you sink right in, and worms with sharp, iron beaks bore into your body and devour it. This situation is the result of sexual misconduct, such as adultery with the partners of others and improper sexual practices, and of constantly seeking for sexual pleasure; since the object of sexual desire is something dirty, the result is rebirth in an environment of similarly filthy nature.[58]

(c) Then there is [the Road of Razor Edges], which looks from a distance like a field in which you can walk freely, but turns out to be made entirely of very sharp knives, with their edges pointing upwards. You have to walk on it, cutting your feet into shreds every time you put them down. [222] Next you come to a forest, which looks as if you will be able to rest in its shade. But as soon as you are under the trees, you find their leaves are sharp swords, which fall down on you and hack you to pieces. [222–3] Then you see a tree at the top of which is a person for whom you feel lust or strong attachment, let us say a woman, although it could be a man. To get to her you start climbing the tree, which is all covered with knife-like thorns.[59] As you climb up, the thorns point downwards and pierce every part of your body. When you reach the top you find the woman (or man) is no longer there.[60] Looking down, you see she is now on the ground below. Driven by attachment, you climb down again, but now the thorns are pointing upwards and again they pierce your body all over and tear the flesh. In addition your flesh is eaten by dogs[61] [and iron-beaked birds].

All these sharp weapons of different sorts are not external objects unconnected with your mind, but just the creation of your negative karma. Despite being cut in pieces, you do not die, but through the power of your karma you continuously experience the same sort of suffering.

(d) [223–4] [The fourth type of supplementary hell is the River Vaitaraṇī ("Fordless"). See the root text.[62]]

All these situations are created entirely by ourself. There is no other person forcing us into them. We are free to engage in the actions that cause them, and we are free to engage in the practice of Dharma and rid our mind of such imprints. It is entirely up to us whether we spend our life tiring ourself out with work, earning money, or amusing ourself, until one day we die and there is nothing more to be done, or alternatively, undertake worthwhile practice.

Sometimes when people are dying, a sign indicates the form of their next rebirth. If a dying person feels unbearably hot, crying out for fresh air and taking off all his clothes and bedclothes, as I have often seen happen, this indicates he is likely to be reborn in a cold hell. If instead he feels extremely cold, even though he is in bed, covered with many blankets, in a well-heated room, this is a sign of a coming rebirth in a hot hell. In the West one has little opportunity to observe these phenomena now, because when a dying person is distressed he is immediately injected with a drug such as morphine and becomes hazy or unconscious.

4a.3 *How to meditate on the suffering of the cold hells*

Further examples of the countless types of suffering that result from the limitless possible wrong actions are described in connection with the cold hells. Whereas the hot hells result mainly from killing other sentient beings, the cold hells result principally from holding wrong views, such as disbelief in past and future lives, and destroying representations of the Three Jewels, such as Buddha images and scriptures. We accumulate these negative karmas light-heartedly and do not notice their imprints on the mind, but still they ripen in the form of such a hell existence.[63]

[226] When born in a cold hell, you find yourself on an extensive ground of ice, surrounded by very high, snowy mountains. All around, blizzards rage continually. It is not a pleasant place, like the mountains where we go skiing, but all dark, bitterly cold, and very oppressive and frightening. There is no difficulty in being born there; you do not need a mother and father, you just appear there spontaneously.

[227] In this terrible cold, you are completely naked and shivering. Soon hundreds of thousands of blisters come up on your body, filled with liquid. When the cold becomes more

intense [in the second cold hell], the blisters burst and the liquid runs out on to your body and freezes. If you scream, no-one will hear your voice. There is nothing to do, you just have to remain there.

Our mind is full of imprints that will lead us into such situations, unless we practise now the means to be rid of them. The choice is ours.

In the unbearable cold, you make various noises, as we do now when cold, but they come out as frightful, inhuman sounds which indicate you are dying of cold [only you cannot die]. When it is colder still, your teeth stick together as if they were glued and you cannot make any more sounds.[64] In Tibet, people frozen to death when attempting to cross high passes would die in just this way, with their teeth clenched together as if they were smiling. A later traveller would call out to the victim, "Don't just stand there laughing!" then when he got closer would realize it was a corpse.

When [in the sixth cold hell] the cold becomes even more terrible, your body becomes blue and all hard like ice, and starts to crack. Next, it cracks more and becomes red. From the many open cracks, all the body fluids flow out and freeze. On the mountains of Tibet, one sometimes hears in the night a sudden loud noise, almost like a bomb exploding, from the cracking of a great mass of ice. In these hells, similarly, your body cracks with a loud noise.

[228] We do not like to spend even an hour in a cold room, but the suffering of the cold hells goes on for countless years, longer even than that of the hot hells. You cannot die, and it is impossible to do Dharma practices that would purify the karmic cause: you just have to stay there until it is used up. If your karma is not exhausted when the time comes for the world (including this hell) to be destroyed, you are simply reborn automatically in a similar hell in another world.

We do our negative actions ourself, and we suffer the result ourself: no-one can share it with us.

Just as being trapped in a forest fire bears some resemblance to being in a hot hell, so there are very cold places on Earth, full of ice and snow, on high mountains and elsewhere, which resemble cold hells. There may be hell beings there, experiencing that suffering, but we cannot see them, because our karma is so different.

4b HOW TO MEDITATE ON THE SUFFERINGS OF THE PRETAS

[229] If we are reborn as a preta, it is not through someone else sentencing us to this destiny as a punishment, but through our own mental imprints alone. The main causes are avarice, a form of clinging to one's possessions, not wishing to let them go, whether they are large or small, and also the related attitude of covetousness, wishing to possess what belongs to others. These respectively prevent us from practising Giving, such as helping others with material gifts, and provide us with strong desire for material possessions and enjoyments. The result similar to the cause is thus that the preta, though obsessed with the desire to obtain food or possessions, is always prevented from obtaining them.

The dominant result, or the environment into which the preta is born, is a featureless desert plain, without anything pleasant to see such as mountains, trees, grass, lakes or rivers. The preta's body is exceedingly repulsive to look at, black like a burnt tree-stump and with a very big belly, a very thin neck, and tiny limbs.

[230] There are different kinds of pretas. Some suffer mainly from external problems, some through problems involving their own body. As a preta, you cannot have positive thoughts, but your past habits compel you to be overwhelmed with some concern such as wanting to eat, wanting to drink, or wanting to wear clothes.

A preta obsessed with desire to drink sees a mirage of water in the distance and runs towards it, but when he gets there there is no water to be seen. One desperate to eat sees a vision of food some way ahead, but when he comes close it changes into glowing embers or fire; or he sees a fruit tree, and runs up to it, but just as he is about to pick the fruit, armed guards appear and drive him away. Just as his avarice stopped him being generous to others before, now he experiences the suffering of being unable to obtain material enjoyments.

[231–2] An internally-obscured preta can find food and put

it in his mouth, but then it turns into poison, or flames, which burn him inside. He cannot vomit it as a human being would, but must keep it inside and experience the pain. Various similar sufferings are mentioned in the text. All have the same pattern of wanting something intensely and being frustrated in attempts to get it, so that the mind becomes extremely depressed. As in the hells, the suffering is so great that you cannot think of the Dharma, feel regret for your past actions, or remember your Spiritual Friend.

[233] There are other unpleasant physical sensations. For example, in winter, when the sun is shining we feel a welcome warmth from it, but in a preta it produces a sensation of extreme cold. In the summer, whereas we find moonlight cool and pleasant, to a preta it feels excruciatingly hot.

If we look at our mind, we can see we have avarice and attachment to things. When we go to a restaurant, for example, we check carefully through the menu, rejecting what is not so good and trying to get the best for ourself. We should remember that the result of such an avaricious attitude is life as a preta. Already we have many mental imprints of this type, which will ripen unless we remove them.

Normally we cannot see pretas, but sometimes pretas who live in the same place as human beings can see and be seen by them. "Ghosts" can be manifestations of deceased persons who have become pretas and appear in a form similar to their previous one; or it can be that the person died because of harm by a preta, and this preta is now returning to the person's relatives to cause further harm and confusion. The great hells also are invisible to human beings, but there exist "individual hells" (*pratyeka-naraka*) on Earth, some of whose beings can be seen; some such hell-beings appear in the form of trees, other plants, or rocks.

Our mind is full of imprints waiting to give rise to future destinies, like a department store full of goods ready to be bought. If we wish to improve our situation, we must eliminate our negative imprints now, by confession with the four forces (see p. 70 above). If we have no confidence in this method but continue to be caught up in worldly involvements, these imprints will not go away.

4c HOW TO MEDITATE ON THE SUFFERINGS OF ANIMALS

We all see animals and know they exist. At zoos and in aquaria we can see many different types which live on the earth or in the sea. We may think that animals are a separate category of beings from us, that we cannot be reborn in such a state: this is a mistake. They are beings like us, reborn as animals because of certain actions they committed. If we accumulate that sort of karma, we too are sure to take animal rebirth. For example, if other people who have just eaten with us die of food poisoning, then we know we are going to die the same way, it is only a matter of time. Likewise, we and other beings have created the karma for animal rebirth; they happen to have become animals before us, but it is only a matter of time before we follow them.

While many types of action can lead to an animal destiny, the main type is probably sexual misconduct – sexual activity with an improper object, in an improper manner, at an improper place, or at an improper time.

Although animals have a great many sufferings, their principal problem is being stupid. My dog, Norbu, for example, is always here when I am teaching; but although he is just like us in that he is constantly developing attachment, anger, pride and jealousy, he cannot understand a single word. If I speak loudly he probably thinks I am scolding him. Animals just have no chance to learn the Dharma. We should think about this point and understand that we must practise Dharma now in order to avoid falling into that state when this very short life is over.

[235] Most animals live in the ocean. Some dwell in dark holes, or in insecure homes which are liable to be destroyed in a moment.

[236] Not having houses, they suffer from heat and cold and from the wind. They are in a perpetual state of war with each other; sometimes large animals eat thousands of small ones, and sometimes an army of insects or other small creatures kills a bigger animal.

[237] The animals living among human beings are usually very badly treated. We kill them so that we can eat their meat or wear their skins; we take the milk of cows, which was intended for their calves; we use them for our sport. While in the West

we have cars, tractors and lorries which we can use instead of animals, in poor countries like India animals are made to carry excessively heavy loads. We are shocked to hear about the sufferings very similar to these that were inflicted on human beings in the Nazi concentration camps or by the Chinese in Tibet, but animals do not receive the same consideration. A Buddha or Bodhisattva, however, is not partial like this, but regards all sentient beings, human, animal, or whatever, in exactly the same way.

Thus animals do not have any peace or rest, but are always afflicted.

[238] We often complain about our problems even in this human life – difficult family situations, illnesses, headaches and so on – but this is nothing compared with the bad experiences that other sorts of beings must undergo. We must consider that since we cannot tell what karmas we do or do not have, it is quite possible that we could be reborn as an animal; if we are, the many sufferings and the stupidity characteristic of animals will be very hard to bear.

Meditation 5
The Practice of Taking Refuge

[5a THE CAUSES BASED ON WHICH ONE GOES FOR REFUGE][65]

[239] Since we are carrying on our mind the imprints of past unwholesome actions, which will in future lives lead us into the realms of woe, we must now engage in the practice of Dharma to remove them. Then, even if many people are praying that we should go to Hell, we shall not be reborn in any ill destiny. Otherwise, even if we do not wish to and others are praying that we should not, we shall.

The first step in eliminating these karmic traces is to recognize very clearly that the past actions were mistaken. Secondly, based on this recognition, we must resolve not to be seduced by habit into repeating these actions. This is what we can do for ourself. Then, by going for Refuge to the Three Jewels, we can unite their liberating power with our own effort and become able to overcome the causes of unfortunate rebirth.

Just as a person does not feel he must go to a doctor unless he is aware of having some sickness even if others advise him to, so we cannot take Refuge effectively unless we are aware that the ill destinies at least are of the nature of suffering. Thinking about the actions one has done in the past and the possibility of being reborn in ill destinies, one can develop the genuine attitude of seeking Refuge.

[5b THE OBJECTS TO WHICH ONE GOES FOR REFUGE]

[240] A mere verbal Refuge, just reciting the words, is not sufficient. One takes real Refuge when one's mind is turned completely towards the Three Jewels of Refuge with perfect confidence.

(a) *The Buddha Refuge* is a being in whom all faults have been eliminated and all good qualities perfected. Such a being, with his unobstructed Wisdom-knowledge, his impartial Compassion and his effortless Power, is concerned only to benefit others. His very purpose is to serve as a Refuge, and he is perfectly adapted to it.

We may wonder how it is that so many Buddhas have arisen, all perfect Refuges, and yet we are still suffering. Why have they not liberated us? In fact, the Buddhas always wish to help sentient beings, but the sentient beings have to make this possible by establishing a connection. It is like the way the sun shines everywhere it is allowed in, but cannot shine into a house whose doors are all closed and windows all shuttered. There is no failure on the sun's part in not shining there.[66]

We should think of ourself in relation to the Buddha as a sick person who is seeking treatment from a doctor.

(b) *The Dharma Refuge* is the realizations in the mind of an Enlightened Being, and his abandonments, the Truth of Cessation. These are the actual liberating Refuge because when we can generate them in our own mind, they liberate us.

Dharma is from the Sanskrit root *DHRI*, "to hold", so means holding oneself away from experiencing suffering.

The Dharma corresponds to the medicine or treatment prescribed by the doctor: by developing within oneself the Dharma that the Buddha has taught, one is liberated from the sickness of samsaric suffering. This requires effort from us: we have to practise. Just as the patient will not be cured merely by sleeping in a room full of medicines but must actually take the medicine prescribed, so we cannot be liberated just by wishing and sleeping in a room full of Buddhist texts. Practising the Dharma does not involve any external show but is a slow, internal process of changing one's mental orientation.

(c) *The Sangha Refuge* is the Ultimate Sangha, all the beings who by practising the Buddhist Path have become *Āryas*.

Saṃ-gha (from *sam* + *han* "to strike, come into contact") means literally "in contact together", "in close contact". An *Ārya* being, besides having direct understanding of the ultimate nature of persons and *dharmas*, is able to abandon in succession layer after layer of faults and obscurations of the mind, with their causes; he may be said to be "in close contact with", or inseparable from, these qualities of realization and abandonment.

Such *Ārya* Sangha are our undeceptive friends or helpers in the practice of the Dharma. Other beings are of unstable, constantly changing mind, and liable to degenerate; if we take refuge in such people we are likely to degenerate with them. Therefore we must instead take as our companions the *Ārya* Sangha.

[5c THE MANNER OF GOING FOR REFUGE]

[241] The Three Jewels are thus capable of acting as our Refuge, but from our own side we must develop faith in their power and turn our mind completely towards them. Then the thought of Refuge will arise in our mind.

We need be in no doubt that through this thought of Refuge we shall be able to accumulate a vast amount of merit and eliminate all possibility of being reborn in realms of woe. As was stated above (commentary on verse 19), if the merit of taking Refuge had form, the whole world could not contain it. It could not easily be exhausted – one might as well try to empty the ocean by taking one spoonful of water each day.

Once a god of the heaven of the Thirty-three perceived that he was about to die and be reborn as a pig. Generating regret for the action which was to cause this rebirth, he took Refuge in the Buddha, Dharma and Sangha and was able to avert it.

Faith in the Three Jewels is the basis of all Dharma practice. Without faith, our practice cannot succeed, therefore we must develop it.

[242] Aware that samsaric existence in general is suffering

and that the three ill destinies in particular are extremely terrifying, we must take Refuge now in the Three Jewels, which will guarantee our avoiding these destinies. [243] So to prevent our entering the realms of woe, we take Refuge in the Buddha as the Teacher, in the Dharma as that which we must develop in our mind, and in the Sangha as our helpers.

[5d THE METHOD TO BE PRACTISED AFTER GOING FOR REFUGE]

[244] Having taken Refuge, one must follow the practices of Refuge, otherwise there is little point in taking it.

[5d.1 *The individual practices*]

[Towards each of the Three Jewels of Refuge individually,] there are positive and negative practices, things to do and things to stop doing. Some of these will seem rather dubious to those who do not have real motivation to practise these teachings, but if you have studied this course from the beginning and sincerely intend to transform your mind, there will be no problem.

(a) [245] Since we have taken Refuge in the Buddha as our ultimate Teacher, we should abandon all refuge in teachers of a different line. This is not just sectarianism but is to avoid the dangers of confusion and losing sight of the Goal. If one loses one's way when driving in the countryside, one stops and asks someone. If after following his route a little way one begins to doubt him and asks someone else, who gives different advice, one will soon be more lost than ever. Similarly if one takes advice from several different teachers at once, one runs the risk of becoming confused about the way to practise. When you are faced with two roads, you cannot take both at once; in spiritual practice also, one has to stick to one tradition.

The other danger is that one may find a teacher or a god who can give temporary help, and because he seems to be helping one very much, come to feel that he is better than the Enlightened One. When one thus takes ultimate refuge in someone else, one's Refuge in the Buddha is lost.

This is the negative practice.

The positive one is to respect any kind of image of the

Buddha, even a reflection in a mirror, as the Buddha himself. We must not put such an image on the floor, stand our plate on it, sit on it, put it under our bed, or treat it in any other disrespectful manner, as this will degenerate our Refuge and leave negative imprints on our mind. We should be careful not to buy more images than we are able to look after respectfully. We can keep one or two on our altar, but if we buy all the nice statues we come across we shall soon find we have nowhere suitable to put them.[67]

(b) [246] The negative practice in relation to Refuge in the Dharma is to avoid acting in a way altogether contrary to the Dharma. If part of our mind takes Refuge in the Dharma but in our everyday life we continue behaving in a way completely opposed to it, this taking Refuge is of little meaning. Of course, we are led by our mental defilements into many actions that are against the Dharma; this is natural and we should not think it makes our Refuge worthless. But what we must avoid are the intention of harming other sentient beings, and actual actions that harm them. This abandonment of harming must not be partial, covering only certain beings close to us, or only human beings, but must extend to every living being without exception, be it human, animal, or anything else.

The positive practice is to respect any written or printed words explaining the Dharma as if they were the Dharma [Refuge] itself. This applies to any Dharma text or notes, even a single page or a single letter.[68] We are much exposed to the danger of disrespect to the Dharma since we have many texts and are always writing things down. If we have notes which are no longer of use to us, we should burn them rather than throw them away with ordinary rubbish. If we use a bag containing Dharma books or notes to sit on, this shows our mental attitude is mistaken. Such actions lead to rebirth as an animal.

(c) [247] When we have taken Refuge in the Sangha, the negative practice we should follow is to avoid relying on people who do not follow the Buddhist Path. This does not mean we should not be friendly with them – certainly we should be friendly with people who practise any religion – but we should not place ourself in their hands and follow their advice, as this will eventually lead us out of the Buddhist Path.

Of course, none of our relationships with others, especially with religious persons, should be based on attachment or aversion.

The companions in whom we can really trust are the *Ārya Sangha*, the realized beings on the Buddhist Path.

[5d.2   *The common practices*]

There are also [six] practices that relate to all the Three Jewels.

(a) [248] [We should go for Refuge again and again, recollecting the differences and the qualities of the Three Jewels.]⁶⁹

(b) Remembering the kindness of the Three Jewels – whatever good situation we are in is due to them – we should offer them the first part of whatever we eat and drink. Some people claim that there is a major difference between Christianity and Buddhism in that the Christian is helped by the grace of God, but the Buddhist is left to his own resources. In fact, the Buddhist practitioner receives from his Refuges an inspiration very similar to the Christian "grace", except that it comes not from God but from the Buddha, Dharma and Sangha.

(c) [249] Living among friends and relatives who do not practise the Buddhist Path, we should be very compassionate towards them, recognizing how unfortunate they are to be spending their lives without the precious teaching. Without being too much of a missionary, we should try skilfully, especially by our own example, to lead them towards the Buddhist Refuge.

(d) When in difficulty, we should turn to the Three Jewels, praying to them with confidence that their power will enable us to solve our problems. If instead we ignore these Objects of Refuge and try to overcome the difficulty by other, worldly means, such as other people or material things, we shall not succeed.

(e) [250] As the benefits of taking Refuge are limitless (see above and next two verses), we should try to generate the thought of Refuge every day, and recite the formula six times, three times each day and three times each night. If we recite the Six-session Guru-yoga, that satisfies this commitment.

(f) We should be careful not to make jokes involving the Three Jewels. Also we should not swear by them, to try and convince someone that what we are saying is true (even if it is).

[251] [According to the oral tradition, eight benefits accrue from taking Refuge and should be remembered when carrying out practice (e).]⁷⁰

(i) To have generated the thought of Refuge is the measure of being a Buddhist. Whatever one says, one is not Buddhist if one has not generated this thought. Thus Refuge is called the door of the Doctrine.

(ii) It is the basis for taking the three kinds of vows – *Prātimokṣha*, Bodhisattva and Tantric vows. Having Refuge in one's mind, if one takes these vows they will be firm and steady.

(iii) Even if we do not undertake such practices as prostrating and reciting mantras, taking Refuge has very great power to eliminate negative imprints, and (iv) to accumulate a vast amount of merit.

(v) Taking Refuge thus closes the door to the realms of woe, by removing the causes for being reborn in them.

(vi) Many people complain of being afflicted by spirits, unable to sleep and so forth, but if we take Refuge sincerely then the power of the merits it generates will make it impossible for spirits to harm us.

(vii) [252] [Whatever one wishes is realized.]

(viii) We quickly approach Buddhahood.

It is important to meditate on these teachings on the practices of Refuge, as even if one has already produced the true thought of Refuge, living with people hostile to Buddhist practice can cause one to lose all enthusiasm. We should remember the kindness of the Three Jewels and the benefits of taking Refuge in them, and encouraged by understanding the benefits, try to follow the practices taught here, aware of what we should and should not do.

Meditation 6
How to generate Confidence in the Laws of Actions and Results

[253] Having meditated on the sufferings we would experience as an animal, preta or hell being, we should ask ourself whether we really wish to take such a rebirth. If not, we should consider that our situation is just like that of someone who has been arrested as a thief and told that he will be tortured with red-hot irons the next day, for we are in imminent danger of entering these ill destinies. But there is no-one outside ourself who forces us into them; it is solely the result of using wrongly our three doors of action. We must therefore examine how we use our three doors, watching always lest our thoughts, speech and actions of body be directed by wrong motivations.

If, for example, we eat too much of some food we are particularly fond of, we make ourself sick – this is just the result of our own greed and was not forced upon us by anyone else. To avoid making ourself sick the same way again and again, we must become strongly aware that eating that food leads to sickness, and try to stop eating it. In the same way, we must be watchful of our actions, in order to avoid unfortunate rebirth.

What we must observe is our state of mind, since this is what determines whether our actions (*karma*) are positive or negative, "white" or "black". If we can give a positive direction to the mind, then the actions of body and speech will follow. So if we discover our mind is in a positive state, we should rejoice as if we had found a precious jewel and resolve to keep it that way as much as we can. If we fall into mistaken conduct, we should feel regret, recognizing we have made a mistake, and put our mind back in the right direction. Also we should try to purify the mistaken action. In short, then, we should try to develop right actions of body, speech and mind and diminish wrong ones.

In a worldly activity such as business, if we make a mistake we immediately start to worry about the problems it will cause, such as running out of money. But if we fall into mistaken actions while practising Dharma, we are less likely to feel like that. In fact the situations are very similar, but in the former case we can see the results of the mistake in this life, while in the latter we cannot, so we tend not to believe in them very strongly.

So we should train in mindfulness, awareness and watchfulness over our motivation.

[254] The practice of religion is not like a worldly task, where you can ask someone else to help. We are born alone and we die alone; we alone are responsible for our actions, and we alone experience the results.

All the suffering we experience, in this life and in future lives, is the direct result of our own mistaken actions. Hence by guarding our motivation with mindfulness and awareness, and so stopping mistaken actions, we can avoid suffering in the future. If we keep our mind properly oriented, the worst anyone can do to us is kill us, but even a whole army cannot make us take an unfortunate rebirth. If on the other hand we fail to keep our mind positively directed, and constantly engage in unwholesome actions, we are accumulating the causes for rebirth in a realm of woe. Therefore we must keep a check on our motivation, rejoicing when it is good, and feeling regret and purifying it when it is bad.

Perhaps we become depressed when we think we are close to death and have accumulated many negative actions that will result in an unfortunate rebirth. There is no point in this. We are completely free to practise Dharma and eliminate the imprints of our negative actions – we do not have to pay anyone for this.

[6a HOW KARMA IS DEFINITE]

[255] If we sow different sorts of seeds in a field, such as wheat, barley and peas, each will develop into its own kind of sprout. A barley sprout arises only from barley, and so on. [256] Just as a seed cannot grow into a plant of a different type, so our actions can produce only results of their own type. An unvirtuous action can only give rise to suffering, and a positive action can only give rise to happiness. This order can never be mixed up.

In more detail, also, a particular type of positive (or negative) action will give rise to a particular type of happiness (or suffering).

An action may come to fruition (*vipāka*) by "throwing" us into a particular state of existence [e.g. man, pig, etc.], or it may act as "completing karma", determining some detail of one's body, surroundings or experiences in the new existence. Every detail, such as each colour in a peacock's tail, has its karmic cause. The throwing karma of a life is analogous to the outline drawing of a deity when one is painting a thangka, and the many completing karmas correspond to the various colours with which the outline is filled in. In this way our actions shape our next existence.

Therefore, if we want a better existence in the future, we must be mindful of our actions now. Of course we have to engage in some worldly work, to eat, look after our family and so forth, but we must also try to give part of our mind to the Dharma.

We should contemplate together the certainty of karma and our mortality (Meditation 3): we are sure to die, but we cannot tell when, therefore in the time we have left we should use this body for the practice of Dharma. Combining the two topics is very beneficial for one's practice. So in *Bodhisattva-caryāvatāra* [Chapter II], for example, these two are alternated.

[6b THE GREAT INCREASE OF KARMA]

[257] We may think that if we have done something wrong, it will indeed lead to some unpleasant experience for us but it will probably not be too bad. But this is not so. From one cherry seed grows a big cherry tree, which every year produces thousands of cherries, besides leaves, [blossom] and the rest. Likewise a single action, positive or negative, can produce many fruits of the corresponding type of experience, over a very long time. From one negative action can come an extremely long existence in hell, experiencing very intense suffering. Conversely, from the positive action of taking Refuge, as was stated above, accrue merits so limitless that one could empty the ocean by taking a spoonful of water each day sooner than one could exhaust them. This is because the positive karma of taking Refuge increases.

Therefore, we should be aware that karma increases, and understanding well that even a small positive action can bring a great positive result for a long time, we must try to accomplish even the most trivial virtuous action whenever we have the chance. Also, since a single bad action can bring a heavy and long-lasting painful result, we must try, with constant watchfulness, not to let our actions become negative for a single moment.

[6c ONE DOES NOT MEET KARMA ONE HAS NOT CREATED]

[258)] The principal cause of the cherry tree is the seed. [If there had been no seed, no tree could have grown.] However, the seed alone cannot grow into a tree and produce fruit – co-operative conditions are also needed. The seed must be planted in a fertile field with warmth and moisture. If any one of these conditions is lacking, if for example the field is dry, the seed cannot give rise to a sprout and eventually a tree.

This applies also to the spiritual life: to allow our virtuous actions to come to full fruition, we must provide them with the right conditions. A good way to do this is to dedicate all our merits towards the Enlightenment of all beings.

[6d CREATED KARMA IS INEVITABLE]

[259–260] [If the seed has been sown and all the conditions for its growth are complete, then it will certainly grow.] However, there can arise obstructive conditions which destroy the potential for giving fruit: [if the cherry seed is burnt, it will never grow into a tree; or] if the cherry tree is burnt, it will produce no more fruit. The power of virtuous karma can be destroyed by anger and by wrong views about the spiritual Path, such as denying Liberation and Enlightenment. We must therefore be careful to avoid these states of mind. We should note that anger is particularly likely to arise when one is suffering from *lung* (see Introduction, pp. 20–22).

[261–2] Therefore we should spend this life in worthwhile activities, dedicating our merits to provide them with the conditions they need to bear their maximum fruit as fortunate rebirths, and avoiding the mental states that prevent their ripening. [262–3] On the other hand, we should avoid all unvirtuous actions, and try to create the conditions that destroy their power to ripen as unfortunate rebirths.

One such method is to develop regret for one's past wrong actions, being strongly aware that they are negative. It does not matter if thinking of one's wrong actions makes one feel depressed and guilty, the important thing is to recognize them as wrong.

Another method is to recite at least twenty-one times the mantra of Vajrasattva. Even if this does not eliminate completely the imprints of negative actions, it can stop them increasing.

Unlike a seed, which once it has been sown may rot, be eaten by a bird, dry up, or be blown away by the wind, the traces of negative actions can never be made powerless by accidental circumstances – we have to do it ourself.

To sum up, we must try to turn towards virtue, to increase the power of virtue we already have, to turn away from non-virtue, and to purify the imprints of non-virtue we have already created.[71] As we shall die alone, we ourself must do these things, by the methods explained above.

It is very beneficial to combine our study of the Dharma with meditation on the *Lam rim*. *Lam rim* is the essential ingredient that gives flavour to the whole practice. If one just studies, without applying the *Lam rim* to one's mind, one will just become more and more inflated with pride.

The Actual Practice

Part Three Path of the Intermediate Person

Meditation 7
The Sufferings of the Happier Realms and the General Sufferings of Samsara

To practise the Path of the intermediate religious person, one must develop Renunciation. This is a state of mind that understands that all types of samsaric existence are unsatisfactory and lacking in freedom, and aims at the attainment of Liberation.

To develop a strong desire for Liberation, it is essential that wherever we look in samsara we see no situation fit to stay in. If we have clinging to any state such as the human state or a divine state, we cannot wholeheartedly aspire to Liberation. Therefore this teaching lays much stress on becoming aware of the faults of all possible samsaric rebirths.

7a THE SUFFERINGS OF THE THREE HAPPIER DESTINIES
7a.1 *How to meditate on the sufferings of human beings*

[265] In the meditations of the Path of the inferior religious person, one recognizes the sufferings of the ill destinies of hell beings, pretas and animals, and by contemplating Refuge and Karma one learns how to avoid such rebirth. But pressing the meditation further, we find that even the higher states of samsaric rebirth are unsatisfactory. They are transitory by

nature and even if one is born into such a state one can fall back into an ill destiny.

Four great sufferings are bound up with human existence – birth, aging, sickness and death. In the course of our rebirths we experience these again and again.

(a) *The suffering of birth*. [266] From the moment of conception on, the embryo is already a human being. Though smaller than us, it has feelings, and given its situation, it will experience suffering most of the time and happiness only on rare occasions. We can easily see that to be constricted in such a narrow, dark, wet space as the womb must be unpleasant. Being very feeble, its bones not properly formed and hardened and its skin very tender, the foetus is extremely sensitive to the sufferings of its environment.

[267] After nine months of this suffering, the baby has to leave the womb – when the time is ripe, he can no longer stay inside. Coming out through the tight passage, squeezed between bones, is very difficult – sometimes the baby has to be pulled out by a doctor or midwife. And while the mother may have access to pain-killing drugs, there is no injection of morphine or the like to make it easier for the baby, although he is much more delicate and sensitive. This time is therefore one of very great suffering. For animals too, birth is suffering – a lamb being born, for example, has no midwife to catch him, but just falls on the ground. We cannot remember being born. We think that death will be great suffering, but actually the suffering of birth is much worse.[72]

We should not listen to this as a story about someone else, but take it as applying directly to ourself. We have been through this in the past and will have to go through it again. The reason we cannot remember our birth is the very intensity of the suffering, which inhibits the memory of it. We can observe the same phenomenon with regard to intensely painful situations that we experience later in life – sometimes we cannot remember such an incident at all; sometimes the memory is unclear.[73]

(b) *The suffering of aging*. [268] With every day that passes we come closer to our death, the appearance of our body gradually approaching that it will have when we are dead. This gradual change is aging. We can all see the changes outwardly: we lose your youthful complexion, our hair whitens or turns grey, our body bends so that we cannot stand straight, and we walk unsteadily even on flat ground. When we are young, our flesh is firm and fills out the skin, but as we age, this pleasant appearance is lost and our skin hangs down in wrinkles so that our face, limbs and body are like an uneven field. Our teeth fall out, so that although we crave for nice food, it is very hard for us to eat it. Our speech that was once strong becomes quavering so that others can hardly understand what we are saying; our mind is less clear than it used to be, and we tend to be forgetful.

[269] All our faculties lose their power – we cannot see or hear clearly, sitting down and getting up are difficult. Wherever we go, people think "He's just an old man," and treat us with scorn. We can no longer eat the food we like, because our digestion cannot cope with it. When we were young and good-looking, people were happy to be our friends, but now we are old and unattractive, no-one cares. We see that most of our years have fled and are constantly aware that death will soon be upon us. Maybe we still want to go out and have fun, climbing mountains and so on, but we are no longer able to – we are just stuck in a room in an old people's home.

This is our situation – if we die, the problem is we do not know what kind of existence will follow; but if we live on as an old person, that too is difficult. Thus samsaric existence is by nature difficult, and we must direct our mind towards Liberation.

We should not limit our contemplation to the words of the text, but imagine the whole situation we may experience as an old person. For example, if we married when we were young and beautiful, just looking at each other and seeing how our partner has deteriorated makes us feel depressed.

(c) *The suffering of sickness.* [270] Sickness can come upon us suddenly, the elements of our body becoming unbalanced so that our body becomes full of pain and we must stay in bed, unable to move. Day and night we groan with pain that seems to go on for ever. Perhaps we shall die suddenly from a car accident or a heart attack, but otherwise we inevitably face a painful process of death from disease. Nowadays the pain of terminal sickness may be relieved by drugs such as morphine, but these do nothing to cure you.

One is not allowed to eat the food one likes, because the doctor says it will be harmful; instead one is given food one dislikes. To try and cure the sickness quickly, doctors may operate, but in serious illness the chances are this will not help, but bring only more suffering.

[271] When our health is disrupted by serious illness, to see our friends, possessions, house, servants or relatives no longer makes us feel happy, but they seem like enemies, disturbing to our mind. There is also the constant worry that maybe this illness will lead to our death.

We must contemplate these teachings again and again, thinking that although we may be young and healthy at the moment, still we are subject to sickness. When there are just a few blue patches in a cloudy sky, one is sure that if one is in sunshine at the moment, this will not last more than a few minutes. Our present situation of being free of sickness and not in the process of dying is like this brief sunny interval. We attach a lot of importance to trivial shortcomings in our food or our living place, but these things are negligible compared to the realities of our situation, which we ignore.

(d) *The suffering of death.* [272] We age quickly and are bound to die. It is useful to imagine the ways we could die. We may meet a sudden death, or a slow one, with a gradual physical worsening. [In the latter case,] we get into bed for the last time; medicine is no longer any use, having prayers said and pujas offered will not prevent death coming. Those who look at us can see we are close to death, and we ourself also understand this. With all hope of living cut off, our mind is full of sorrow; whether we are at home or in a hospital ward, our relatives who visit us weep, and we too cry, from our present suffering and from fear as to what will happen to us.

[273] Some people have no chance to speak when dying – some indeed are unconscious – but some are able to pronounce a few last words, tell their wife to look after the children or whatever. At present we can speak freely, but close to death the tongue becomes hard and blue and one cannot move it, or even

if one can move it a little the sounds that emerge are unintelligible. Seeing that the person we are trying to speak to does not understand makes us more frustrated and sad. When others try to speak to us, even if they speak right into our ear their voice seems to come from very far away and we cannot grasp the meaning. As the visual faculty degenerates, the people around our bed seem to be very remote, as if we were looking up at them from the bottom of a deep hole.

As the elements of the body are gradually absorbed – its solidity, its moistness and cohesion, its heat and power of transformation, and its motility[74] – various signs manifest, such as the nose becoming smaller, the mouth drying up, and the eyes becoming fixed, staring rigidly into space. Watching many people die, I have often observed these signs myself.

Breathing becomes difficult; exhalation is stronger while inhalation weakens and eventually stops altogether. Recognizing that one is separating from friends, relatives, possessions and all one holds dear brings acute sorrow to the mind. In addition, one feels regret for the mistaken actions one has committed and one's failure to make the best use of this human life. Spirits can gather round, trying to make us die as quickly as possible and steal our remaining life for themselves. We may experience signs of our future destiny. This can be seen in a dying person from the sounds he makes, his facial expressions, and the way he moves his arms and legs about.

To avoid regret at the time of death, we must spend all our time in worthwhile actions while we can, mindfully avoiding mistaken ones. When we reach the point of death, it will be too late to do anything.

For a Dharma practitioner, too, it is better to die alone, not surrounded by friends and relatives who disturb one and make one feel frustrated, but contemplating the Dharma. One should keep the mind tranquil, free of attachment and regret and conceptualizations. Milarepa said:

> Without a vigil around my corpse,
> Without lamentation over my death,
> If I could die in solitude,
> The aim of this yogin will be fulfilled.[75]

While it is hard for us to practise as Milarepa, we should try in accordance with our capabilities to see this life meaningfully.

(e) *The suffering of meeting the unpleasant.* [274] These sufferings of birth, aging, sickness and death would not be so bad if we only had to experience them once, but we are forced by the power of our defilements to undergo them constantly, again and again. In fact, there are all kinds of unpleasant situations that we do not desire but still are subject to – for example, experiencing physical pain or mental distress, being deprived of our possessions, or our friends or our country being harmed. Our country suffers in war, our family is afflicted by quarrels, individually we suffer pain and disease, all regardless of our wishes. These troubles weigh us down and make us confused and depressed. This is the fundamental nature of samsaric existence. Understanding this, we should realize how samsaric existence is unsatisfactory.

(f) *The suffering of separation from the pleasant.* [275] When with people we like, we wish to stay with them always, yet although we do everything to avoid separation, it is certain that it must come. We would like to be always together with our wife and children whom we love very much, but conditions arise that force us to separate from them. We live in a pleasant country that we do not want to leave, but somehow we are forced to go elsewhere. Even if we do not have to part from our family, country and so forth before death, it is certain that we shall have to do so when we die. This is our situation.

(g) *The suffering of seeking what one wishes and not obtaining it.* [276] There are many things we wish for, but these wishes are hard to fulfil. We may wish for possessions and not get any, wish for work and find none, wish to accomplish something and be baulked. A farmer works his fields and wishes for a good harvest, but fails to get one. One marries, hoping to raise a prosperous family, but it does not work out. Unable to accomplish their aims, people become depressed; some even become crazy or kill themselves.

Meditators too may decide to practise in order to achieve certain realizations, then be unable to meditate as they want. Then they become depressed, strain too much, and develop *lung*.

Not only do we fail to meet our aims, but situations we do not want fall on us all the time. We must understand that all this is of the nature of samsaric existence – there is no state of happiness in samsara that we can call satisfactory.

These sufferings [of human beings] we can experience directly. But now the sufferings of other types of existence are to be described – sufferings that we cannot perceive at present.

7a.2 How to meditate on the sufferings of asuras

[278] The special characteristic of the asuras is that they are always jealous. To have jealousy in one's mind stops one being happy. Jealousy is an attitude of being unable to bear the advantages and fine possessions of others. Thus if we are jealous, every time we see someone else living well – perhaps wearing finer clothes than ourself – we create our own suffering. In addition, being jealous of what others have brings in its train hatred towards them, following jealousy like a dog following its owner. Jealousy is often compared to a snake, always moving about and trying to harm other beings.

The asuras, whose minds are so permeated with jealousy, live within sight of the realm of the gods, which is superior to their own; consequently they suffer intensely from jealousy of the wealth and good qualities of the gods. Besides this, they feel impelled to fight against the gods, whom in fact they are incapable of defeating, and so they experience the additional misery of being beaten in battle.

The asuras are very intelligent and clever, but their pervading jealousy makes this intelligence quite useless [for Dharma practice]. Outwardly they look like gods, but inwardly, an asura's mind is so lacking in peace that it would be better to be a cow.

Therefore, understanding that the existence of an asura is unsatisfactory, we must wish not to be born as one, but direct our mind towards full Liberation.

7a.3 How to meditate on the sufferings of gods of the Desire Realm

But there do exist divine states of existence that are very pleasant. To attain such a state, the mere wish is not sufficient

– one must accumulate many wholesome actions and dedicate the merit towards being reborn in such a pleasant realm. However, this is a mistake, which we should avoid. Instead we should dedicate our merits towards the attainment of Liberation.

[279] Since being a god is the result of positive actions, it allows a certain, temporary happiness. But you cannot remain in that state as long as you wish. Since it is conditioned by your karma, when the power of this positive karma is exhausted you have to die. It is like being a bird who can fly very high in the sky, but must eventually come down again when her strength runs out.

The gods do not age the same way we do, but still when they come close to death they show particular signs of aging, not as gross as ours. Normally they are of divine appearance, their bodies shining with light and adorned with garlands of flowers [which are always fresh]; the place they live in is very comfortable, and everything and everyone they see is beautiful and delightful. But when death approaches, they become nervous and restless, unable to stop in one place, much as we feel when we have *lung* and neither staying in our room nor going for a walk makes us feel right. Their flower-garlands start to wither, the body loses its radiance, and other signs that their positive karma is nearing exhaustion manifest, so that their appearance gradually deteriorates.

[279–280] When these signs occur, they understand that they are about to die and separate from their pleasant existence, and this makes them very frightened and agitated. They foresee the time of their death and have clairvoyant vision of the next rebirth that awaits them. This clairvoyance is of no benefit to them but greatly enhances their fear and anguish, for they see that, now their merits are exhausted, a past bad action is to ripen and throw them into one of the realms of woe. They are in the position of someone forced to emigrate to another country and whose money has almost run out – hard times loom ahead.

[281–2] Therefore we must avoid wishing for the delights of rebirth as a god, for although it brings some pleasure for a time, in the end it can only give rise to great suffering.

7a.4 *How to meditate on the sufferings of the gods of the two higher realms*

[283–4] We may think that since in the Form and Formless Realms one does not experience these signs of death that afflict the gods of the Desire Realm, perhaps it is all right to wish for rebirth there. But this wish also is to be abandoned, for it obstructs the desire for Liberation.

It is true that the Form and Formless Realms are free of gross sufferings. One is reborn in them as the result of the practice of *dhyāna* concentration [with appropriate dedication]. One then dwells there in that concentration for an extremely long time, experiencing happiness. But when the positive karma is exhausted, this life must cease and one will probably be reborn in a lower state of existence.

Therefore we must become aware that in all samsara there is no place to rest, and must dedicate all the energy of our meritorious actions to attaining Liberation.

7b THE GENERAL SUFFERINGS OF SAMSARA[76]

[285–292] When we become aware that we are going to have to die, we feel a certain unease and fear. But we must realize that it is not only in this life that we shall die, but we face the same prospect again and again, until we attain Liberation. This is surely rather frightening.

We have to die, and after death we have to reappear in another state of existence. Our body will not always be of agreeable aspect like our present human form; when we see certain creatures, we may be struck by their grotesque and repulsive shape, but we must understand that at some stage we too are liable to be born with a body like that. As long as we are governed by defilements, we are bound to experience death and rebirth, time after time.

In this cycle of rebirths, there is no certainty whether we shall be high, as gods, or low, as animals [or worse]. Sometimes we shall be very high, experiencing many pleasures and drinking nectar; at other times we shall be so low that we are forced to eat filth. At present, as human beings, we protect our bodies and keep ourselves warm with clothes, and when they wear out we buy new ones; but when we are in the ill destinies, that will not be possible, and our naked bodies will be tormented in manifold ways. Such unfortunate states of existence are perfectly possible for us, for in this life we are creating the causes to be born in them.

We sometimes feel sad because of loneliness in this life, if we lack a husband or wife or friends. But in fact we are always essentially alone in samsara — we are born alone and we die alone.

Friends and enemies are uncertain and can change from one moment to the next. Today someone is a close friend whom we see every day, confiding in him all our problems and secrets; but later, with one incident of bad behaviour towards us, even a few words, he becomes an enemy we want never to see again, and if so much as a thought of him comes into our mind we quickly push it away. Another person is an enemy whom we have constantly wished to harm, and even sworn to kill on sight; but sometimes he too can turn into a good friend.

There is nothing stable and reliable in this samsaric existence. Friends and enemies are uncertain, when this life will end is uncertain, whether we shall [then] be in a high or a low state is uncertain. Therefore it is better to devote our mind to the practice of Dharma.

Even within one human life, our status is uncertain. A powerful king can become a starving, homeless beggar, mistreated by all – our standard of living can switch from very high to very low even overnight.

We may think we know the people around us well, but really we hardly know them at all. We have no idea how we were related to them previously. They may have been our father, our mother, our child, our enemy, our employer, or anything. The Arhant Shāriputra once came upon a young couple with their child and dog. The husband was eating a fish from the pond nearby; the dog came [to chew the bones], and he beat it with a stick. In fact, the fish was his father, reborn as a fish as a result of himself catching fish in that pond, and the dog was his mother, reborn as the family pet through attachment to her offspring. Meanwhile, his wife was nursing their child, who was in reality the reincarnation of his bitterest enemy – a former lover of hers, whom he had killed in jealousy, now reborn as her son because of attachment to her. Seeing all this, Shāriputra remarked:

> [He] eats [his] father's flesh and beats [his] mother;
> [She] holds [their] mortal enemy in [her] lap;
> The wife is gnawing at [her] husband's bones –
> At samsara's features, one wants to laugh.[77]

Thus our present life is only part of the story: when we take other lives into account our relationships are completely mixed up.

Such is samsara. Since no samsaric situation is satisfactory, we must turn our mind away from samsara and towards the attainment of Liberation.

Meditation 8
How to Think about the Process of Functioning of Samsara and Practise the Path to Liberation

8a THE FUNCTIONING OF SAMSARA

[297] There are six classes of samsaric existence, the three ill destinies and the three happier ones. We circulate from one to another without end, as if travelling endlessly back and forth among six great cities. We career around at such a hectic pace that one can hardly say where we are at a particular time, just as when a burning firebrand is whirled round rapidly, one can see the circle traced by the flames but cannot make out the position of the brand itself.

Circling in samsara means taking rebirth again and again. Taking rebirth is not pleasant, but accompanied always by suffering, whether actual physical or mental suffering or the omnipresent type of suffering, which is a latent potential for [actual] suffering. Thus we never find a samsaric existence that is completely free from unsatisfactoriness.

Conventionally we speak of a baby as "young" and an aged man as "old"; but when every being has been circling in samsara since beginningless time, one can hardly distinguish young and old. Suppose a man of ninety lives near a ten-year-old boy; after a while the "old" man dies and is reborn as a baby, still near the boy, who is now a man – which is really the elder? Every person in the world has already been through numberless lives.

With no control we circulate in samsara – we do not want to grow old, we do not want to die, but nevertheless we have to. We must therefore analyse the cause of this circling and of the suffering it entails.

[298] If someone insults us, saying, for example, "You are dishonest and cunning," then there arises in our mind a strong sense of self, "He is insulting *me*!" When we answer back, our words are accompanied by this impression of an inherent 'I' within ourself. Likewise if we are praised or flattered, this sense of I comes up and the words of praise seem to refer to something solid and definite. This is not confined to human beings, let alone to people trained in a particular philosophical system: it can occur just as well in a cow. If you try to take away the carrot that my dog, Norbu, is eating now, he will be angry and think, "He's taking away *my* carrot!" With this "my" there is the strong sense of ego [that we are concerned with]. This sense of ego is a manifestation of spontaneous, "innate", self-grasping, a grasping of inherent existence of the person that does not depend on any special condition such as philosophical training.

Innate self-grasping is an aspect of ignorance. We may feel that our mind must be completely full of this ignorance, for we are always saying "I have to do a job," "I have to study," "I need to go into town." But this is not so. We must distinguish between correct use of "I" and the sense of I that is faulty. The I we speak of normally in everyday activity – "I am going shopping," etc. – involves a correct way of apprehending the person. It is only on certain occasions, such as when we are praised or criticized, that the strong sense of ego, grasped as the [inherently existent] object of the praise or blame, arises.

Based on this [illusory] appearance of a strong ego, there develop additional mistaken attitudes. We grasp part of the world as belonging to ourself and to be cherished, seeing some people as our friends, for example, and we reject another part as threatening and hostile, and try to push it away. Thus because of dividing ourself from others by ego-grasping, we develop an attached view of external objects, distinguishing strongly between things [and people] we like and those we dislike.

When our mind is pervaded with greed towards some things and hatred towards others, many mistaken ways of thinking develop; our speech and our bodily actions too are influenced by greed and hatred – we run after objects of attachment, abuse people, and the like. Thus we create wrong actions with our three doors of body, speech and mind. These actions leave imprints on our mental continuum, which in the future, when they meet the appropriate external conditions, generate unpleasant situations. [In particular, they throw us into new states of samsaric rebirth.] In this way, we circle in samsara, experiencing suffering.

8b THE PATH TO LIBERATION

[299] The way to end this process is to destroy its origin, the false sense of self. First we must recognize it, then eliminate it. If we can do this, it is like cutting off the flow of a river at the source: everything that comes afterwards, the greed and hatred, karmic imprints and the unpleasant situations that grow from them, will be stopped.

How can we destroy innate self-grasping? No external means can do this. All the military might in the world will not suffice to destroy our ignorance. The way to do it is to use Wisdom and recognize that the inherently-existent ego that is grasped by innate self-grasping simply does not exist. Once we understand this, the basis for grasping an inherent self vanishes, and spontaneous self-grasping must cease.

This process is likened to [an experience familiar to all who have lived in countries where snakes are common]: one is out walking when the light is poor, and one catches sight of something long and thin, with variegated markings, lying in coils on the ground. Thinking "That is a snake!", one becomes afraid and perhaps jumps back,[78] but then, looking more closely, one sees it is not a snake but just a coloured piece of rope. Then the mind grasping it as a snake ceases, as does the resultant fear.

Meditation 8: The Functioning of Samsara, and the Path

Therefore we should rely on a Spiritual Friend who is skilled in teaching how the person is not inherently existent, and following his instructions, gradually develop the necessary Wisdom.

[300] To be able to investigate in a sustained manner the non-inherent-existence of the person, we need a certain stability of mind. Therefore we must train in concentration (*samādhi*).

[301] This concentration cannot be achieved without moral discipline, avoiding unwholesome actions. Based on such restraint, one can develop strong concentration, through which the Wisdom realizing Selflessness can be produced.

[302] The causal relationship between Morality, Concentration and Wisdom is illustrated by a simile. In a field, one can sow barley seed, from which grow barley plants, and these produce many more grains of barley. The field is analogous to Morality, the tall barley plant to Concentration, and the grains produced to the Wisdom realizing Selflessness. Just as the grain can be ground and made into bread that satisfies our hunger, so the Wisdom of Selflessness satisfies us by eliminating all sufferings.

[303] The three Trainings of Morality, Concentration and Wisdom do not arise in us spontaneously, but demand effort. First we must receive Dharma teachings from our Guru; then, having understood them, we must practise them assiduously. Without understanding how to practise, there can of course be no result. With continuous effort in application, we can eventually develop the three Trainings.

[304] Wrong actions of body, speech and mind occur through one or other of four conditions, just as a thief who has entered a house with four doors must have come through one of these four. They are as follows.

(a) *Ignorance*, not knowing what is right or wrong. Then one engages in actions without discrimination. This ignorance will not vanish of itself – it will always remain unless we do something to get rid of it. What we must do is listen to the teachings of a Spiritual Friend, and thus learn to discriminate good from evil. For example, a foreigner who comes to live in Switzerland may wish to behave correctly, in accordance with all the Swiss laws and regulations, but if he does not know these rules then despite his good intentions he will be sure to infringe them.

(b) *Strong defilements*. Sometimes greed, hatred or another negative attitude arises in one's mind so strongly that one is drawn helplessly into committing an action that one knows is wrong.

(c) *Recklessness*. Sometimes we know what is good or evil, but we simply do not care about trying to practise what is good, and just do anything, like a mad dog. Such behaviour is very destructive, like a river that is not confined between banks but flows anywhere, on fields, through houses, and so on. With this attitude we create most of our mistaken actions.

(d) *Lack of respect* for Dharma teachings, one's teacher, etc. A *Lam rim* text, for example, contains valuable advice; if we treat it with respect, this is a positive action, in conformity with having taken Refuge in the Dharma, but if we have no respect, if we throw it on the floor and do not take care of it, this is a negative action. Lack of respect for one's teacher, for symbols of the Buddha, and in general for all sentient beings, leads to unwholesome actions and [hence] problems.

Avoiding these four conditions, we should try to practise the advice of the Buddha, and establish in ourself the root of the Doctrine, i.e. establish ourself in a positive direction. If we can do this, it will be beneficial for us in this and in future lives.

The Actual Practice

Part Four
The Path of the Superior Person

Meditation 9
The Development of Bodhicitta

9a HOW TO THINK ABOUT THE REASON ONE MUST ENTER THIS PATH

[305–6] Through the teachings of the preceding chapters, one becomes aware of the impermanence of this life, then generates the wish to be free of the sufferings involved in samsaric existence. By practising the three Trainings of Morality, Concentration and Wisdom, one can indeed attain one's individual Liberation from samsara; but this is not sufficient. To aim at one's own Liberation alone is very small-minded. It means forgetting the other sentient beings who are suffering in samsara, and not trying to help them.

It is as if we and our elderly mother were in prison, and we took a chance to escape alone, just leaving our mother inside. Anyone who would do this is a bad, inconsiderate sort of person. Likewise someone who strives only for his own Liberation from samsara has a very inferior type of motivation, not caring much about others. This is not a correct way of training one's mind in the Dharma.

Therefore we must remember the other sentient beings around us, and strive to go beyond a wish for individual Liberation towards a wish for a Liberation in which all beings participate.

9b TRAINING IN BODHICITTA BY THE SEVEN INSTRUCTIONS OF CAUSE AND EFFECT[78a]

9b.0 *How to achieve evenmindedness*

[307] When one develops the wish for shared Liberation, one naturally asks oneself why one is unable to bring other sentient beings to the Path, although one wishes to. The reason would seem to be that we lack an even mind towards others, and this obstructs our benefiting them.

This lack is due to our narrow outlook, confined to this life. When someone occasionally relates positively to us, we develop attachment for him and want him to be closer to us. When we meet people who sometimes disagree with our opinions, or harm [us] a little, we develop hatred towards them, hold them as enemies, and try to avoid them.

Even within this life, we only consider a short period. A person may have been harming us for years, but this week he has been good to us in some way, perhaps given us a present: then we start to cherish him, and forget about the previous harm. Another person takes care of us for many years, but this week a disagreement has arisen: we start to fight and quarrel with him, forgetting about the years of kindness.

This narrowness of outlook brings many quarrels and unpleasant situations, some of which we have to be ashamed of.

Thus our mind is not even towards other people, but discriminates among them – it is as uneven as the Alps. We should learn to recognize clearly this unevenness in our mind, and then try to transform it.

[308] This is how we should transform it. There are many people we dislike at present, the reason in each case being something quite recent – in the last week or the last month, say. But this is not our only life. In the course of many past lives, the same people we now dislike have cared for us with limitless kindness. If we react shortsightedly against them and hold them as enemies on the basis of a few days' bad behaviour, we are lacking in any sort of consideration and conscience.

We can also transform our attitude towards those we dislike by thinking that in the future our relationship with them can change: they may become close friends who help us very much. This too helps to overcome our aversion.

Meditation 9: The Development of Bodhicitta 141

[309] On the other hand, there are people to whom we are attached. We may bear them in mind constantly, thinking about them all day. This exaggerated attitude too is completely baseless. Although such a person is dear to us now, in the past he may have been our chief enemy, and it is quite possible that a year from now he will have turned against us, treated us very badly, or broken off the relationship. We can observe that between husband and wife, between other family members, or between groups of people, things do not stay good or bad for ever; for a while they may be good, then they turn bad, or vice versa. To make changes in the material world can take a lot of work, but relationships with people are easily transformed – one word out of place and the relationship can be ruined.

Therefore we must try to see that enemies and friends are not different as we grasp them, but are all people, and quite equal.

[310] A third attitude that often occurs in us is to feel completely unconnected with certain people, and not to care what happens to them. We must recognize that this way of thinking is also mistaken. Although these people seem unrelated to us now, it was not always so, and there is no reason why in another moment, or next year, they should not be closely related to us.

We should not regard any group of sentient beings with indifference, but realize the impermanent nature of relationships and develop the wish to help them also.

[311] Up to now we have, quite naturally, discriminated among beings, without thinking about the Dharma. Because of this uneven attitude we have experienced many problems. But now we have received these teachings, we can apply them and get used to this way of thinking. In this way it is possible to level our uneven mind and cut off much of our hatred and attachment, so that our mind becomes much more peaceful and relaxed.

The essence of the Mahāyāna motivation is Compassion. But the water of Compassion cannot stay on the jagged mountains of an uneven mind. Just as water remains only in a flat place, so Compassion demands an even mind.

Transforming our mind is not easy. We probably think, "But So-and-so is really bad, I cannot possibly develop evenmindedness or liking towards him." When this happens, we should turn the thought round and ask ourself, "What about me? Am I not bad like that person?" We do not want to think of ourself as bad, but this person, our enemy, no doubt thinks we are. There are thus two people with almost the same thought: I think of him as bad and he thinks of me as bad – who is right? On analysis it is very hard to say. Questioning ourself in this manner is one way gradually to diminish our dislike for a particular person.

Another method is to eliminate dislike by meditation on Emptiness. This person, my enemy, thinks I am bad. Who am I, then? What is this person whom he hates? Analyzing throughout our [five] aggregates we can find nothing of which we can say, "Here is the me that is harmed, or hated." Then since there is no object for that enemy [to act against], the feeling we have towards him will vanish.

Developing evenmindedness is of immediate benefit: one is no longer disturbed by other people, but feels relaxed and can put up with disagreement. It would be superfluous to speak of the long-term benefits.

Some practitioners who think of themselves as yogins look down on the Hīnayāna as an inferior vehicle. This is an incorrect attitude and shows that they lack evenmindedness. Hīnayāna Arhants have completely realized evenmindedness. If an Arhant had a person on one side cutting his body with a knife, and another on the other side anointing him lovingly with perfume, he would have exactly the same attitude towards both. With us, of course, it is quite different – when somebody attacks us we immediately respond in kind, while the loving person we will try to keep close to us.

We must promise ourself to try and make our mind even, and consider those we now see as enemies, those we see as friends, and those to whom we are indifferent, without discrimination as all being people and all equal.

[312–3] In battle, an army first shoots the enemy troops in the front line, then having killed those it advances and attacks those behind. Likewise, having developed evenmindedness, we must take a further step to increase the power of our mind. Seeing all other people as being equal is good, but not sufficient.

Meditation 9: The Development of Bodhicitta 143

We must now try to give a positive nature to our evenmindedness, not only seeing other people as equal, but feeling impelled to work for their benefit. Our feeling that we are independent of others must be transformed into a feeling that we are closely related to every living being.

9b.1 *How to meditate on recognizing beings as one's mother*

To feel this close relatedness we contemplate as the main example the closest relationship between human beings, that of mother and child. One first recognizes that all sentient beings have been one's mother, then remembers the kindness of mothers, and thus sees the kindness of all sentient beings.

However, it is not easy to practise this method effectively. There are two contemplations thought to be particularly difficult – to have a proper relationship with one's Guru, seeing him as Buddha (Meditation 1b), and this one of seeing all sentient beings as one's mother. This meditation depends on the conviction not only that we are subject to rebirth, but that we have existed since beginningless time and taken countless births in the past, and will take countless more in the future. This conviction is based on an understanding of the nature of mind as something not created by material causes and which migrates from existence to existence. If we have this strong conviction then we can engage effectively in this meditation to generate *Bodhicitta* by way of recognizing all sentient beings as our mother. If not, then we can practise the other method, Exchange of Self and Others (see 9c below).

[314–317] Despite its difficulty, we should practise this contemplation of all sentient beings being our mother, if we can. First we must think of the nature of our mind. Our mind comes from the past and moves from one existence to another: it has taken rebirths without number. In the future too we shall take numberless lives. Although there are types of birth that do not depend on parents,[79] birth from a womb and birth from an egg do. Therefore since we have taken birth numberless times, it follows that every sentient being has been our mother and our father, and also that we have been the father and the mother of every sentient being.[80]

So we should try to see every sentient being as our mother, and that we have been closely related to every one. If we cannot do this, then at least we should develop evenmindedness towards them.

9b.2 How to meditate on remembering their kindness

We meditate on the kindness of other sentient beings so as to generate Compassion and the energy to go through difficulties for their sake. A child who recognizes the kindness of his mother, for example, will do whatever he can to please her. If we dislike our mother, of course, this meditation is difficult.

[321] At the beginning of our life, our mother kept us in her womb. Some mothers now have their child aborted, but we are talking about a good mother. For nine months she carried us there, as carefully as if she was holding a precious jewel, [322] avoiding all behaviour that might harm us. For example, she would eat only food that was good for her baby, avoiding other food; in this way she put aside her own desires for our benefit.

Some people in the West say there is no kindness involved in the mother's keeping her child in the womb, giving birth to it, and taking care of it once it is born, because this is no more than her responsibility. However, although it is her responsibility, there are many who do not accept it, and if she had not taken care of us we would probably be dead by now; therefore our mother did have great kindness in carrying out her responsibility.

[323] When our mother gave birth to us, she suffered a great deal of physical pain. Though nowadays medical aid may allow the mother not to feel too much pain, still, many times we have been born from a mother who was suffering intensely; but she was unconcerned about her own pain and cared only that her child be healthy.

[324–331] When we were born, we were just a tiny lump of flesh, [helpless and] very delicate: if we had been left half an hour alone in the cold, without clothes, we would have died. Perhaps we think that the staff of the maternity hospital did more to help us just after we were born than our mother did, but in most of our numberless births we have been entirely dependent on our mother.

Meditation 9: The Development of Bodhicitta   145

Besides her kindness of keeping us well when we were very young, even our present activities such as study or trying to practise the Dharma depend on our mother's kindness. But we find it hard to recollect this kindness, because being always involved in busy activity we do not notice what really happened to us.

It is accepted in Buddhism that we have not been born only as humans but as animals and other types of being. This is not a mere belief but actual fact. [Animal mothers too are very kind to their offspring.] Once I saw on television some baby sealions being caught and killed by fishermen. Although there was nothing the mother could do, her mind was so full of kindness and the wish to care for her babies that she still followed their bodies. Another time I saw birds defending their eggs – to protect their young that are about to hatch, they will do anything they can, even fight with animals that are stronger than themselves. We should not see the kindness of animals to their young as something unconnected with us, but as something we too have experienced. In numberless lives we have been born as animals and cared for by our mother of that time in the same ways we see now with other animals.

Animal and other mothers in general show great kindness, more concerned with the sickness of their children than with their own sickness. If her children are behaving well and are successful in their studies at school, a mother is very pleased and happy, but if they behave badly and do not study well she is very concerned. This is not for her own sake, but from thinking of the future welfare of the children. Many other examples are given in the text.

Many people say they cannot remember their mother's kindness because she treated them very badly and they do not like her at all. It may be true that our mother has beaten us or mistreated us some time, but in this meditation when we are seeking to generate compassion, we should completely disregard such things and think only of our positive relationship with her – this is the true relationship. It is the same as with the practice of devotion to the Spiritual Friend: if we see faults in our teacher, this obstructs the development of a proper respect towards him. We must therefore ignore altogether whatever faults appear to our eyes, and pay attention only to his good qualities; then our faith and respect will grow, and, as a result, our own qualities.

We may think that indeed our mother was very kind to us, but we do not see the same kindness in other beings around us. In fact, all sentient beings are kind, like our mother, but we do not see it because of our limited view, restricted to a narrow range of time (see above, 9b.0). If we look on the long term, we have had numberless past existences. In them we have had to face countless problems, which we were not able to overcome without the help of other sentient beings. Since beginningless time we have continually been helped by other sentient beings, and in the future, until we attain freedom from samsaric rebirth, we shall have to depend on other sentient beings to help us solve our problems.

If we investigate, we can see this kindness of other beings in a great many situations. For example, the sweater I am wearing now results from the kindness of perhaps two hundred beings – the animals who gave the initial material, and many human beings doing various jobs. So I am benefited and kept warm by the kindness of all these beings.

Actually, if we really wish to meditate on *Bodhicitta*, there is scarcely a limit to the ways in which we could recollect the kindness of all sentient beings. We have received their kindness in previous lives and will in the future, and all our practice of religion and progress towards Liberation and Enlightenment depends on other sentient beings. Since all the practices are based on them, the sentient beings are like a staircase to Enlightenment. Therefore Shāntideva said:

> When Buddha-qualities are accomplished
> Through sentient beings and Conqu'rors alike,
> How can I not respect the beings
> Just as I do the Conquerors?[81]

9b.3 *How to meditate on repaying their kindness*

[332–4] Shāntideva continues,

> Also, what else can repay

The non-dissembling Friends, [the Buddhas,]
Who have helped immeasurably,
Apart from pleasing sentient beings?[82]

At present we cannot really benefit other sentient beings, but we should try to develop awareness of the kindness with which each one has related to us in the past.

Remembering their kindness would be enough if they were happy, but we can see that they are not happy. They are crazed by the demon of emotions that dwells within them, and afflicted all the time by the three sufferings.

Furthermore, they are blind to good and evil, completely confused about what should be done and what will only bring harm to themselves; and they lack the guidance of a spiritual teacher. If we look at Vevey,[83] for example, although many of the people have a certain temporary, material happiness and comfort, very few of them, perhaps two or three, are able to discriminate what should and should not be done in order to develop themselves spiritually, and a similar number relate to a spiritual teacher. This would not matter if they were sure to go on living in comfort in the future, but it is far from certain that they will – in fact most are heading for quite an unfavourable future.

Therefore, since sentient beings have been very kind to us and are in a miserable situation, it is unworthy to forget about them and be concerned only with ourself. What we have done in the past cannot be altered, but from now on we should try to abandon our selfish attitude and, remembering the kindness of other sentient beings, try to use our entire existence, our body, speech and mind, in order to benefit them. This is the attitude of repaying their kindness. We must wish to help every being, from human beings down to insects, and whenever an occasion arises when we are able actually to help them, we must do so. For example, in winter there are many birds who cannot find food, so to give them food is a beneficial action.

But the action most beneficial for sentient beings is not the giving of temporary, material aid, but freeing them entirely from samsara and placing them in the ultimate bliss of Liberation.

9b.4 How to meditate on Loving-kindness

[335–7] When we cannot place ourself in the bliss of Liberation, it is very hard to set all other sentient beings there. But we are practising the Dharma and performing many positive actions such as recitations, prayers and meditation. At the end of each such action we should try to gather up the merit accruing from it and dedicate it towards all sentient beings' attaining ultimate happiness.

It is very good to meditate on Loving-kindness and Compassion – we should do so, and at the end of the meditation dedicate the merit for the benefit of all sentient beings.

Such dedication is very beneficial. On the one hand it really benefits sentient beings, and on the other it benefits ourself. Since our life is being used up like a burning candle and will quickly finish, we should use what we have left of this existence positively, by meditating and practising the Dharma and dedicating the merits for the happiness of all sentient beings.

9b.5 How to meditate on Compassion

[338–341] Loving-kindness and Compassion are linked in such a way that when we develop one, the other also develops. Loving-kindness is the wish that all other beings be endowed with happiness; this naturally brings about the wish that they be free of suffering, which is Compassion.

9b.6 How to meditate on the Superior Intention

[349–352] We should practise the meditations in sequence, first remembering the kindness of all sentient beings, then noticing their miserable situation, then developing Loving-kindness, the wish to see them happy, and then developing Compassion, the wish to see them free of suffering. Practising them one after the other will strengthen our mind until it comes to generate the Superior Intention.

The Superior Intention arises in our mind when the power of Loving-kindness and Compassion builds up, just as the heat of burning gas can warm up water and then boil it. It is the thought, "By myself, without asking the help of any other sentient being, I shall free all sentient beings from suffering and establish them in the state of happiness [and perfect Enlightenment]."

Many stories of the Buddha's previous lives are available in English translation,[84] which explain clearly his practice as a Bodhisattva, including the way he developed the Superior Intention to liberate all sentient beings by himself.

9b.7 *How to meditate on the generation of* Bodhicitta

[353–366] It is on the basis of the Superior Intention that *Bodhicitta*, the "Thought of Enlightenment", arises. When one has the strong determination to establish all beings in Enlightenment by oneself, one is still aware that in reality one lacks the ability to do this.

On consideration, one realizes that one would have the ability if one attained a state that is endowed with all qualities and powers and completely free of any fault or obstruction. This is the state one wishes to reach in order to help all sentient beings – namely, Buddhahood. In Buddhahood, one really can help all sentient beings effectively. Even a part of one's speech or one's mind, or one ray of light emanating from one's body, is able to benefit others infinitely. When we see this, *Bodhicitta* is beginning in our mind.

At this point, it is useful to understand what the qualities of the Buddha are. Many are described in the text.

9c HOW TO MEDITATE ON BODHICITTA BY EXCHANGE OF SELF AND OTHERS

The other method of developing *Bodhicitta* was taught by Shāntideva in the *Bodhisattva-caryâvatāra*.

[342] We have already been closely linked with every other sentient being, the only difference being the time, some earlier and some later. If we think deeply about it, every one of these beings has been extremely kind to us. In these circumstances, the attitude of being concerned only with one's own welfare, ignoring the welfare of the other sentient beings, is completely incorrect.

[343–6] It is incorrect not only in relation to the other sentient beings, but as regards oneself: the attitude concerned only with one's own benefit is the source of all the sufferings we experience. We know that because of one thing and another we always have endless problems – all these problems are due to cherishing ourself alone. Realizing this, we should now change this attitude and think that since self-cherishing is the cause of all our sufferings, from now on we shall cherish other sentient beings instead.

We maintain the self-cherishing attitude because it is supposed to benefit us, but actually it brings us only problems. But the Arhants, Bodhisattvas and Buddhas enjoy unceasing, great happiness, and their attainment is due to cherishing other sentient beings instead of themselves. For this reason too, cherishing only oneself is completely wrong.

The text gives several arguments, but the main point is that we should compare our present situation with that of the perfectly enlightened Buddhas. Because of self-cherishing, we live in a turbulent sea of sufferings; while through developing the attitude of cherishing others, the Enlightened Beings have attained complete perfection, accomplishing the benefits of both themselves and others. Recognizing this great difference between ourself and the Buddhas, we should try to effect a transformation.

[347] Going on to the actual practice of Exchanging, first we should generate the very strong, sincere wish to take upon ourself all the sufferings and difficulties of other sentient beings.

[348] Next, we should generate the very strong, sincere wish to dedicate all we have – that is, our body, speech and mind – to the service of others. We should develop the attitude that Shāntideva describes:

> Since I have given this body up
> To all sentient beings to do as they will,
> At their pleasure, they may always
> Kill it, abuse it, strike it and so on.[85]

In addition, we should dedicate to the benefit of other sentient beings all the merits we have accumulated through our practice of the Dharma, whether by reciting mantras, meditating, prostrating, or in any other way.

If we try, we are all quite capable of training our mind to

Meditation 9: The Development of Bodhicitta

develop this attitude. This is one way accessible to us of using our body, speech and mind to help sentient beings. [At Tharpa Choeling,] we try to sit in meditation for some minutes each morning. If at that time, instead of just thinking nothing, we try to develop the attitude of helping sentient beings, and then dedicate to their benefit all the merit accumulated through this mental effort, through our recitation of prayers, and through the meditational posture of the body, then we are beginning to do something wholesome. We can meditate as we wish in the morning: if we practise mindfulness of breathing, for example, this is good for calming the mind, but if we combine such meditation with training in this virtuous attitude, it is much more powerful and the effects can last all day long. If we combine our meditation with the practice of Giving and Taking,[86] it is very beneficial.

Meditation 10
How to Train in the Six Perfections

[367] The aim of Meditation 9 is to develop *Bodhicitta*, the powerful desire to attain Enlightenment for the benefit of all sentient beings. But this goal cannot be accomplished just by wishing. For example, if on top of a certain mountain is a ski station, with a good restaurant and other facilities, that we very much want to go to, we cannot get there simply by wishing every day, "May I get to the top of that mountain!" Actually to get there, we must either try to get a lift, or use our own money and take the funicular, the train and everything.

The work we must engage in to actualize the desire for Enlightenment is the practice of the Perfections (*pāramitā*).

To practise the Perfections formally, we should first take the Bodhisattva ordination. In fact, most of us [here] have already taken this ordination many times, as it is included in Tantric initiations. It involves taking the vow in front of one's Master [and all Buddhas and Bodhisattvas] to abandon eighteen root downfalls and forty-six secondary downfalls, turn one's mind away from such actions, try to avoid the negative causes that produce these downfalls, and try to accumulate all positive causes.[87]

[10a GIVING]

[368] The first Perfection, that of Giving, is here divided into three types.

(a) *Giving of Dharma*. If one gives a Dharma teaching motivated by the wish for some reward, such as offerings of money or gifts, respect, or reputation, that is not Giving. But if one gives the teaching solely for the benefit of other beings, then it is Giving of Dharma.

(b) *Giving of Safety*. If we find any being, human or animal, in great danger, especially in danger of its life, and are able to rescue it from that danger, this is Giving of Safety. Opportunities for such Giving are not rare – on a walk in the woods, one may encounter some small creature that lives on dry land but has fallen into water, or vice versa; if with Compassion one removes it from that danger then one is practising this Giving. Also one can buy live animals that are to be killed, such as fish, and release them in a suitable place.[88] This too is Giving of Safety.

(c) *Material Giving*. [369] Most people think giving material things is the only meaning of Giving, but [as we have seen,] this is not so. Still it is an important part of the practice of Giving. Whether or not the gift of a material object is real practice of Giving depends on the motivation. If one gives with hope of return, such as wishing for a bigger gift from the recipient or for good treatment from him, that is not really Giving, only a form of business. But if the motivation is a pure wish to help, then even though one gives very little, perhaps a few seeds to a bird, it is a pure practice of Giving.

Material Giving can be practised at any time, whether or not one actually gives a material thing; for the actual Giving is not the thing one gives but the mental attitude, the determination to give for the benefit of sentient beings, without any attachment to one's own welfare. This applies to all the forms of Giving.

The Perfection of Giving, here explained very briefly,[89] is the first of the Perfections because it is the easiest to practise.

[10b MORALITY]

(a) *Morality of Vows.* [370] This is threefold: *Pratimokṣa*, *Bodhicitta* (or Bodhisattva) and Tantric vows. When one takes a tantric initiation that involves Tantric Vows, there are certain tantric precepts one must follow; when one takes Bodhisattva ordination, or any *Pratimokṣa* ordination (whether as a lay follower or as a monk or nun), again there are corresponding vows to be observed. The Tibetan word for "vow", *sdom pa*, literally means "to tie". Just as a bunch of flowers will stay together if tied with a string, and fall apart if this tie breaks, so one's body, speech and mind need the restraint of vowed discipline to keep them under control.

If one has not taken any vows, there is still the basic practice of Morality to follow, which consists of abandoning the ten non-virtuous actions.

(b) *Morality of Collecting Positive* Dharmas. [370–1] This means trying to accumulate with our body, speech and mind as much virtue as we can, through prayers, recitations, prostrations and all forms of virtuous action. It includes all our study and practice of the Dharma, which is our principal task.

(c) *Morality of Helping Sentient Beings.* [371–2] This is using our body, speech and mind to try and help other sentient beings as much as possible, in whatever way we can.

[10c PATIENCE]

This Perfection also is threefold: unconcern with the harms one receives, willingly bearing suffering, and certain thought about the Dharma.

(a) *Patience of Unconcern with Harming.* [373] Normally when another being, human or otherwise, harms us, our mind becomes agitated. All the time, our mind is under the domination of the three poisons – greed, hate and delusion – but sometimes they are strongly manifest and sometimes not noticeable. They are like a wound that normally one is unaware of but which gives a lot of pain if it touches anything. So usually our mind is fairly peaceful, but when it meets certain conditions then a defilement such as anger manifests.

Anger can arise for a positive reason, when one is angry for someone else's benefit, as when a mother is very concerned about the welfare of her child; or one can be angry on one's own behalf. Anger arises very easily in us. This is natural, but when it happens, we should think it is not correct to let anger arise, because from beginning to end it is harmful. When it arises it destroys our peace of mind and makes us unhappy for a time; and besides this it leaves a negative imprint on our mind, which will eventually give rise to greater suffering in the future.

In addition, we should think that we are seeking to emulate the Bodhisattvas. They, when another being harms them, are not upset and do not react at all, but remain peaceful and even return help for harm. As followers of the Bodhisattva Path, we should do likewise.

This is easy to say but very difficult to practise. Anger is not easy to control. Still, to attempt the practice of Patience in such situations, not reacting to harm, is very beneficial. Even from the worldly point of view, someone who can remain peaceful and unaffected by harm is considered a good person. Also, if we practise Patience and do not react, it will eventually calm the anger of the other person, who will realize his fault and generate regret.

(b) *Patience of Willingly Bearing Suffering*. [374] This is concerned with all the other types of suffering we experience, not necessarily caused by beings – such problems as not finding food or work or a place to stay, or problems with our mind or our body. When we encounter such a situation, then instead of being upset, we should realize that it has not come about without cause, but is in fact the result of our own self-cherishing attitude. Constantly holding self-cherishing in our mind brings endless troubles.

(c) *Patience of Certain Thought about the Dharma*.[90] [375] This means an unchanging faith in the Buddhas, the Teaching and the other [objects of devotion], and determination concerning the practice.

[10d ENERGY]

(a) *Armour-like Energy* [376] is a very strong resolve to engage in any action, no matter how vast or profound and difficult, for helping other sentient beings and for realizing the Ultimate Goal.

(b) *Energy of Collecting Virtue*, [377] like the second Morality, means trying to accumulate as much virtue as one can with one's body, speech and mind.

(c) *Energy of Helping Sentient Beings* is helping other sentient beings, like the third Morality.

The general meaning of Energy (*vīrya*) is joy in the practice of virtue. Strenuous effort put into mundane actions is not Energy, only hardship.

This joy in the practice will arise naturally if one meditates correctly. Practising correctly, one soon experiences great peace and happiness in the mind, and this leads immediately to the development of Energy. If one has practised meditation for a long time but it remains a strenuous effort and does not arouse joy in the mind, then something must be wrong with one's way of meditating, and one should find out what.

[10e DHYĀNA]

[379] *Dhyāna* is a type of meditative concentration. From the point of view of its nature, it is divided into (a) samsaric *Dhyāna*, or *Dhyāna* in the mind of a samsaric being, and (b) Supermundane *Dhyāna*, *Dhyāna* in the mind of a being who has attained Liberation, i.e. an Arhant.

By way of class, there is *Dhyāna* falling into the class of Quietude (*śamatha*), that falling into the class of Insight (*vipaśyanā*), and that which is a Union of Quietude and Insight.

From the point of view of its function, *Dhyāna* is divided into three:

(a) *Dhyāna* that is not focussed upon an exalted topic, but brings about physical and mental bliss.
(b) *Dhyāna* that acts as a basis for qualities: when one concentrates on such objects as the Four Noble Truths,

or Selflessness of the personality, many qualities can be developed within one.[91]
(c) *Dhyāna* of benefiting sentient beings [380], [i.e. *Dhyāna* accomplishing the aims of the eleven ways of helping].[92]

[10f *WISDOM*]

[381–2] Wisdom is here divided into three:

(a) Wisdom perceiving the Ultimate Truth.
(b) Wisdom perceiving the conventional, which is skilled in the Five Sciences of grammar, logic, medicine, arts and crafts such as architecture, and "inner knowledge", or knowledge of religious philosophy.
(c) Wisdom that understands correctly how to accomplish without mistake both one's own benefit and the benefit of others.

Meditation 11
How to Train in the Four Means of Attraction

Sometimes one speaks of ten Perfections, adding to the six discussed briefly above the Perfections of Skill in Means, Vow, Power, and Wisdom-knowledge. Here, however, the four Means of Attraction (*saṃgraha-vastu*) are described instead. Whereas the six Perfections are primarily a means towards one's own Enlightenment, although of course they also benefit others, the four [Means of Attraction] are directed principally to the benefit of others.

(a) [383] In order to attract beings to be trained, so that he can teach them, a master should first give them material things such as food or whatever they need.

(b) Then he should teach them the Dharma, speaking in a pleasant, soothing manner.

(c) Just speaking pleasantly is not sufficient. When the disciples are relaxed, he should introduce them to actual practice of the Dharma.

(d) [383–4] In addition, he should be consistent with his own teaching, not only telling his disciples what to do but setting an example by practising it himself. Without such an example, they will not have any enthusiasm to practice.

These four Means of Attraction are the best way of benefiting others. The first two are not completely necessary – one may have no material wealth to share with potential converts, or one's voice may be rather harsh and not particularly pleasant – but the last two are indispensable.

Meditation 12
How to Meditate on Quietude

Now the text explains in more detail [the main parts of the fifth and sixth Perfections,] the meditations of Quietude (*śamatha*) and Insight (*vipaśyanā*).

[385] What we must have, in order to be free from samsara, is the understanding of Emptiness, the Ultimate Mode of Being of [oneself and all] phenomena. Without this, there can be no Liberation. [386] Furthermore, this Ultimate Mode of Being must be understood with a very stable, powerful mind, since if the mind is wavering [or weak] this understanding will not have the power to liberate us. To develop the necessary strength and stability of mind we must get rid of the two main hindrances, agitation and fading, and attain the one-pointed concentration of Quietude.

[387] In developing Quietude there are [five] faults, which we must overcome successively by applying the corresponding antidotes:

(a) Laziness, which does not let our mind be happy in the meditation, but leads it elsewhere.
(b) Forgetting the object: for example, if one is trying to concentrate on [a visualization of] a deity, the mind fails to continue recollecting the object, which disappears com-

pletely.
(c) Agitation and fading.
(d) Not applying the remedy of fading or agitation when one of these is present.
(e) Applying a remedy when the fault is not present.

[388] For these five faults, there are eight remedial actions.

(a) To get rid of laziness, there are four remedies:
 (i) Faith in the practice of this meditation, which one develops by contemplating its benefits. Stable, one-pointed concentration is very beneficial for oneself and also enables one to help others very much.
 (ii) Such faith in the meditation induces the desire to strive in its practice.
 (iii) When one has developed this desire to practise and attain *samādhi*, one is prepared to make much effort in it — that is, Energy (*vīrya*) arises spontaneously, as with any job one likes doing.
 (iv) [389] As a result of energetically pursuing the practice, a blissful Tranquillity (or relaxation) (*praśrabdhi*) of body and mind arises.
(b) To counter forgetfulness of the object, one must develop Mindfulness.
(c) To avoid agitation and fading, one must use Awareness, constantly checking to observe whether one or other of these hindrances is arising in the meditation.
(d) [389–390] If fading or agitation is present, then [with one's Will] one must apply the corresponding remedy.
(e) If neither is present, then one must keep the mind in a state of Unconcern, or Equanimity. Applying an antidote when the fault is not present is of no help, but only interferes with the meditation.

[391–3] The development of Quietude is further explained in terms of nine mental stages, which are developed in succession, using six powers and four types of attention. This explanation comes from two texts of Maitreya, *Mahāyāna-sūtrālaṃkāra* and *Madhyânta-vibhaṅga*,[93] but we need not go into it here.

Meditation 13
How to meditate on Insight

[394] We could practise meditation of Insight into Emptiness (*vipaśyanā*) straight away, but our mind is as unstable as the flame of a butter-lamp in the wind, so our meditation is constantly disrupted by random thoughts and forgetfulness. Therefore to be able to meditate forcefully on Emptiness, we must first develop one-pointed concentration. When we have achieved this, we shall be able to meditate on Emptiness or on any object we wish – our mind will be like a heavy stone, which stays just where you put it.

[13a *THE ROOT OF SAMSARA*[94]]

[395] We are samsaric beings, and thus constantly attacked by an endless series of problems and sufferings, which we are powerless to arrest. Sometimes we claim we are free and can do anything, but on analysis we can see this is untrue, for although we wish to be always happy and untroubled, troubles keep coming.

Sometimes, wishing to be happy and recognizing that the cause of happiness is virtue, we begin to practise virtue. But then obstacles arise, from external conditions or from within us, which interfere with this practice, and it is unsuccessful.

Furthermore, if a wrong view concerning the spiritual Path arises in our mind, this can completely destroy our roots of virtue. Outside we might look the same, but inside we should be totally different and in a miserable situation.

We engage in non-virtues with body, speech and mind, but the heaviest are the mental ones. We are shocked to hear of the Nazis exterminating millions of people, and indeed this is a heavy karma, but it happens to be a visible action. It is stated in the Sutras that the negative karma of wrong views about the Dharma is far heavier than that of killing people.

Until we reach a certain stage of spiritual development – the stage of Summits on the Path of Preparation – we are subject to our roots of virtue being destroyed by wrong view. This illustrates the extent to which we lack real power over our existence. It also shows that in our Dharma practice we should proceed slowly and carefully, not undertaking what is beyond our capacity, otherwise there is danger of error.

Since we are so helpless in samsara, then, we must investigate the cause for our being there. What is the source of our problems, and how may we eliminate it?

Generally we seek the cause of suffering outside ourself. Sometimes, indeed, external factors act as a condition for our experiencing suffering, while sometimes we just project this upon them, but in fact the most fundamental cause lies within us. Similarly, if we plant a seed in the ground, warmth, moisture and the rest act as conditions for its growing into a sprout, but the main cause of the sprout is the seed itself.

For example, if someone looks at us in a way we do not like, we get angry, and put the blame on that person, but really we should blame our own anger.

[396–7] The basic problem is a type of confusion present in us, which grasps the manner in which we exist in a way that does not conform to reality. On the basis of this, defilements start to grow within us, which leads towards problems. It is like starting a business with a fundamental mistake in your plans – everything goes wrong, you do not get what you wanted, and you get into trouble with other people as well.

Our mind is not defiled by nature, but neutral. However, when we meet certain external conditions, for example when somebody criticizes us or praises us, there arises a sense of an 'I' or ego that seems to be the real I, existing autonomously within us, there from before and not dependent on anything else such as external conditions. If we go into an old church and see a carved crucifix on the wall, this crucifix appears to be there from its own side, from long before, autonomous and not dependent on the fact that we are seeing it: the way the I appears is similar to this. The feeling of I seems to grasp directly something that we consider our person, as definitely as an arrow hitting its target with a THUNK.

In fact, there is no inherently-existent, autonomous I as that sense of I grasps it – its appearance is a fabrication of ignorance. This does not mean we do not exist at all – we do exist, and engage in various activities such as studying this teaching – but we do not exist that way.

This spontaneous sense of an inherent self is something that every sentient being possesses, even an insect; it is not an intellectual acceptance of the existence of a self, such as may occur through thinking about it, training one's mind in a particular philosophy, or being taught that there is such a self. That sort of speculative self-grasping presents its own problems, but it is the spontaneous, innate sense of self that is most responsible for the sufferings we experience.

Innate self-grasping is present in our mind all the time, but it is usually latent. It manifests itself strongly on such occasions as someone's insulting or praising us.

Based on this innate sense of self, we divide the world into two – "mine" and the rest. To our body, our aggregates, our possessions, our friends, and all that we consider "mine", we develop attachment. Towards people we regard as enemies, things we do not need, ideas contrary to ours, and everything else on the side opposite to ours, we develop hatred and aversion.

Motivated by attachment and hatred, we act with our body, speech and mind. Arising out of negative states of mind, all these actions are unwholesome and can bring only suffering as a result. For example, thousands of animals are killed every day, and the people who killed them are motivated by attachment to themselves and their families – wanting food or money, they kill many sentient beings and accumulate bad karma. While many of us do not kill animals, we create other wrong actions. Our speech is largely motivated by attachment and hatred, and leads us into many problems.

When these actions finish, they leave negative imprints on our mind. Although these imprints are not something material that can be seen or felt as a weight, we have many of them, and when they meet the right conditions they will ripen and give rise to suffering results. They are the seeds of suffering referred to above, just waiting for the right conditions so that they can germinate. Every day we accumulate such imprints, which can cause only difficulties in this life and later lives.

Hence we circle, life after life, in the six samsaric realms, so that if we ask where we have been one can hardly say [more precisely than "in samsara"], just as when a lighted incense stick is twirled rapidly in the dark, all one can see is a red circle. As we spin, a continuous series of unpleasant experiences come one after the other, like ripples on water stirred by the wind.

[398] If we wish to eliminate this suffering of our samsaric existence, we must uproot its cause, the innate sense of an inherent self. To do this, we must realize that in reality there is no inherently existent self; then the grasping of such a self will be destroyed and the main cause of suffering will no longer be there. After that – just as when there is no seed in the ground, no amount of sun and rain will produce a sprout – no conditions, external or internal, will be able to make us experience suffering.

[13b *HOW TO MEDITATE ON SELFLESSNESS OF THE PERSONALITY*]
[13b.1 *First point, ascertaining the object of negation*][95]

[399] The innate self-grasping mind being immaterial, we cannot excise it by surgery, or even destroy it with bombs; we cannot catch it like a thief and throw it in gaol. What we must do is apply analysis to it in meditation.

First, we must make ourself very clearly aware of just how the inherent existence of the self appears to us. It may be useful to think about unpleasant situations in which people abuse us, or pleasant situations in which people praise us, and learn to recognize the manner in which the sense of an autonomous ego then appears.[96]

It is very important to understand this manner of appearance clearly, before we go on to investigate whether the self really exists like that. If we have not ascertained the manner of appearance at the beginning, then subsequent analysis is like trying to interrogate a thief when you have not caught him and have no idea who is the thief. Asking in an empty house, "Have you been stealing?" and so forth, is so much wasted breath. So, first catch your thief.

[13b.2 *Second point, ascertaining the major premise*][97]

[400] Once we have a clear image of the inherently existent self, we can begin to check whether it exists as it appears. Still it is not useful to negate its existence straight away – this does not help to eliminate one's ignorance. First we must investigate where it appears. If there does exist such an inherently existent I, then [there are only two possibilities:] either it exists within our aggregates (i.e. our body and mind) or it must exist outside them.

[13b.3 *Third point, ascertaining freedom from oneness (with the aggregates)*][98]

[401–3] If this I exists inherently as one with our aggregates, we must be able to find it either in our body or in our mind. So we should investigate, does it exist in our body?

Is my head the I? This is impossible, for the I is a person, whereas the head is not a person. Are my arms my self? They cannot be, because my self is a person, but my arms are just a part of the body that the person possesses, not a person.

We continue this analysis, analyzing many parts of the body – legs, flesh, bones, fat and so on – and see that each one is not a person, just something the person possesses. We find that there is no particle of our body that can be considered to be the inherently-existent I that appears so strongly.

So it is not in the body; that leaves the mind. We may think the mind is the inherently-existent I — then we must check whether there is such an I in the mind. The mind includes six types of consciousness, five sensory and one mental – is any of these the I? Clearly [the sensory consciousnesses] are something we possess, and not our person. The mental consciousness, if we investigate, is not a single unity but has many different aspects, such as conceptual [and perceptual minds and different moments], whereas we are only one person. If we accept that the mind, or the mental consciousness, is the person, then it follows we are many people, which is absurd.

The mind and the person are quite distinct in nature – the mind is clear and knowing, while the person is an impermanent entity which is neither matter nor consciousness.

[13b.4 *Fourth point, ascertaining freedom from plurality (in relation to the aggregates)*][99]

[404] Thus there is not such an I within either our body or our mind; and if we look outside the body and mind, we also cannot find an I separate from them, a metre to one side or anywhere.

[405] Thus our analysis arrives at a kind of empty space, where we realize that the appearance of the ego was baseless – from the beginning, the inherently-existent person has not been there, but still there has been the illusory appearance of an inherently-existent person.

This analysis must be performed in meditation. And it is not sufficient to do it once and reach the space where there is no appearance of an inherently existent I, then say "Right, there is no inherently existent I," and leave it there. The mind grasping an inherently existent self is so strong that it cannot be overcome just by one analysis. Rather, we must repeat the analysis many times, first recognizing the manner in which the inherent I appears to the mind, then applying various sorts of analysis[100] to find that there is no such inherent I present, and arriving at the space of Emptiness. With repeated analysis, the mind grasping an inherent self will weaken.

When we go into a dark room at night, we may see a vague shape we think might be a burglar. We are frightened; then, cautiously investigating, we find it is only a grandfather clock, so our mind grasping it as a burglar vanishes, and with it our fear. In the same way, repeated practice of this analysis leads us to understand thoroughly that the inherently existent I, which was so clear to start with, is not there at all, so consequently the mind grasping it gradually disappears, and with this the defilements, which were based on that confusion. When our mind is no longer polluted by defilements, our actions become pure and unmistaken, and no imprints will be left on the mind to create future suffering. In addition, we can by various methods purify the imprints already on our mind, and so cut completely the way to suffering.

When we reach the empty space devoid of appearance of I, we must not think that we do not exist as a person at all. Although there is no inherently existent I in us, still we exist conventionally as a person; otherwise there would be no-one to experience the world, go here and there, and create problems for himself out of his delusion.

[13c HOW TO MEDITATE ON SELFLESSNESS OF DHARMAS]

[The text repeats the four-point analysis, applying it to (a) the body (verses 406–9) and (b) the mind [410–13]. Then [414] it indicates the extension to all *dharmas*. This analysis being so similar to that for the person, Geshe Rabten did not comment on it.]

[415] *Dharmas* (or phenomena), then, do not exist from their own side; they appear to exist as autonomous and self-supporting, existent from their own side, or truly existent, but in reality they do not exist in accordance with this mode of appearance.

[416] But still they are not non-existent: they do exist, because we experience suffering and happiness and engage in activities. That is to say, they exist empirically. To elucidate the mode of existence, the text quotes some analogies – they exist in the manner of dreams, illusions such as an appearance of a horse conjured up by a magician, echoes, or a reflection of the full moon in water. All these things appear in a certain way but do not exist as they appear.

[417] We should understand these examples clearly. A dream is not real, [for example, a house in a dream is not a real

house,] but still it is there, and comes about because of the ripening of various mental imprints while one sleeps; when these imprints are finished, the dream ceases. A reflection of the moon in water is not a real moon, but still that appearance is there, arising from [a collection of] such conditions as the pool of water and the moon. An echo of a voice is not an actual voice, but still it is an echo, it exists and comes about because of certain conditions. [418] In the same way, all *dharmas*, although not truly existent, exist in dependence on a coming-together of conditions.

[419–420] *Dharmas* exist in this way, but if we investigate them using ultimate analysis, such as we applied above to the person, then it is impossible to find them. What such analysis reveals is the lack of a truly and independently existent person [or *dharma*], not that the person [or *dharma*] does not exist at all.

When this ultimate analysis is applied in meditation, one arrives at the experience of an empty space, where the object of negation no longer appears.

[421–2] But then, when one rises out of that concentration, one again sees *dharmas*, such as forms, but in a special way. Although they still appear as existing truly, from their own side, one can see that they do not exist in the way they appear. Thus in the post-meditational period one sees phenomena as like dreams, echoes, and the rest.

[423] The meditation on Emptiness, using ultimate analysis to arrive at the experience of space, is of twofold purpose. On the one hand it serves to eliminate our habitual bad tendencies and latent impressions created through actions based on self-grasping, and all our defilements. [That is, we gradually abandon our negativities and obscurations.] On the other hand, through this meditation on Ultimate Truth we accumulate the collection of Wisdom. In addition, in the postmeditational period we see *dharmas* as like dreams, echoes, [or illusions,] appearing as truly existent but not existing the way they appear. Through this understanding, we can act in accordance with reality, practise the Dharma, and so accumulate the collection of Merits. This also is necessary for the practice of the Path. Thus by these two practices, the ["Space-like yoga" of] concentra-

tion of Emptiness, and seeing phenomena as existing in the manner of illusions, we can gather the two collections, of Wisdom and Merits. That is, we develop what is positive.

The practice of the Path consists in the abandonment of the negative and the actualization of the positive. The best way to accomplish this twofold task is through the practice explained here, of meditation on Emptiness combined with seeing objects as like illusions.

Meditation 14
How to Enter the Adamantine Vehicle

Now the text discusses very briefly when and how to enter the Adamantine Vehicle, the Vajrayāna.

[424] Before entering the Vajrayāna Path, one must have developed the three ordinary Paths of Renunciation, *Bodhicitta*, and Right View of Emptiness. When one has these three, one should seek a qualified Vajra Master, both learned and realized. Having found him, one must rely on him with unwavering faith, and request initiation at his feet.

[425] Taking an initiation, or empowerment, involves accepting certain commitments and vows. The commitments are specific to a particular empowerment – reciting the *sādhana* and so forth – while the vows are the general requirements for tantric practice. Too often we observe the commitments of recitation etc., but forget the most important vows. Really we should keep all the vows well.

First one practises the Generation Stage, then [when that has been realized,] the Completion Stage, until finally one attains the stage of Unification, or Buddhahood.

This completes the teaching of this text, the *Essential Nectar of the Holy Doctrine*. I have not commented on it word by word, but explained the condensed meaning. If you wish to see just how each subject is explained in the text you can look at the translation.

The Text

The Essential Nectar of the Holy Doctrine
Dam chos bdud rtsi'i snying po

by Kongpo Lama, Yeshe Tsöndrü

How to practise
the profound instructions
on the Stages of the Path
to Enlightenment,
in verse

The Essential Nectar of the Holy Doctrine

To my Glorious, Holy Root Guru and those of His lineage, combining in one all the Conquerors of the three times, I prostrate and go for Refuge. May They look after me inseparably in all my future lives!

Here I shall describe concisely, in verse, how fortunate tamable beings may practise the profound instructions on the Stages of the Path to Enlightenment.

[THE PREPARATORY PRACTICES]

3a FIRST, THE STAGE OF TAKING REFUGE

1   Before me, midst a cloud-sea of wondrous off'rings,
    Upon a throne which eight mighty and powerful
    Lions uphold, precious and very wide,
    On a lotus-flower and great discs of sun and moon,

2   Is my Root Guru who shows the unerring Path,
    Indivisible from the Lord, the King of Sages,
    Shining like the peak of a golden mountain,
    With the Marks' and Signs' glory, and clad in the three
        monk's robes.

3   His right hand earth-touching, his left, in contemplation,
Holds an alms-bowl, brim-full with *amṛita*.
His body, a mass of splendour whose sight never palls,
Sits radiantly amidst a web of light.

4   Around this matchless and exalted Teacher
Sit all the Gurus of the three lineages,
Just as the stars of the lunar constellations
Surround the disc of the Moon upon all sides.

5   Surrounding these direct and lineage Gurus
Are *Yidam* deities, Buddhas of the ten
Directions, Bodhisattvas, Hearers, *Pratyekas*,
And hosts of *ḍākinīs* and Dharma-Protectors.

6   To each one's right and left, on well-made tables,
Are volumes of the pure teachings which have come
Out of his mouth, every letter of which
Proclaims the song of the Dharma, in its own sound.

7   From the bodies of these objects of Refuge,
Light-rays spread throughout the ten directions.
The end of every light-ray emits countless
Emanations, who ripen sentient beings.

8   With compassionate eyes they gaze upon me:
"Son of good family, if you wish to be free
From samsaric suffering, I will help you,"
They say, as with smiling face they comfort me.

9   Surrounding me, my parents and all sentient beings,
Afflicted with sufferings of the six classes of beings,
Looking everywhere, desperate for refuge,
Wailing in torment and lamenting, are set.

10   Alas! from beginningless time until the present,
I have been circling among the six realms of existence,
Tortured always by a hundred sufferings,
But never finding a way to escape from them.

11   Now I've a good means, this opportune rebirth,
And have met the Master and the Excellent Doctrine;

But since to drive back beginningless habit's defilements
Is hard, I've had no hope of taking their permanent stronghold.

12 There is no assurance I will not die today.
    Where I'm reborn is not in my control.
    So if I fall in th' abyss of the realms of woe,
    Think – can I bear their suffering for a moment?

13 Though I win the rare, high state of a human or god,
    Hundreds of suff'rings, like birth, age, sickness and death,
    Still torment me incessantly; since I shall fall
    Again to ill destiny, how trust in high estate?

14 So, having now gained the favoured, opportune birth,
    And been received by an excellent Path-showing Guru,
    Now seeing samsara's faults and Nirvana's virtues,
    I must quickly free myself from this dreadful samsara.

15 But liberating myself is not enough.
    Since all these migrating beings, lost in samsara,
    Are none other than my own mothers and fathers,
    I must free them all from samsara too.

16 So, since there is not a single Refuge and helper
    Who can free all sentient beings, myself and others,
    From the vast and endless ocean of samsara
    Apart from these three Exalted Ones, therefore:

17 I and all migrators, boundless like space,
    Henceforth, until the Perfection of Enlightenment,
    Go for Refuge to the direct and lineage Gurus.
    We go for Refuge to the Buddhas, the Revealers.
    We go for Refuge to the Dharma, both scripture and insight.
    We go for Refuge to the Sangha, the host of *Āryas*.

Say this verse three or seven times, or as desired.

18 This Taking Refuge pleases all the Objects
    Of Refuge; streams of nectar pour from their bodies,

Washing away my own and other beings'
Sins, veils, diseases, and conditions hostile to life;

19   Purifying faults with regard to the Three Supreme Ones;
Greatly increasing life, merits, and virtues
Of scripture and insight; admitting all sentient beings,
Myself and others, to Refuge in the Three Jewels.

3b GENERATION OF BODHICITTA

20   Just as I am bound in samsara's prison
By fetters of karma and *kleśa*, and tormented,
So too are those who've repeatedly been my mothers,
Nursing me kindly – all suffering sentient beings.

21   The burden of freeing these beings falls on me;
But my present condition being what it is,
So much for my liberating others –
There's no knowing where I'll migrate myself!

22   Gaining either Arhantship would not complete
My own benefit, and is trifling help to others.
So, to perfect both my own and others' benefit,
I must certainly win the rank of a Conqueror.

23   If I win that most exalted rank,
All weakness stops, and every virtue's perfect,
So that I can help without an effort
My wand'ring old mothers, wherever space extends.

24   Therefore I must attain without delay
The station of a Perfect Buddha. For
This reason, undismayed, I must train in turn
In all the powerful actions, such as Giving.

25   Through my rousing thus the Supreme *Bodhicitta*,
The Gurus, Conqu'rors and their Sons are delighted.
From the King of Sages' body, a replica
Dissolves into me, cleansing all obscurations and sins.

26   I am transformed into a Sage-King's body.
From my body, light-rays spread to the ten directions,
Removing all faults of the impure world and its beings,

So only purity fills the Universe.

3c THE FOUR IMMEASURABLES

27 Alas! though all these wandering sentient beings
    In countless lives have been each other's parents,
    They know it not, and so through greed and hatred
    Heap up bad deeds, and experience only sorrow.

28 If now, free of mutual greed and hatred,
    They dwelt in equanimity, how wonderful!
    May they so dwell! I will make them dwell thus!
    Please inspire me so that I can do this!

29 Alas! though all these wandering sentient beings
    Always want only happiness, nevertheless,
    Since they don't know that happiness' cause is virtue,
    Of if they do, are unable to achieve it,

30 They're destitute of happiness. If they now
    Had happiness and its cause, how wonderful!
    May they have it! I will make this happen!
    Please inspire me so that I can do this!

31 Alas! though all these wandering sentient beings
    Never in any way want suffering,
    Very deluded, mistaking right and wrong practice,
    They're always absorbed in negative, sinful actions;

32 So suff'ring afflicts them. If they now were free
    Of suffering and its cause, how wonderful!
    May they be free! I will make this happen!
    Please inspire me so that I can do this!

33 Alas! if all these wandering sentient beings
    Were free of all sufferings, general to samsara
    Or particular to ill destinies, and their causes;
    Then attaining in order the bliss of high estate

34 And Liberation, were never separate from
    Unsullied Supreme Bliss, how wonderful!
    May they be unseparate! I will make this happen!
    Please inspire me so that I can do this!

3d SPECIAL GENERATION OF BODHICITTA

35   Especially, to free all space-wide sentient beings,
I must quickly, quickly become a Buddha.
Therefore, I'll practise the deep instructions on
The Stages of the Path to Enlightenment!

4 VISUALIZING THE FIELD OF ACCUMULATION.

For ease of practice, the same Refuge Objects visualized previously may be retained here by memory, and not absorbed. At this point, it is taught, one should do the Invocation and Bath Offering, as follows.

5 TRAIN THE MIND WITH THE SEVEN LIMBS
INVOCATION

36   Direct and Lineage Gurus in fields throughout space!
Hosts of *Yidam* deities, Buddhas, Bodhisattvas!
Hearers, *Pratyekas*, heroes, *ḍākinīs*, guardians!
All of you, with compassion, please listen to me!

37   Forget not your Vow, when for our sake, in
       measureless eons,
You generated the supreme *Bodhicitta!*
Like the garuda in the celestial vault,
With compassion, through your magical powers come
       here!

5a BATH OFFERING*

38   Behold this bath-house, filled with scented fragrance,
With floor of crystal, clear and shimmering!
Graceful pillars of sparkling gems it has,
Spread with a canopy of glowing pearls.

39   Just as, at the Holy Birth,

---

*Not given in full in the text. Verses 38, 41 & 43 are from *Bodhisattva-caryâvatāra* II. 10–12, the others from various puja texts, hence a certain lack of continuity.

>Gods made offerings of baths,
>I, with purest, heavenly water
>Offer you this bath likewise.
>OṂ SARVA-TATHĀGATA-ABHIṢEKATASAMAYA-ŚRĪYE ĀḤ HŪṂ!

40 Though the body, speech and mind of Conquerors lack defilements,
May off'ring this bath to the Conquerors' bodies, speech and minds
To cleanse beings' obscurations of body, speech and mind
Make pure beings' obscurations of body, speech and mind!

41 *Tathāgatas* and your Sons, I offer to you
This bath, with numerous vases of precious substance
Filled to the brim with pleasant, perfumed water,
Accompanied copiously by songs and music.

42 Since it's an excellent, glorious bath,
With matchless water of Compassion
And inspiring Wisdom-knowledge water,
Please grant whatever attainments I wish!

43 I dry your bodies with a matchless cloth,
Clean and anointed with the finest perfume.
OṂ HŪṂ TRĀM HRĪḤ ĀḤ KĀYA-VIŚODHANAYE SVĀHĀ!

44 In order to train my mind, I offer you
Various garments, exquisite and precious,
Blissful to touch and as sparkling bright as rainbows.
May I be adorned with the excellent garment of Patience!

45 Since Conqu'rors are naturally adorned with the Marks and Signs,
One cannot seek to adorn them with further ornaments;
But through my offering of the finest of jewels,
May all beings win the Body with Marks and Signs!

46 A surround of love, with pennants of sweet words,
With *samādhi* as canopy, clear light of quick wits —
These worthy requisites, excellent conditions, I offer.
May beings attain the purest wisdom-knowledge!

47 From your compassion for me and all beings,
By the might of your magical powers,
As long as I am performing this puja
Please remain, O Conquerors!

5b THE SEVEN LIMBS COMBINING THE POINTS OF PURIFICATION AND ACCUMULATING MERIT
5b.1 Prostration

48 "I must guide the beings of the Age of Conflict
Whom infinite other Conquerors have not tamed!" —
So with the three secrets, in this field you manifested,
Guru, King of Sages — to you I prostrate!

49 Most skilled in the means of the Vast and Profound
    Instructions
Of Sutra and Tantra, you lead those sunk in despair
In samsara's ocean to the steps to the Precious Three
    Bodies,
Direct and Lineage Gurus — to you I prostrate!

50 If anyone zealously practises and reveres you,
You grant in an instant the level of Unification,
Hard to find in many eons, O *Yidams*
Of the four classes of Tantra — to you I prostrate!

51 Through countless eons' practice of the two
Accumulations, you exhausted all faults and perfected
Every virtue. O Teachers, Buddhas whose deeds
Are spontaneous and unceasing, to you I prostrate!

52 Whoever relies on you, you cleanse of all faults,
And grant without exception every perfection
Of high estate and Definite Goodness. Holy
Dharma of Scripture and Insight, to you I prostrate!

53   Not thinking of your own happiness even when
        dreaming,
    With courage regardless of even your body and life
    You always work only for others' happiness,
    Exalted Sons of the Conqu'rors – to you I prostrate!

54   Seeing all samsaric states as like a fire-pit,
    Riding in the litter of the Three Trainings
    You travel to the city of Liberation,
    Hearer and *Pratyeka Āryas* – to you I prostrate!

55   In four and twenty supreme holy places
    You always think in compassion of practitioners,
    And appear in a dance of varied emanations,
    Assemblies of heroes and *dākinīs* – to you I prostrate!

56   Fulfilling the wished-for hopes of all who practise
    The Holy Dharma correctly, as they want,
    You pulverize tribes of intractable, hindering demons,
    Sworn Protectors of Dharma – to you I prostrate!

57   In short, to all who are worthy of prostration,
    I manifest bodies as numerous as the realms,
    And hymning their virtues with oceans of lyric praise,
    With firm faith and great devotion I prostrate!

5b.2 *Offering*

58   Ample, precious vessels, well-ordered and perfect,
    I fill with a water-off'ring of deathless nectar.
    On the banks of a pool adorned with delightful lotuses,
    Swirl fine streams, with the eight properties, to wash
        your feet.

59   A myriad lovely flowers, such as *utpalas,*
    Kumudas, and lotuses, fill the earth.
    From different kinds of medicinal spices, clouds
    Of fragrant, burning incense fill the air.

60   Everywhere shine the lights of suns and moons,
    Of glowing jewels and lamps of purest butter.

	Full of the scent of sandalwood and camphor,
	Flows gently wave after wave of cool, perfumed water.
61	Abounding in hundreds of flavours, scents and colours,
	Are laid out food and drink for gods and humans.
	Varied sounds of music, such as lutes,
	Cymbals, flutes and drums vibrate the three worlds.
62	The best of forms, sweet sounds, fine smells and tastes,
	Infinite kinds of pleasing tangibles, and
	Superb royal gems, the seven precious things,
	And the eight lucky symbols, arrayed, fill all the realms.
63	Trees, flowers and lakes and other pleasant things
	That no-one owns, any offering things there are,
	My own and others' bodies and all our enjoyments,
	Unattached, fearless and joyful, I offer to all.
64	All merits I've heaped up from hearing, thinking and meditating
	On the Sage's ocean of Sutra and Tantra teachings;
	And masses of marvellous off'rings, produced by my power,
	Like All-Good's off'ring-clouds, filling all realms, I offer.
65	Thus I offer this sea of clouds of manifold off'rings
	Produced by faith, conviction and *samādhi*.
	Please accept them in compassion, and rain
	Siddhis and all we want on me and all wanderers.

5b.3 *Confession of sins*

At this point, do the *Confession of Downfalls (Appendix 1)* and so on, or not, as you wish.

66	The only cause of all my measureless sufferings,
	My negative actions of body, speech and mind,
	Which I have done before, or ordered done:
	Each one I confess from the heart, and will make cease.

5b.4 *Rejoicing*

67 In every good action of the supreme direct
 And lineage Gurus, of the infinite Conquerors
 And of their Sons, in past or present or future,
 I rejoice with great devotion and sincerity.

5b.5 *Requesting the Turning of the Wheel of Dharma*

68 To me and the wanderers fallen into the depths
 Of the frightful abyss of samsara, overcome
 By dense darkness of suffering, knowing not what to do,
 Please show the light of Dharma, the Path of Freedom!

5b.6 *Asking the Gurus to remain*

69 With Skill and Compassion, may all the Form Bodies you manifest
 To universal tamable beings to tame them
 Please remain as protectors for each of these beings
 Till every wanderer reaches Supreme Enlightenment!

5b.7 *Dedication*

70 All my heaped-up virtues, shown by this,
 I dedicate so that I quickly win Highest Enlightenment,
 To set forever these wanderers, my old mothers,
 Tired of samsara's path, on the Path of Bliss.

6a THE MANDALA OFFERING

At this point, offer a mandala.

6b MAKING REQUESTS, IN ACCORDANCE WITH THE ORAL INSTRUCTIONS

71 O my Root Guru, glorious and precious,
 Sitting on lotus and moon upon my crown,
 Please take care of me through your great kindness
 And grant the attainments of body, speech and mind!

72 Amid the thousand Guides of this fortunate eon,
    You excel in compassion for beings of this Age of Strife,
    O Great Guru, King of Sages, Vajradhara!
    I request you: please inspire my mindstream!

73 Following deity yogas of the Great Secret,
    The lucky you lead in one life to Unification,
    Assembly of Gurus who inspire the Practice!
    I request you: please inspire my mindstream!

74 The points of the Vast Path, th'Perfection of Wisdom's hidden
    Meaning, moved by Compassion, you teach to migrators,
    Gurus of the Lineage of Vast Conduct!
    I request you: please inspire my mindstream!

75 Embodied beings who ramble in ignorant error
    You fix in the Path of Deep, Unbusied Peace,
    Gurus of the lineage of Profound View!
    I request you: please inspire my mindstream!

76 Holding both traditions, of Vast and Profound advice,
    You spread in Tibet the Supreme Vehicle's Teaching,
    Assembly of Gurus of the Kadam Lineage!
    I request you: please inspire my mindstream!

77 You teach well all explanations of Sutra and Tantra
    Combined in one person's Path to Enlightenment,
    Assembly of Gurus of the Ganden Kagyü!
    I request you: please inspire my mindstream!

78 Very Compassion of all the countless Conqu'rors
    Turned into the form of excellent, Path-showing Friends,
    O Root Gurus, endowed with such great kindness,
    I request you: please inspire my mindstream!

Next, recite the *Yon tan gzhir gyur ma* (Appendix 2: 14 verses), or if you feel inclined to do something slightly longer, [continue with the following prayers for success in the Stages of the Path].

79   May the thought that high Gurus, who show the unerring Path,
Have ordinary faults, arise not for a moment!
Seeing you act well, mindful of your great kindness
Let me practise as you teach – inspire me thus!

80   Let me quickly stop reckless, unconcerned, wrong attitudes,
Which uselessly squander this excellent, opportune birth,
And earnestly minding its rarity and value,
Seize its most useful essence – inspire me thus!

81   Free of the grasping at permanence, that I'll endure
A hundred years, although I see death's uncertain,
Let me be earnestly mindful of my nature –
I'll die soon, but when is uncertain – inspire me thus!

82   Let me eradicate thoughts and actions which fail
In the least to dread the unbearable threefold abyss;
When I just recall what I've seen or heard of ill destinies'
Nature, let terror arise – inspire me thus!

83   Though I see the great danger, I still might not seek the Protectors –
Let me cast out such thoughts, and quite free of this attitude
Take Refuge earnestly in the Three Supreme Jewels,
The sole non-deceptive Refuge – inspire me thus!

84   Let my stubbornness cease, which will not trust although
I've seen and heard hundreds of kinds of cause and effect!
Let me find real confidence in the laws of white
And black actions and their results – inspire me thus!

85   Free of the mind that sees sundry samsaric places,
Bodies and objects as pleasant, and is attached,

Let me understand all three realms are like pits of fire,
And develop a strong wish for Freedom – inspire me thus!

86 Let me banish this foe, self-grasping, which has bound me
Since time without beginning in samsara's gaol;
And be skilled in the Three Trainings' practice, the complete, unerring,
Supreme Path of Release – inspire me thus!

87 Let not low motivation arise, which abandons migrators
And strives for my own nirvanic bliss alone,
But the highest sort grow very quickly, which shoulders the burden
Of benefit of others – inspire me thus!

88 Let me drive out this chronic disease of cherishing self,
Sole cause of all problems of samsara and beyond,
And grow skilled in cherishing others more than myself,
Sole way for our full joint perfection – inspire me thus!

89 In carrying out the ocean of Buddha-son's deeds,
Let me not be fainthearted even for a moment,
But train in the Six Perfections, as in the stories
Of Heroes who dwell in the Stages – inspire me thus!

90 All main obstructions to realizing pure *dhyāna* –
Agitation, fading, conceptions, and signs – allayed,
May I develop effortless concentration,
Controlling at will any object – inspire me thus!

91 With wrong views, extreme or perverse, which deviate from
The deep meaning of the Conqueror's thought, not arising
Let me soon realize truly the primordial mode of existence,
Alliance of Void and appearance – inspire me thus!

92 Devoid of the falsely-based mind that seeks the
      Quick Path
    Discouraged at the Buddha-sons' powerful deeds,
    Let me enter the Great Secret Vehicle with the
      intention
    Of rushing to free all migrators – inspire me thus!

93 Removing all stains of downfalls and faults
      transgressing
    Major and minor promises made at empowerments,
    Let me see that commitments and vows are the Path's
      foundation,
    And cherish them like my life – inspire me thus!

94 Without the fears of ordinary birth, death and *bardo*,
    Which while in samsara always join me to suffering,
    Let me master the Two Stages, seeing surroundings
      and beings
    As the Three Bodies' vajra play – inspire me thus!

95 For the moment, also, all sign of inner and outer
    Obstructions that hinder the good Path's practice
      quelled,
    May the good collections and all advantageous
      conditions
    Come spontaneously, without effort – inspire me thus!

96 In all future lives, may I gain the opportune rebirth
    And meet a Guru who teaches the Path like this,
    And by hearing, thinking and meditating, rush
      through
    The Stages and Paths, win Omniscience, then free all
      beings!

Making requests like this, one practises also the stages of visualization of *Opening the Door of the Supreme Path* and requesting many inspirations, according to the oral instructions. Then one either absorbs the Field of Accumulation, as given in *bDe lam*, or not, as given in the *Oral Precepts of Mañjuśrī* (*'Jam dpal zhal lung*), as one wishes. (These are *Lam rim* texts by the First Panchen Lama and the Fifth Dalai Lama.)

THE ACTUAL PRACTICE: BASICS
MEDITATION 1
GURU DEVOTION
1a.1 The advantages of devotion to one's Spiritual Friend

97 Proper adherence with thought and action to
One's holy Spiritual Friend, who demonstrates
The whole, supreme, unerring Path to *Bodhi*,
Has benefits which are inconceivable.

98 With hundreds of efforts for oceans of countless eons,
Great Unification is hard to find, but it's taught
That if one relies on one's Guru's power, it's easy
To win it in one short life of degenerate times.

99 When one correctly adheres to one's holy Guru,
The thought that one will quickly be freed from samsara
Deeply gladdens the minds of all the Conqu'rors,
Like mothers who see their children will succeed.

100 When as disciple one rightly adheres to one's Guru,
The Conquerors happily enter the Guru's body
Even without invitation, accept all one's off'rings,
And also inspire one's mindstream, it is taught.

101 Then, through the inspiration of all the Buddhas
Entering by the opening of faithful mind,
One's unharmed by hosts of *māras* and *kleśas*, and insights
To Paths and Stages instantly grow and develop.

102 If one always relies on him with devotion,
Misdeeds and defilements all cease of themselves
And positive traits spontaneously develop,
So one finds extensive happiness here and hereafter.

103 By the fruit like the cause of duly pleasing one's Guru
In this life, in every later life one will
Encounter excellent Spiritual Friends, and hear
The holy Doctrine, complete and without mistake.

104   In short, by Guru-devotion, one temporally
Finds good birth as human or god, free of the unleisures;
Ultimately, all samsara's sorrow exhausted,
One wins the holy state of Definite Goodness.

1a.2   The disadvantages of not being devoted

105   Thus the advantages of proper devotion
To one's Spiritual Friend are inconceivable.
Likewise, wrong devotion and lack of devotion
Have inconceivable disadvantages too.

106   It's taught that in one's own Guru appears the work
Of all the Spiritual Friends and Conquerors;
Disrespect to him is thus disrespect to all Buddhas.
What could have heavier karmic fruition than that?

107   So many moments of anger towards one's Guru:
So many eons' collected virtues destroyed.
Those moments, says the *Kālacakra-Tantra*,
Mean the same number of eons' rebirth in hell.

108   If one's done grievous sins, like the five immediate, still
By relying on Tantra, the Goal can be reached in this life.
But one who has heartfelt contempt for his Master, it's taught,
Though he practice for eons, can win no attainment at all.

109   Says a Tantra: a person who's fond of despising and blaming
His Path-showing Guru may try the highest tantric
Practice, abandoning dullness, sleep and distractions;
It's as if he were practising for the realms of woe.

110   If one is without respect for one's supreme Guru,
Virtues will not arise; those arisen decay.
In this life come sickness, untimely death, and so on;
In future lives, endless wand'ring in realms of woe.

111 If, by some fluke, one finds a happy rebirth,
     Through the result like the cause of disrespect
     One is born in the leisureless states, and never hears
     Even the words "Holy Dharma" or "Spiritual Friend".

112 In short, if the way one adheres to one's Guru is wrong,
     One will wander forever, tasting only suffering,
     In samsara in general, woeful realms in particular,
     With no chance of gaining high rebirth or Liberation.

113 Since such benefits and disadvantages transcend thought,
     And the roots of my good collections are seen here too,
     Unless thoughts of faults no longer cross my mind
     I am certainly not adhering with faith and devotion.

1b.1   The development of faith, which is the root

114 Just as one and the same moon in the sky
     Appears at once, without effort, reflected in
     Every body of water in the world;
     So too my Path-showing Spiritual Friends, says a Sutra,

115 Are one and the same wisdom-knowledge of the Buddhas,
     Appearing at once, without effort, in the forms
     Of Emanation, Enjoyment and ordinary Gurus,
     Before pure and impure tamable beings, to tame them.

116 Many tantras, in particular, teach
     That at the end of the age, omnipresent Lord
     Vajradhara himself appears in the form
     Of ordinary Gurus, and guides degenerate beings.

117 Therefore, whatever bodies and deeds they show,
     In fact there's no doubt that all the Conquerors of
     The ten directions display these taming bodies
     To guide us into the Path of Liberation.

118 As for this appearance as of faults:

> The Master, with all faults gone and perfect in virtues,
> Was seen by Devadatta, Lek-pä Kar-ma,
> And the *Tīrthikas* as a mass of faults.

119 Likewise, through my thick cover of negative karma,
Like someone with jaundice seeing a conch as yellow,
I always perceive the faultless as having faults;
Why, just from this, should they really have such such faults?

120 For the sake of sentient beings, it's taught, the Conqu'rors
Show themselves in any form, such as *māras*.
How do I know that this uniform appearance
As faulty is not deliberate show, like this?

121 While I'm not free of this cover of negative karma,
Even if all Buddhas come and stand right before me
I've no chance of seeing their supreme Bodies adorned
With the Marks and Signs, any more than I see them now.

122 Therefore, all these apparently faulty aspects
Of my instructors' actions must be either
Just my mistaken perception from negative karma,
Or alternatively, a deliberate manifestation.

123 Therefore, however they may appear to me,
In fact they're free of faults and perfect in virtues,
Identical with the Conqu'rors, without exception,
Of all the infinite realms, combined in one.

1b.2 *Remembering [the Gurus'] kindness*

124 Not only are these, my Protectors, thus
Of the very nature of all the Conquerors;
In constantly caring for me with the nectar
Of Holy Dharma, their kindness exceeds all the Conqu'rors'.

125 It's as when a man is suffering in prison

      And someone ransoms him from that confinement
      Then has him taken somewhere full of enjoyments:
      Certainly that person does him a great kindness.

126   When, therefore, our Gurus teach to us
      The means of escaping from the three ill destinies,
      Giving us kindness so that we may enjoy
      As we wish, for a while, the glory of gods and humans;

127   And when they then teach us well the unsurpassed means
      Of quelling all troubles of samsara and Nirvana,
      And lead us to the supreme state of the Three *Kāyas:*
      In what way could this kindness not be great?

128   If it's taught that the kindness of teaching a single verse
      Could not be repaid by eons of offering equal
      In number to its letters, how can one measure
      The kindness of teaching the good Path all complete?

129   When we go forth from our homes, like pits of fire,
      Then in solitude dwell, in a sage's righteous conduct,
      And taste the supreme taste of the nectar of Dharma,
      This is the kindness of our precious Gurus.

130   When we meet the Mañjunātha Guru's teaching,
      Hard to find even on searching for thousands of eons,
      And also find confidence in the method he teaches,
      This is the kindness of our holy Instructors.

131   Therefore these, my Spiritual Friends, must be:
      Rescuers, rescuing from the realms of woe;
      Sea-captains, taking me over the sea of samsara;
      Guides, who conduct me to high birth and Liberation;

132   Doctors, who cure the chronic disease of defilements;
      Rivers of water, that put out the great fire of suffering;
      Lamps, that dispel the darkness of ignorance;
      Suns, that show clearly the Path to Liberation;

133   Releasers from bonds in the prison of samsara;
      Rain-clouds, dropping the rain of the Holy Dharma;

Friends and relatives, helping and dispelling harm;
And parents, always protecting me with love.

1c THE WAY TO PLEASE ONE'S GURU WITH ACTIONS

134 In this way, every worldly or supermundane
Benefit is a kindness of the Guru.
Although one can never completely repay this kindness,
For the sake of gratitude one should try to please him.

135 Just as one strives to grow seeds in a fertile field,
Though the Guru's indifferent to honour, why not strive
In respecting this best of fields with off'rings and worship,
To perfect soon my own great accumulation of merit?

136 It is taught that revering a single hair of the Guru
Who's shown one the unerring Path excels in merit
Honour and worship to all the assemblies of *Ārya*
Hearers, *Pratyekas* and Buddha-sons, and all the Buddhas.

137 Many holy men, such as Nāropa, Milarepa,
Drom-tön-pa, Sakya Pandita and Cha-yül-pa,
Giving up body, life and wealth for their Gurus
Without a thought, won qualities. Therefore,

138 Like them, I must strive in the ways of devotion
And honour with body and speech, such as offering all
My cherished possessions, rising, prostrating, giving
Baths and massages, praising and speaking respectfully.

139 But far the best way that one's three doors can please the Guru
Is great effort, never idle, day or night,
In the stages of the complete, unerring Path.
I must please him by offering practice just as he teaches!
Please inspire me so that I can do this!

MEDITATION 2
THE OPPORTUNE, FORTUNATE REBIRTH
2a RECOGNITION OF THE OPPORTUNE, FORTUNATE REBIRTH

140   From the beginningless past until the present,
      I have been circling in the three realms of samsara,
      Taking countless bodies as a hell-being,
      Preta, beast, or human, whose suffering

141   Only sometimes paused, when I found happy rebirth.
      Even then, most of my births were in dark eons, lacking
      Teachings. Sometimes I roamed in border countries.
      Sometimes I was an idiot or the like.

142   Sometimes, again, I've been someone who holds perverse views,
      Sometimes, one whom bad friends lead astray.
      Certain times went by with specious doctrines.
      Sometimes I was stultified by delusion.

143   This time, through the compassion of my Gurus:
      Dwelling free of the fears of the realms of woe,
      Gaining the best human body, in Jambudvīpa,
      Meeting a good eon, in an age with light;

144   Born in a land where the glorious Dharma extends,
      Intellect not defective, senses complete,
      Having found confidence in the three "baskets" of Scriptures,
      Meeting a Guru just like an actual Buddha;

145   Getting advice on the complete, unerring Path,
      Clear understanding of what's to be done and what's not,
      Mind strongly turned towards the Holy Dharma,
      All good conditions like food, clothes and money complete;

146   I have now found the excellent human body,
      Which, because of these points, is complete in the eighteen

Factors of opportunity and good fortune.
This is through gath'ring an ocean of previous virtue.

2b THINKING ABOUT THE GREAT VALUE OF THE OPPORTUNE, FORTUNATE REBIRTH

147 This body, the complete, opportune, fortunate basis,
Is of immense value, in no way to be conveyed
Even by such an example as finding a system
Of realms thrice-thousandfold, all full of precious
    jewels.

148 Temporally, whatever I want of the wealth
And plenitude of the high states of gods and humans,
With this excellent basis, I can attain it
Just as I wish, without any trouble or hardship.

149 With this basis, I can easily gain, if I wish,
Not merely high samsaric estate, but also
A karmic fruition with eight virtues, fit as foundation
For achieving the glorious level of Definite Goodness.

150 Whichever totally Pure Land I may wish to go to,
Beyond the impure states of world and beings,
Such as the realm of Tushita, wide and blissful,
With this basis, I am able to do so.

151 This is not all. Should I wish to find even the bliss
Of Liberation, every samsaric suffering –
Birth, aging, sickness, death and the rest – appeased
Forever, with this excellent basis, I can achieve it.

152 Even the state of the Perfect, Spontaneous Three
    Kāyas,
Complete in every good quality, pure of all
Faults – the two obscurations, including their imprints–
I can achieve with this basis, if I practise.

153 In particular, with this basis composed of six elements,
If I rely on Highest Yoga Tantra,
I can attain that very stage, of Unity
Of the two Supreme Bodies, in this short life.

154   Since this excellent, opportune, fortunate basis, because
        Of these points, has very great value, whether one looks
        At its temporal or at its ultimate value, therefore
        The Gurus have said it excels a wish-granting jewel.

155   In this case, having met with such a basis,
        To be attached to fruitless work for this life
        And not to practise the Path for high rebirth or Freedom,
        Is, if I think well about it, truly crazy.

156   If now, allowed to accomplish the twofold benefit
        Or whatever I wish, I do not very quickly practise,
        Then I am like a man who reaches the Land
        Of jewels, but does not take any wish-granting gems.

157   Now, casting actions for this life far away,
        Let me train my mind, regardless of day and night,
        In the Stages of the Path to the Goal, Enlightenment,
        And make worthwhile my winning this opportune rebirth!

2c THINKING ABOUT THE RARITY OF THE OPPORTUNE, FORTUNATE REBIRTH

158   Although I have come to acquire such a basis, it's like
        Threadball the cripple's once riding upon a wild ass:
        Apart from just this single present occasion,
        I shall not find it repeated again in the future.

159   Just to gain, in general, upper-realm rebirth,
        One has to collect its various virtuous causes.
        Since it is hard to generate virtuous attitude,
        Gaining an upper-realm rebirth is also hard.

160   To gain the opportune, fortunate birth in particular,
        Each factor's cause, of the eighteen, must be achieved.
        Since achieving the causes like this is exceedingly rare,
        How could the fruit, complete opportune birth, not be rare?

161   If, by a fluke, I've already achieved all the causes
        Of gaining the opportune birth, without any missing,

My mind still contains very many conditions
   destructive
Of them, such as anger, wrong views, and abandoning
   Dharma.

162 Even if such conditions do not destroy them,
Since my defiled mind and incorrect conduct are strong
While positive mind and desirable conduct are weak,
Don't I know which result is going to ripen first?

163 Our Lord, the Conqueror's Doctrine appears in the
   world
Only from time to time, like a star in the daytime.
If we reflect on this point too, to gain
The excellent, opportune, fortunate birth's very rare.

164 Did not th' infallible, truth-telling Master say
That the beings of lower realms are as the dust on the
   Earth,
While the beings above, who've gone to happy
   migrations,
Are as the dust-particles on a finger-nail?

165 He taught that, compared with the limitless number of
   beings
In hell, in preta and in animal destinies,
Those reborn in good destinies, with the bodies
Of gods or humans, are counted in ones and twos.

166 How many befuddled, animal sentient beings
Are in the ground in the space taken up by a tent?
And again, how many people in a city?
Even in large ones, only a few hundred thousand.

167 Among human beings, consider the few who have
   entered
The door of the Dharma, the multitude who have not!
Even among those who boast of practising Dharma,
Are there many or few with the perfect, opportune
   birth?

168 Thinking about these points, the Conqueror taught,

With many examples to make the meaning plain –
Such as the turtle, putting its neck through the central
Hole in a yoke which is drifting all over the ocean;

169   A pea attaching itself to the side of a glass-house;
A star being seen at midday in a blue sky;
And mustard-seed staying on the point of a needle –
How rare is this body, the opportune, fortunate basis.

170   Thus, by way of cause, effect and examples,
The excellent basis is very hard to find.
Can I afford to wait and not grasp the essential
Value in this which is obtained only once?

171   At this time when I've found the opportune, fortunate basis,
Thoroughly free from the eight states of no opportunity,
Letting appearance distract me, I don't reach the essence,
But start to return to the realms of woe again.

172   This is like returning to one's own country
Empty-handed from the Land of Jewels.
Where is there an action more deluded?
What severer loss could there possibly be?

173   In general, gaining the opportune birth is thus rare.
In particular, meeting a Manjunath's teaching is rare.
A fully qualified Guru as Refuge is rare.
The Dharma, complete and unerring both, is rare.

174   To have inner analytical wisdom is rare.
A mind that is fit to be used in the Dharma is rare.
Friends who are striving for Liberation are rare.
The conditions, subsistence consistent with Dharma, are rare.

175   At this time when so many rare things have come together,
If I don't abandon all thoughts and all actions of this life
And practise the Path for high rebirth and Definite Goodness,

Then nothing could be more regrettable.

176 So now, without falling under the power of distraction,
For the sake of helping mother sentient beings,
Who time and again have cared for me with kindness,
I must practise the deep Path to its end.
Gurus, please inspire me for this purpose!

THE ACTUAL PRACTICE: PATH OF THE INFERIOR PERSON

MEDITATION 3
DEATH

3a *THINKING ABOUT THE CERTAINTY OF DEATH*

177 This excellent basis, always hard to find,
And if one finds it, very great in value,
Is not permanent: it will quickly perish,
Like a drop of dew on the tip of a grass-blade.

178 Whatever kind of body I receive,
In happy or woeful destinies in this
Endless samsara of three realms, in the end
It does not go beyond the nature of death.

179 Also, whatever sort of place I dwell in –
High heavenly spheres, on the earth, below, in the sea,
Mount Meru, a hidden rocky cleft, or elsewhere –
I cannot escape this foe, the Lord of Death.

180 Not in former ages of Perfection;
Not now, when the five degenerations are spreading;
Nor in the future, is there a time in which
There's a chance that the Lord of Death will not oppress me.

181 No means whatever, including Brahma, Shiva,
Vishnu, an emperor's mighty armies, a sage's
Power of truth, inner magical things, or mantras,
Or miraculous powers, can turn back Death.

182 Not to be bought off with a ransom of worlds

Thrice-thousandfold, filled entirely with wealth and
   riches;
This foe, the Lord of Death, can't be repulsed
By medicines prepared by the very King of Doctors.

183   Of all beings, high or low, who've appeared in the
         past,
      If one checks now, only names remain.
      Of all the sentient beings living at present,
      The time will also come when not one's left.

184   Nothing is being added to my life:
      Finish it must, not tarrying an instant.
      If it's like the example of a burning lamp,
      What chance is there now of remaining without dying?

185   From one's first appearance in the womb,
      One travels towards death, without interruption,
      Like a stream descending a steep mountain.
      Is it not mistaken to think "I'll remain alive"?

186   If a man is being hurriedly led
      To his place of execution, and on the way
      Someone pays respect with the five sense objects,
      Will this be a cause of pleasure for him?

187   When I am hastening, as in this example,
      Towards my death, without a moment's pause,
      Should I meet even hundreds of sense pleasures,
      Is this something I should be pleased about?

188   If, in a short time, I must leave behind
      My present home, my relatives and friends,
      All my possessions and even this body, and go,
      Why be attached to this present, like a dream?

189   If my years, my months, my days, my hours,
      Like the shadows cast by the setting sun,
      Cannot be permanent, but must go in a moment,
      What chance have I of not dying soon?

190   Before, until now, my years have just gone by;
      In the rest of my life, too, the time for practising

Dharma,
When sleep and the like don't divert me, is but a moment.
So is this a time for activities of leisure?

191 If, moreover, I check what fraction of
A single day I'm thinking correctly of Dharma,
And what distracted, then it becomes clear:
Thinking in this way too, I've no time to spare.

192 From these points, in the end I'm certain to die,
There being no condition that can stop it.
If, moreover, I'll die soon, without respite,
How can I not strive truly now in the Dharma?

3b THINKING ABOUT HOW THERE IS NO CERTAINTY AS TO WHEN I SHALL DIE

193 Not only am I sure to die in the end:
There is no certainty that this very day
I shall not be deprived of life, my body
Left in a graveyard, and my mind reach the *bardo*.

194 Of yore lived sages with lifetimes of countless years;
One day the maximum life will be ten years;
Now there's no fixed order of old and young.
What is certain now about lifetime in Jambudvīpa?

195 I am here in the morning, gone in the afternoon;
Or here at bedtime, gone when it's time to get up.
Now I exist, and now I don't exist.
This way that life's impermanent is indeed frightening.

196 I might collide with something, fall over a cliff,
My boat might capsize, I might be burned by fire,
My house could collapse, I might be thrown from a horse,
My body and limbs can be broken or wounded by weapons.

197 Harm by enemies, human or non-human;
Diseases, of four hundred and four varieties;
Eighty thousand kinds of evil spirits:

Such outer and inner conditions for death are many.

198 It's a growth-time for the five degenerations,
So ways of extending life are hard to practise.
As the power of external medicines is also failing,
Therefore conditions for staying alive are few.

199 Food can be unwholesome and turn into poison;
Medicine can fail and become a cause of disease.
Thus even conditions for living become death's causes –
How can one trust in conditions for living here?

200 Again, life is like the guttering flame of a lamp
In the wind of all the varied conditions for death.
To have plans as if my life could last forever
Is grasping at permanence. Certainly it will finish.

201 This human life and body of mine are like
The example of a bubble in the water:
Even a tiny cause destroys it, so
Harbouring hopes of long life is most mistaken.

202 Even collections very hard to destroy,
Like the Earth, Mount Meru, four continents, and the ocean,
Will be destroyed, so what certainty is there
That this body, like a clay pitcher, won't perish right now?

203 Though today I am well and free from sickness,
Since this foe, the Lord of Death, will come
All at once, unsuspected, like a cloud in the sky,
This is no time for staying in mental ease.

204 As I have no news of which is coming first –
The hour when tomorrow dawns, or the body and mind
Of the intermediate state of my next existence –
Is it not worthwhile to practise the Dharma quickly?

3c THINKING ABOUT HOW NOTHING EXCEPT THE DHARMA CAN HELP AT THE TIME OF DEATH

205 When I am seized by that foe, the Lord of Death,

Even if all beings of the three realms of existence,
Who are my friends and relatives, surround me,
I am powerless to take with me a single one.

206   Even though I owned thrice-thousandfold worlds,
All filled to the brim with the seven precious things,
Of all that wealth I'd have no means to take
To my next existence even a sesame seed.

207   Even this body, together with which I was born,
Is left behind on my bed and bedding, while
By the wind of good and bad karma my mind is carried
To its unique place within the six realms of existence.

208   Consequently, at the hour of death,
Body, possessions and friends no longer help.
What is useful at that time is only
The holy Dharma, the infallible Refuge.

209   Therefore I now must turn my back upon
Dreamlike, worthless activities of this life,
And through the *Lam rim*, essence of the Dharma,
Strive for the glorious state of Enlightenment!
Please inspire me so that I can do this!

MEDITATION 4
THE SUFFERINGS OF THE REALMS OF WOE
4a HOW TO MEDITATE ON THE SUFFERINGS OF THE HELLS
4a.1 *How to meditate on the sufferings of the hot hells*

210   Alas! This rare and precious body
    is impermanent; soon 'twill perish.
After death, where I'm born is controlled
    willy-nilly by my karma.
If, through very strong negative karma
    and feeble positive karma, I fall
In the frightful abyss of the realms of woe,
    shall I be able to bear that suff'ring?

211   Underground, many leagues from here,
    are the so-called hells of sentient beings,

Red-hot, burning iron ground below,
   the sides surrounded by burning iron walls;
The air above all full of flames.
   Each individual hell also
Is of burning iron, encircled with
   a wall and enclosure, closed with four gates.

212   In the Reviving Hell, the beings
   get very angry with each other.
With various weapons, produced by karma,
   they strike one another and fall unconscious.
A voice comes from the sky, announcing
   "Be cured, all of you!", and straightaway
They revive again, get up, and then
   as before, undergo the cycle of suffering.

213   In Black Line Hell, held firmly by
   swarms of Yama's frightful henchmen,
You lie on the red-hot, burning iron ground.
   They stretch your limbs out like a ground-sheet,
Then when they've marked your cherished body
   with black lines, in many crosses,
You enjoy the suff'ring of being cleft
   and cut up thereon with various weapons.

214   In Crushing Hell, you're massed 'tween huge
   iron mountains, like lions' or tigers' faces.
The two mountains clash, and squeeze you out,
   so that a river of blood then flows.
Thrown into a vast iron machine,
   you are thoroughly pressed, like sugarcane,
Then huge rocks, like mountains, fall from the sky,
   squash you, and grind flesh and blood to dust.

215   In those called Howling, sentient beings
   run around, looking for somewhere to stay.
They enter single and nested buildings,
   made of iron, that burst into flames.
Straight away, the doors slam shut,
   so that there's nowhere to escape to.
Flames consume their bodies entirely.

They pass day and night in howling and wails.

216 In the Heating Hell, you are cooked like a fish
    in a gigantic cauldron of blazing hot iron.
With a stake of one point, burning with fire,
    you're impaled so it comes out the top of your head.
Then from all your sensory openings
    very broad flames come flaring out.
You are laid on the blazing iron ground
    and beaten with a hammer of iron.

217 In Intense Heating, you are impaled
    with a blazing stake of three sharp points,
And your body is wrapped up in a sheet
    of very hot, red iron, like a garment.
In a large iron pot, you are cooked in boiling
    molten copper. When your bones
All fall apart, they are spread on the ground,
    flesh and skin regrow, then you're cooked as before.

218 In Avīci, from all four directions
    come blazing fires, in a great heap,
And burn your skin, flesh, bones and tendons,
    right to the marrow, like a lamp's wick.
One can only tell you're a sentient being
    from your shrieks of direst torment.
A searing iron basket is put in your hand,
    and you're made to winnow blazing coals.

219 On a high mountain of red-hot iron
    you fall down and have to climb up again.
Your tongue is pulled out of your mouth, much
    stretched, and staked out there with iron pegs.
Yama's men throw you down on your back
    and open your mouth with red-hot pincers.
They thrust in red-hot cannon-balls
    and pour boiling, molten bronze down your throat.

4a.2 *How to meditate on the sufferings of the Supplementary Hells*

220 Moreover, outside every door

of each of the eight types of hot hells
Are so-called supplementary hells,
   where there are many terrible fears.
In the Pit of Hot Coals, when you put your foot down,
   it sinks to the knee, and the skin and flesh
Are lost, but regrow as soon as you raise it,
   then you suffer that cycle again.

221   In the Swamp of Excrement, stinking of corpses,
   you fall in and sink right up to the neck,
And sharp-beaked worms who live in that swamp
   bore in and devour you, right to the marrow.
On the Road which is Full of Sharp Knives, their edges
   pointing upwards, when you put
Your foot down, it's cut into mincemeat, and when
   you raise it, it regrows, and so goes the cycle.

222   When you arrive at the Sword-leaved Forest,
   if you linger and keep in the shade,
Many sharp swords from the trees come towards you
   and hack off your limbs and minor parts.
When you faint to the ground from the pain of your
   wounds, dogs tear the flesh from your body, and eat it.
In the forest called Shālmalī,
   you have to climb up and down the trunks

223   Of iron trees, bristling with iron thorns.
   When you go up, the thorns stream downwards,
When you go down, they bristle upwards,
   piercing your limbs and minor parts.
Many iron-beaked magpies perch
   on your head, and peck your eyeballs.
The River Vaitaraṇī is
   a vast stream of searing molten bronze.

224   When you fall in its boiling billows,
   flesh, blood and skin are all consumed;
And on the bank of this blazing river,
   people brandishing cudgels and hooks
With their cudgels, stop you getting out,

and with the hooks, drag you out, throw you down,
  And ask what you want. If you're hungry and thirsty,
    they give you iron balls and molten copper.

225 Thus, the suffering of the great hells
       is totally unbearable.
     Moreover, it's not just for a short while,
       but experienced for countless eons.
     You are unable to die as long
       as that non-virtue is not exhausted.
     If, hearing this teaching, you're not scared crazy,
       is your mind made of matter or something?

4a.3 *How to meditate on the sufferings of the cold hells*

226 But this is not all. Ten thousand leagues
       beyond the place where the hot hells are
     Are what are called the Eight Cold Hells.
       Their floors are full of blocks of ice.
     Snowy mountains surround all sides.
       Above, snow swirls in [endless] storms.
     All is covered in blackest darkness.
       A cold wind rises fiercely. There,

227 The denizens' naked, unclothed bodies
       shiver and bend and shrivel right up.
     The wind raises hundreds of thousands of blisters;
       they all burst, and serum oozes out.
     One emits noises, "Brrrr" and "Boo-hoo",
       wails, and also one's teeth lock.
     With the fearful cold one's body turns
       blue, then red, and cracks in pieces.

228 Nor is this terrible cold experience
       only a few days: it is taught
     That to empty a great store of eighty quarters
       of sesame, taking a seed each century,
     Is the measure of life in the Blistering Hell;
       in the other seven, each twenty times more.
     What assurance I'll not be reborn in such places?
       Think! If I were, could I bear it or not?

4b HOW TO MEDITATE ON THE SUFFERING OF THE PRETAS

229 Moreover, five hundred leagues below
       this continent are the beings called Pretas,
   Who come from the fault of avarice.
       The ground of their place is of red copper,
   As if sun-scorched. On a vast desert plain,
       devoid of sense-pleasures, they [roam] dejected,
   Each one's body like a burnt tree-stump,
       with parched mouth, big belly, and tiny limbs.

230 Those with outward obscurations
       see water or fruit, say, and run to enjoy it;
   But as when a mirage's water's pursued,
       it becomes invisible anywhere;
   Or else it looks full of glowing embers
       or foul bits of pus, blood, excretions and whatnot;
   Or guardians brandishing various arms
       protect it and stop them from using it.

231 Those with internal obscurations
       have bodies with bellies the size of mountains,
   And mouths as small as the eye of a needle,
       which burst into flames and are blocked with goitres.
   Should they find food or drink, it won't fit in their mouths.
   If it does go in, their mouth burns it with fire.
   It can't pass their throat, since that's blocked with the goitre;
       if it does go down, it won't fill the belly.

232 Those obscured towards food and drink
       are called "the ones with garlands of flames";
   Whatever they eat and whatever they drink
       bursts into flames and starts to burn them.
   For those who eat filth, such foul-smelling refuse
       as excrement, urine, spittle and snot,
   Pus, blood and vomit is all they enjoy.
       ·They lack any chance to have good food and drink.

233   With their minuscule limbs and big bodies, moreover,
        they're worn out with rushing about after food.
    In summertime, even the moonlight is hot;
        in wintertime, even the sunlight is cold.
    When they just look at the sea, it dries up.
        Some are obstructed by knots in the neck.
    Their bodies and minds are so tortured by hunger,
        they even cut off their own flesh and eat it.

234   They don't even hear tell of food and drink,
        but are always afflicted by violent pangs
    Of terrible hunger and thirst; and it's not
        for a short time only: in fact it's taught
    That for five hundred, sometimes five thousand,
        or even ten thousand of their years,
    Of days like our months, they cannot die.
        If born in that place, what on earth would I do?

4c HOW TO MEDITATE ON THE SUFFERING OF ANIMALS

235   The hidden home of the very deluded,
        the animals, is in the ocean, from
    The water's surface down to the floor.
        Their size, shape, colour and so forth are
    Indefinite, numberless in kind,
        like heaps of grain piled up on boards.
    One pressing another, so they can hardly
        move, they live in lightless holes.

236   Scattered ones roam in the lands of gods
        and humans, some plagued by hunger and thirst;
    Some suffer from sun and wind, hard to bear;
        some pass their lives entirely in darkness.
    Some make a home in heaps of dust;
        others breed in swamps of sewage.
    Sometimes bigger ones gulp down small ones;
        or armies of small beasts devour a large one.

237   Variously killed for their meat, skin and so on;
        slaughtered in all sorts of different ways;

Helplessly laden with burdens too heavy
    to carry, exploited, ridden, and struck;
Their hair and parts of their organs cropped;
    or used for ploughing, milking and so forth –
They're oppressed day and night, without interruption,
    by many great sufferings, hard to endure.

238   Further, their lifetimes may be lengthy,
        up to an eon, not sure to be short.
    They are disturbed by many kinds
        of personal sufferings, through their karma,
    But all are very deluded and stupid,
        not knowing what should be done or abandoned.
    O woe! Alas! Born even an instant
        in such a body, how could I bear it?

MEDITATION 5
THE PRACTICE OF TAKING REFUGE

239   Thus, the unbearable sufferings of the hells,
    Of pretas and of beasts are hard to endure.
    Whoever else I go to for Refuge, except
    The Three Supreme Ones, cannot protect me from
        them.

240   How can I be protected by the Three Jewels?
    The Dharma's the actual Refuge, which saves from
        these fears,
    The Buddhas are the Teachers of this Dharma,
    The Sangha, my helpers in the Dharma's practice.

241   If, therefore, I do not rely from my heart on the
        threefold,
    Infallible, Supreme Refuge as my protector,
    I've no means of freedom from special and general fears
    Of ill destinies' dreadful abyss and of samsara.

242   From this moment, moreover, I must strive to keep
    This Refuge; if I fall to a realm of woe,
    Then wailing and calling out hundreds of cries for help,

I'll still find no protector there at all.

243   Therefore, from now on, I and all other migrators
      Go to the Buddhas, the Supreme Teachers, for Refuge;
      We go to their Teachings, the holy Dharma, for Refuge;
      We go to the Sangha, who practise it, for Refuge.

Say this verse, the actual taking of Refuge, three or seven times, or as desired.

244   Having thus vowed Refuge in the Three Jewels,
      I must train correctly in the Refuge practices.

245   So, having taken the Master as Refuge, I cannot
      Take refuge in other teachers, or worldly gods.
      With conviction, avoiding disrespect, I must worship
      Even the Master's image as the Buddha.

246   Having gone to the Dharma for Refuge, I must stop adhering
      To non-Dharma, actions and thoughts to harm sentient beings.
      Even to letters of the Holy Doctrine,
      I must be respectful, avoiding stepping over them.

247   Having taken the Sangha as Refuge, I may not rely
      On companions with wrong views, such as *Tīrthikas*.
      Not attached or angry, I must revere those who wear
      Even signs of saffron as actual *Ārya* Sangha.

248   Knowing how Buddhist and non-Buddhist differ, I must
      Take Refuge again and again in the Three Supreme Ones.
      Rememb'ring their kindness, I'll always strive in their worship,
      Offering them the first part of my food and drink.

249   Recollecting Compassion, I'll also establish other
      Migrators in taking of Refuge in the Three Jewels.
      I'll avoid other methods, apart from revering the

        Threefold
Refuge on every occasion, and making requests.

250   Knowing the benefits, I must go for Refuge
Three times each day and three times every night.
I may not give up the Three Refuges, even in jest,
Nor for my life, but must keep them on my crown.

251   By going for Refuge, one enters the door of the Doctrine.
It acts as a basis for growth of the three pure vows.
One curbs or exhausts bad karmas, and gains vast merits.
One can't fall to realms of woe, and spirits can't harm one.

252   One achieves what one wishes, and quickly becomes Enlightened.
As it's taught to bring such inconceivable benefits,
I must maintain my Refuge from my heart,
Not transgressing any of the practices.

MEDITATION 6
HOW TO GENERATE CONFIDENCE IN THE LAWS OF ACTIONS AND RESULTS

253   If I fear those sufferings of the realms of woe,
I must examine my own three doors, and train
With steady watchfulness, mindfulness and awareness
In the slightest approach to white and retreat from black actions.

254   Those unbearable suff'rings are only results
Of actions I have accumulated myself;
But since no-one else has made me undergo them,
I must strive now to leave non-virtue and practise virtue.

255   Furthermore, for example, when one sows
In a fertile field, seeds such as wheat or barley,
Peas, rice or millet, shoots of appropriate type

Come up without confusion. In the same way,

256 From karma in gen'ral come pleasure and suff'ring in general;
Pleasure and suff'ring respectively, down to the smallest,
Arise from virtue and non-virtue, never confounded.
From no cause, or discordant cause, they cannot arise.

257 Just as a small seed grows into a big fruit,
So too, from tiny causal virtues and sins,
Boundless resultant pleasures and suff'rings arise,
Such as pleasure and suff'ring for numberless lives.

258 If the seed is not sown, no fruit can grow; likewise,
If the good or bad action is not accumulated,
No happy or painful result whatever can happen,
For there is no meeting with uncreated karma.

259 If a seed is sown, without obstructing conditions,
Its fruit will undoubtedly grow. In just this way,
If a virtue's accumulated, and not destroyed
By some destructive condition, such as anger,

260 Its result, happiness, must unavoidably come.
Likewise, if a created non-virtue's not purified
By purifying conditions, such as confession,
Its result, suffering, must unavoidably come.

261 Therefore, since karma is specifically certain,
Increases, is not met if not created,
And once created is inevitable,
I must devote myself only to virtuous actions,

262 Assiduous in these from the smallest upwards,
Insatiable, like a greedy man gathering wealth,
And trying not to destroy those created with anger.
And I must never commit non-virtuous actions,

263 But practise avoiding them from the smallest upwards,
Fearing them like a poisonous snake in my lap,
With the four forces, sure to purify any committed.
Especially, not satisfied just with high estate,

264 I must practise with effort in all the causes of gaining
    The excellent body with eightfold karmic fruition,
    Since this is more powerful for realizing
        Enlightenment.
    Please inspire me so that I can do this!

THE ACTUAL PRACTICE: PATH OF THE INTERMEDIATE PERSON

MEDITATION 7
THE SUFFERINGS OF THE HAPPIER REALMS AND THE GENERAL SUFFERINGS OF SAMSARA

7a.1 *How to meditate on the sufferings of human beings*

265 If I avoid sin and strive thus in virtue,
        I shall gain higher rebirth; but still,
    As long as I've not won the state of Freedom,
        when samsaric suffering's totally gone,
    Not only do I lack confidence
        since I'll roam again in the realms of woe,
    But even in this birth there's no chance of happiness,
        for its very nature is suffering.

266 In a human womb, it's very dirty
        and evil-smelling, with pus, blood and so on,
    A horribly narrow, dark cavity, crawling
        with vermin – a mass of utmost terrors.
    Your body's constricted as if tied up,
        wrapped in the amniotic sac.
    During a long time you feel many suff'rings,
        due to the mother's behaviour and so on.

267 Then, from the rip'ning of karma arises
        a "wind" that turns you upside down.
    Out of a foul-smelling, filthy passage,
        constricted by bones like some machine,
    You are born, amid a torment
        of hard-to-bear, rough and violent feelings.
    Hence unwanted sufferings pour down like rain;
        fearful indeed is this suff'ring of birth!

268   The youthful body you have when young
           gradually comes to resemble your corpse.
      It bends, the hair whitens, complexion fades,
           even on flat ground your steps are unsteady.
      The flesh losing firmness, you are covered
           in wrinkles, and your skin hangs down loosely.
      Your teeth are few, you crave to eat;
           your speech is quavering, you are forgetful.

269   Your eyes can't see forms, your hearing's unclear,
           rising or sitting's hard, others are scornful.
      It's even hard to digest and enjoy
           food and drink. All people dislike you.
      And the great suff'ring of thinking, "Now
           my youthfulness has become like this;
      Soon I shall die!" afflicts you daily:
           sorrow indeed is this suff'ring of aging!

270   When disease of disordered elements strikes,
           it's hard to move – you're stuck in bed.
      Always groaning with fierce pain of sickness,
           you wail unendingly, day and night.
      Not free to enjoy what you like, you are given
           unwanted food, drink, medicine and so on.
      In constant torment from pains of the sickness,
           still you must suffer bleeding or cautery.

271   A comfortable posture is not to be found.
           You look ill, speak feebly, and cannot get up.
      Because of the sickness, your body, possessions,
           home, friends and servants all seem like enemies.
      Days and nights pass in mental distress.
           You're greatly oppressed by the powerful affliction
      Of misgivings that this illness is fatal.
           Vicious indeed is this suff'ring of sickness!

272   Through physical sickness or other conditions,
           you approach the mouth of the Lord of Death.
      When gripped by your violent fatal disease,
           you lie down on your final bed.
      Doctors can't help, nor rites avail;

        you and others abandon hope of survival.
Friends and relations surround you, weeping.
        Your own face, too, is bathed in tears.

273   Your mouth pronounces your last words.
        Possessions disposed of, your grave is prepared.
Nose contracts, mouth dries up, eyes roll upwards,
        your breath's short and wheezing – what can you do?
Attachment for kin, body, friends and possessions
        afflicts you with sorrow. Misdeeds bring regret.
Your arms and legs flail in your violent agony.
        Fearful indeed is such suff'ring of death!

274   In th' intervals of the torture while
        the four foes, birth, age, sickness and death,
Are turning the wheel, there's still no chance
        of happiness, since there are many suff'rings.
Through meeting what is very unpleasant,
        such as the perils of hostile foes,
Robbers, and beasts of prey, ghosts, fire and water,
        the mind is enclosed in a cell of misery.

275   When you are helplessly parted from something
        greatly cherished and dear to your heart,
Like a relative, friend, possession or servant,
        remembering this, your mind feels great yearning.
You utter all manner of lamentation;
        bedecked with tears, you fall in a swoon.
You toss your limbs and tear out your hair,
        your speech is subdued and you can't even eat.

276   You work your fields, but win no harvest;
        you look after herds, but they don't increase.
You go to do business, but make no profit;
        your hopes of a loan or gift also
Aren't realized. Such wanted things, though sought
        with hundreds of hardships, you do not get.
Unwanted things, like frost, drought, quarrels,
        attachment, and lawsuits, strike like lightning.

277   The destitute suffer in work and labour,

and as the servants or slaves of others.
Those who have wealth have always troubles
    like guarding it and making it grow.
Furthermore, heat and cold, hunger and thirst,
    want and distress, and fighting each other,
And so on, even in human realms,
    are like the suff'rings of realms of woe.

7a.2 *How to meditate on the sufferings of asuras*

278   Asuras also are mentally tortured
    by flames of jealousy, for the wealth
And the perfection of the gods
    prick them like a thorn in the heart;
So they fight with the gods, and feel horrible suffering
    due to desire. Although they're intelligent,
Karmic obscuration deprives them
    of chance of achieving the Path of Freedom.

7a.3 *How to meditate on the sufferings of gods of the Desire Realm*

279   The gods of Desire, at the very moment
    when home, possessions and body are perfect,
Suddenly lose their shining complexion,
    dislike the seat they sit upon;
Their flower-garlands wither, dirt sticks to their clothes,
    and hitherto absent sweat appears.
When seized by such omens of imminent death,
    like humans seized by the signs of death,

280   They know that they are to leave behind
    their homes and mansions of precious things,
Their food of *amṛita,* their dear companions,
    and all that's so very agreeable to them,
And go to the next world. Then by clairvoyance
    they see the place where they'll be reborn,
And long undergo hardly bearable sorrow
    of separation from what is dear.

281   When, too, they fight the asuras' armies,

        they suffer from limbs and minor parts
    Being severed, their bodies rent and killed.
        The gods of less merit are terrorised
    When they see the grandeur of other gods
        who are possessed of vast enjoyments;
    The strong gods force the weak ones out
        Of their homes. They have such sufferings.

282   Extreme attachment to sensual pleasures,
        in short, is like constantly drinking salt water:
    With no satisfaction, you're always in torment,
        so what chance of happiness is there in it?
    Since the elephant, mind, is hopelessly drunk
        with the maddening liquor of sensual desire,
    There's minimal chance of taming it with
        the soothing hook of the holy Dharma.

7a.4 How to meditate on the sufferings of the gods of the two higher realms

283   In the two higher realms, these sufferings
        are not manifest, but they are latent.
    You have defilements, the root of suff'ring
        and faults, together with obscurations.
    At the place of your death, devoid of free-will,
        since your nature is always to be afflicted
    With most painful suff'ring of being conditioned,
        again you will fall: you cannot have confidence.

284   In short, whatever good rebirth,
        divine or human, you have received,
    Just like a bird that flies in the sky,
        when your strength of positive karma's exhausted,
    You'll fall again to the hells, or the realms
        of pretas and animals, there to suffer.
    Alas! Even grandeur of high estate
        is by nature impermanent and deceptive.

7b.1 How to think about the six sufferings

285   If the bodies I've formerly taken weren't lost,

their flesh and bones would equal Mount Meru.
Their blood and lymph, collected together,
would rival the depth and extent of the ocean.
Even my bodies as Brahma, Indra,
world-rulers, common gods and men
Are hard to count, but have all been discarded.
What can you trust about gaining a body?

286 Even implacable foes of past lives
have become friends in this life, and done me service.
Past lives' friends, too, become in this life
real foes, who even attack my life.
Even in this life, from early to later parts,
in every year and month and day,
And moment by moment, friends and foes change.
What can you trust about helping and harming?

287 Sometimes, you're ruler of mighty emperors,
Brahma, or Indra; then servant or slave.
Having been sun or moon, giving light to four
continents, then you must live in a dark interstice.
You enjoy the taste of divine *amṛita*,
then must drink pus, blood or molten copper.
And having lived in a jewelled palace,
you must burn in a house of red-hot iron.

288 Once served with sense pleasures by heavenly maidens,
you're persecuted by guards of hell.
In early life, proud of your strength, wealth and power,
later, you're poor and can find no food.
Though rich in wealth, gems, silks and satins,
when you die you go naked and empty-handed.
Alas! What trust can you possibly have
about the perfections obtained in samsara?

289 I'm familiar, through long acquaintance, with
religious companions, sympathetic
Friends, and pleasant kin and attendants;
but then, one day, all on my own,
Just like a hair pulled out of butter,
I'll roam to a land that's unfamiliar,

>   In the next world. About friends and companions,
>   what then is real and fit to be trusted?

290   Of yore, I've enjoyed the taste of *amrita*,
         celestial mansions, gardens and maidens;
     In human realms, too, I've worn fine clothes,
         enjoyed food and drink, and kept good company.
     Though I've enjoyed the five sense pleasures
         as many times as there are atoms,
     As I taste, craving grows, and much suff'ring's induced;
         what sorrow this suff'ring of no satisfaction!

291   The molten copper I've drunk in the hells,
         The manure I've eaten when born as a worm,
     And the filth I have eaten as dogs, pigs and whatnot,
         If piled up together, would fill the whole world;
     While even the tears I have wept out of suff'ring
         exceed the whole ocean. Since this is taught,
     But still I'm not sick of this sorrow, or frightened,
         is this mind made out of iron, or what?

292   If this whole earth were turned to clay
         and made into tiny pellets, the size
     Of juniper seeds, one might count these,
         but could not reveal a beginning limit
     To my mothers of just one birth, it's taught.
         Think well, therefore! to my rebirths in
     This samsara since the non-existent
         beginning, how could a limit appear?

7b.2   *How to think about the three sufferings*

293   Not only are body and mind afflicted
         with suff'ring of misery, in these ways;
     But ev'ry contaminated feeling
         that seems like pleasure, in samsaric states,
     Isn't pleasure by nature, but only appearance
         of pleasure in a cessation of pain.

In particular, we are always gripped
by the suff'ring of being conditioned, it's taught.

294 In short, just as one has no chance to be happy
while one must carry a heavy burden,
So there's no chance to be happy as long
as I have to hold these *skandhas* I've taken.
These *skandhas* are externally governed
by my previous deeds and defilements,
And they have at all times the seeds of the birth
of all future suff'ring and defilements.

295 Therefore they bring all the reincarnations
and sufferings of future lives,
And are the basis of all the suff'rings
of this life, like birth, aging, sickness and death.
They bring forth the suff'rings of misery
and change in the manner of froth from water.
Under deeds and defilements right from their
formation,
their nature is suff'ring and absence of pleasure.

296 Hence, if I win not the supreme Peace,
exhaustion of all the *skandhas'* suff'ring,
Wherever I'm born in the three realms' six classes
is as if I lived in a pit of thorns.
From the very nature of the three suff'rings,
I have no chance of happiness,
So now is when I shall liberate
myself from this prison of samsara!

MEDITATION 8
HOW TO THINK ABOUT THE PROCESS OF FUNCTIONING OF SAMSARA, AND PRACTISE THE PATH TO LIBERATION

297 What, one may wonder, is the cause of thus
Continually circling, without my control,
Like a whirling firebrand, among the six classes of
beings,

Afflicted by the three suff'rings without a break?

298 Since beginningless time, the great demon of self-grasping,
Thinking "I, I", has dwelt in my heart's recesses;
Marking self off from other, it generates greed and hatred;
With these, karma's heaped up; through karma I spin in samsara.

299 Therefore, if this self-grasping is not expelled,
I cannot be free from samsara. It has to be
Expelled by the wisdom that realizes selflessness. Therefore
I must develop the training relating to Wisdom.

300 If my mind is distracted by fading and agitation,
It cannot see truly how selfless existence works;
So, quelling distractions, I must train in *samādhi*
Dwelling one-pointedly on the deep mode of existence.

301 Since this *samādhi*, in turn, can never develop
If I lack watchfulness, mindfulness and awareness,
I must have the training relating to Morality,
Restraining my three doors with firm awareness and mindfulness.

302 Therefore, since the field where grow the ears
Of the training in Wisdom, bending the tips of the stalks
Of unwavering Concentration, is only Morality,
It's taught that the *Pratimoksha's* the root of the doctrine.

303 So as the ground for my *Pratimoksha* training,
I must hear the advices; develop respect for the Master
And his vows; rely on alertness, mindfulness,
Watchfulness and the defilements' specific opponents;

304 Duly restrain the four doors of production of downfalls;
And carrying out without transgressions the orders

Of the Compassionate, Matchless, Supreme Master,
As I have vowed, establish the root of the Doctrine.
Please inspire me so that I can do this!

THE ACTUAL PRACTICE: PATH OF THE SUPERIOR PERSON

MEDITATION 9
THE DEVELOPMENT OF *BODHICITTA*
9a HOW TO THINK ABOUT THE REASON ONE MUST ENTER THIS PATH

305   If I train well in the three Trainings, as described,
       I shall indeed free myself from the samsaric ocean;
       But striving to free just myself from samsara, not thinking
       About the sentient beings tormented there,

306   Is like leaving one's aged mother shut up
       In prison and getting oneself somehow set free:
       Is there anyone less considerate than that?
       Therefore, I must liberate all migrators.

9b TRAINING IN *BODHICITTA* BY THE SEVEN INSTRUCTIONS OF CAUSE AND EFFECT
9b.0 *How to achieve evenmindedness*

307   Also, although now all these migrating beings
       Appear as friends, foes or neutral, and being attached
       To this, I develop attachment for the friends,
       Hatred for foes, and for neutral folk, unconcern;

308   Still, those who seem to be enemies at present
       Have in the past been my mothers many times,
       They've helped me in such ways as feeding me with their milk
       And lovingly nursing, and guarded me from all harm.

309   All those who seem to be friends at present, too,
       Have in the past been the clearest of enemies –
       Numerous times they have killed or beaten me,
       And even devoured me alive. This also is taught.

310   Also, those who seem to be neutral at present
      In many former lives have variously
      Been friends and foes – they've done me harm in anger,
      And also, infinite times, done me good with love.

311   Therefore, among all these migrating beings,
      Which should I hate, and which should I be attached to?
      Let me now not discriminate liked and hated,
      But have equal mind towards all of them, as my friends.

312   If I should think, "Since friend and foe aren't certain,
      It is not right either to inflict harm
      Or to give aid, but it is right to abide
      Unconcerned," then this is not correct.

313   Since the terrible harm by past lives' foes was deluded,
      Not knowing I was their parents, anger is wrong.
      Since the help they provided in past lives when they were friends
      Resided in truth, why should I not repay this help?

9b.1 *How to meditate on recognizing beings as one's mother*

314   Now if we ask how is it that in fact
      Every sentient being has been my mother,
      It's because there's no commencement to my births,
      And I've taken bodies infinite in number.

315   One may think, if there are infinite sentient beings,
      It is not reasonable all could have been my mother.
      But it is reasonable, since just as beings are numberless,
      So do my rebirths have no finite number.

316   The reason for this is, there's no first point to be shown
      Such that only since then has this mind existed. Thus,
      No limit is seen to the bodies I've taken either.
      But then, apart from the times I've taken birth

317   From heat and moisture, or miraculously,
      Whatever body I've taken, born from womb
      Or egg, must necessarily have had parents,

So it's logically proven all could have been my parents.

318 The Omniscient One, who never taught falsehood, also
Taught that "All beings who wander in samsara
Have not been born in this place in former times,"
Or "They have not taken bodies just like this,"

319 Or "We've never been each other's parents, brothers
And sisters, friends and relatives" – these were not
What He perceived. So, since it's established by scripture,
All these migrating beings have been my mother.

320 For this reason, just as I shall not recognise
Even my parents of this life after death,
Since we're reborn and die, I simply don't recognise beings,
But in fact they are all my mothers who've cherished me kindly.

9b.2 *How to meditate on remembering their kindness*

321 How have they cherished me kindly, one may wonder.
Well, my aged mother of this life
First, for nine or ten months, held me inside her
Just as one holds a precious vessel up,

322 Most anxious, watchful and careful not to harm me
In all her postures, walking, lying or sitting;
Not having just what she liked to eat or drink,
But keeping to helpful things and eschewing the harmful.

323 Then, when she gave birth, afflicted by scarcely bearable
Suffering, yet she did not think of her suff'ring,
But cherished me like a wish-granting jewel she'd found.
Thus she was great in kindness at the beginning.

324 After I was born, my hairs were bristly,
I excreted my filth without being aware,

And did not know in the least what was helpful or harmful,
But with many efforts she brought me up.

325 Also, to nourish my body, she made me drink milk;
To keep my flesh warm, she wrapped me up in soft clothes;
On her back when walking, her lap when sitting, she carried me;
She gave me food with her tongue, wiped my nose with her mouth.

326 Even my filth she cleaned up with her hands;
Saying "my child", she dandled me with her ten fingers;
Protected with loving mind, looked with affectionate eyes,
Called me by nice names, and welcomed me with a smile.

327 She saved me from dangers like water, fire and cliffs;
She preferred to be sick herself than me be sick,
And would rather have died herself than that I died;
Acting thus from the heart, she was indeed most kind.

328 Then, as gradually I grew older, she
Taught me to eat, to drink, to walk, to sit;
When I was cold or hungry, she clothed or fed me.
All her wealth, which she'd gained with sin and suff'ring,

329 She could not use herself, but gave to me,
Without regret. Thus she's very kind at the end.
Not only in this life, but also in many other
Lives, has she protected me with such kindness.

330 Just as she has protected me with kindness,
So all these sentient beings of the five classes
Also, in all the occasions when I've been human,
Have looked after me with such kindness again and again.

331 At the times of my rebirths born from the wombs or eggs

> Of beings other than human, too, they have,
> In accordance with their understanding and ability,
> Helped me and dispelled harms immeasurably.

9b.3 How to meditate on repaying their kindness

332   Thus these migrators have been extremely kind
      To me. If, without repayment, I abandon them,
      That is vile conduct towards my former mothers.
      Therefore, how should I not repay their kindness?

333   Their minds crazed by the fierce great demon, defilements,
      Blind to the Freedom Path, left by their friends and leaders,
      And reeling with misdeeds, they turn towards the abyss
      Of the realms of woe. How could I forsake them, so lost?

334   However, connection with samsaric happiness
      My mothers have undergone many times before;
      Being deceptive, it can't really repay their kindness,
      So I shall set them in bliss of Liberation.

At this point, one may either continue with verses 335 to 341, or if one prefers to meditate on *Bodhicitta* by the method of Exchanging Self and Others, generate Loving-kindness and Compassion using verses 342 to 348.

9b.4 How to meditate on Loving-kindness

335   Also, although these old mothers want to be happy,
      Mostly they don't understand that the cause is virtue,
      And even those who do don't practise it,
      While if they do try, it is useless because of defilements.

336   Therefore, since one does not meet uncreated karma,
      Those in bad destinies always are poor in happiness,
      While even those well-born are lacking in genuine happiness,
      Other than suffering that they perceive as happiness.

337   How wonderful, therefore, it would be if they
       Were all endowed with the Supreme Bliss of
           omniscient
       Buddhas, and its causes, the excellent Paths!
       May they have these! Grant inspiration for this!

9b.5 How to meditate on Compassion

338   Likewise, although they none of them want to suffer,
       Mostly they don't understand that the cause is
           non-virtue,
       If they do, don't avoid it, or if they start to avoid it,
       Cannot succeed. Because they act impurely,

339   And since created karma is unavoidable,
       Hell-beings suffer from intense heat and cold,
       Pretas are greatly afflicted by hunger and thirst,
       Animals suffer from being killed, use, and stupidity;

340   Suff'rings of birth, aging, sickness and death disturb
           humans;
       Asuras are plagued by jealousy and fighting;
       Gods of Desire are grieved by sharp anguish near
           death,
       Form gods and Formless have suff'ring of being
           conditioned.

341   How wonderful, therefore, it would be if they
       Were now free of all these sufferings and their causes,
       Defilements, and the causes [of defilements]!
       May they be free! Grant such inspiration!

Continue at verse 349 below.

9c HOW TO MEDITATE ON BODHICITTA BY THE METHOD OF EXCHANGE OF SELF AND OTHERS*

342   Since, in this way, all these migrating beings

---

*This section, an optional alternative to verses 335 to 341, is printed after verse 366 in the Tibetan text, but is here brought forward to the place at which it is recited.

> Are none other than my own kind parents,
> If I abandon them in the wrong place and
> Cherish myself, then this is not correct;

343 For it is this very cherishing of myself
That has been the cause of all my own sufferings,
And it can be seen that the cherishing of others
Is the cause of all my own happiness.

344 It's taught, too, that all samsaric and nirvanic
Happiness comes from wanting others happy,
While all the troubles there are in samsara and
Nirvana come from wanting oneself to be happy.

345 In short, because the childish cherish themselves,
They are disturbed like this by waves of suff'ring.
Because the Sages practise cherishing others,
Have they not found the stage of Perfect Bliss?

346 Therefore, if I never desire to suffer,
I must reject this cherishing of myself,
And if I desire insatiably to enjoy happiness,
I must strive in the cherishing of others.

347 So, may all these suff'rings and all their causes
Of these beings, who are my ancient mothers,
Ripen upon me, so that they may all
Be liberated from suffering and its causes!

348 May my collection of temp'ral and ultimate happiness,
And whatever virtue I possess,
All ripen upon these migrating sentient beings,
That they may all be endowed with Supreme Bliss!

This is how to meditate on Loving-kindness by way of Giving away (*gTong*), and on Compassion by Taking over (*Len*). Having done this, continue with the Superior Intention, etc.

9b.6 *How to meditate on the Superior Intention*

349 Not satisfied just with the prayer, thinking like that,
"May ev'ry sentient being be devoid

Of suff'ring, and may they all have happiness!",
I myself must act to bring this about.

350　For this reason, as I must make my mother
Of this life happy, and dispel her suff'rings,
So it is I who must act to dispel the suff'ring
Of all sentient beings, and make them happy;

351　For from the side of the sentient beings, they're equal
In wanting happiness and not wanting suff'ring;
While from my side they are all equal in
Having been my mothers and kindly protected me.

352　Therefore, I must shoulder the great burden
Of liberating all these sentient beings
From all the troubles of samsara and Nirvana,
And setting them in the excellent state of Omniscience!

9b.7 *How to meditate on the generation of Bodhicitta*

353　But, one wonders, since I am governed by deeds and defilements,
And can't be sure where I'll be reborn, how can I bear
The great burden of freeing other sentient beings
From samsara, setting them in the highest Enlightenment?

354　Not only do I lack such ability
At present: even if I gained the state
Of Hearer or *Pratyeka* Arhant, I'd never have
The power to set all beings on the stage of Omniscience.

355　Even these two Lesser Arhants have only abandoned
Obscurations of *kleśa*, not those to knowables, so
Their faults are only partially exhausted,
Their virtues are but partially complete.

356　Therefore, while their self-benefit is not complete,
Their benefit of others too is only
Helpful to limited beings, but lacks the power
Of benefiting every sentient being.

357 Well then: who does have the power to free
     All sentient beings from samsara's ocean? –
     This ability only a Buddha has;
     No-one else possesses it at all.

358 Not only others' benefit: none but a Buddha
     Has perfect self-benefit – all the abandonments and
     Realizations. Therefore whichever benefit
     I would win, truly I must gain that supreme rank.

359 If one gains it, one's body has these qualities:
     Adorned with the Marks and Signs, and never
        changing,
     And able to manifest many displays of bodies
     Before ev'ry sentient being, all at once.

360 The qualities of one's speech: should every being
     Ask things at once, it can with a single sound
     Teach all those topics, in each person's language;
     This tuneful speech, too, comes from all parts of the
        body.

361 The mental qualities: while one's Wisdom sees
     Directly the mode of existence of every *dharma*,
     It sees clearly ev'ry particular knowable thing,
     Like something resting on the palm of one's hand.

362 The qualities of one's Love: it's taught that even
     The manner in which one mother loves her child
     Would not be a match for even a hundredth part
     Of the loving compassion one shows to all sentient
        beings.

363 One's divine actions: never moving from
     The Universal Law, one effortlessly
     Appears in taming emanations, just as
     All wishes appear from wish-granting gems or trees.

364 Moreover, these appearances are not limited,
     Sometimes occurring and sometimes not occurring:
     As long as any sentient beings remain,
     One appears with never a break in continuity.

365   How marvellous! If I win that supreme rank,
I shall have such qualities myself,
And also be able perfectly to help
All these sentient beings, my old mothers.

366   Therefore, with the very utmost speed,
I must gain somehow that supreme rank,
Which perfects both benefits, of oneself and others.
May I attain it! Please inspire me to do so!

MEDITATION 10
HOW TO TRAIN IN THE SIX PERFECTIONS

367   Since I won't succeed in attaining such
A Buddha's rank by thinking "May I attain it!",
I must keep *Bodhicitta* vows, strive in the advices,
And enter the ocean of the Buddha-Son's conduct.

368   Giving of Dharma is teaching whatever Dharma
Is fitting, regardless of gain or honour and so forth.
Giving of Safety is protecting from harm
By human or non-human, or by the elements.

369   Material Giving is giving all necessities,
Not with the hope of return or karmic results.
Henceforth I shall train with diligence˚
In the practice of these three aspects of Giving.
Please inspire me so that I can do this!

370   Morality of Vows is acting in vows,
Not transgressing the rules of the advices
Of the three types of vows, as one has promised.
Morality of Collecting Positive *Dharmas*

371   Is to produce in one's mindstream positive *dharmas*
Like the Perfections, and make those produced increase.
Morality of Helping Sentient Beings
Is benefiting beings correctly, through

372   The eleven ways of helping sentient beings.

Henceforth I shall train with diligence
In the practice of these three types of Morality.
Please inspire me so that I can do this!

373 Patience of Unconcern with Harming is,
When all beings rise up as enemies and abuse you,
On top of analysing and not getting angry,
To practise helping them, in return for the harm.

374 Patience of Willingly Bearing Suffering is
To accept with joy being lacking in food and clothing,
Dwelling and so on; unwanted things, such as disease;
And sufferings that arise for the sake of the Dharma.

375 Patience of Certain Thought about Dharma is
To generate heartfelt confidence and conviction
About such devotion-objects as the Three Jewels.
Henceforth I shall train with diligence
In the practice of these three aspects of Patience.
Please inspire me so that I can do this!

376 Armour-like Energy's being joyful, not sad,
When one must dwell many eons in realms of woe
For every sentient being, or stay a long time
In samsara to realize every Buddha-quality.

377 Virtue-collecting Energy's striving to gather
In one's mindstream, positive *dharmas* like the Perfections.
Energy of Helping Sentient Beings
Is striving in the eleven ways that help them.

378 Henceforth I shall train with diligence
In the practice of these three aspects of Energy.
Please inspire me so that I can do this!

379 By nature, *Dhyāna* is twofold: samsaric, beyond.
By class, it is threefold: Quietude, Insight, Union.
By function, abiding in mental and physical bliss;
Dhyāna that acts as a basis for qualities, and

380 *Dhyāna* of benefiting sentient beings.
Henceforth I shall train with diligence

In the practice of these three aspects of *Dhyāna*.
Please inspire me so that I can do this!

381 The Wisdom perceiving the Ultimate, knowing True Nature;
That which perceives the Conventional, knowing five Sciences;
That which correctly understands how to accomplish
Unerringly both the benefits of migrators:

382 Henceforth I shall train with diligence
In the practice of these three aspects of Wisdom.
Please inspire me so that I can do this!

MEDITATION 11
HOW TO TRAIN IN THE FOUR MEANS OF ATTRACTION

383 Skilfully Giving material things to attract;
Teaching the holy Dharma with Pleasant Speech;
Helping to enter the practice of what I have taught;
Consistency with my teaching, I too conforming

384 To practices to which I have introduced others:
Henceforth I shall train correctly in
The practice of these four Means of Attraction.
Please inspire me so that I can do this!

MEDITATION 12
HOW TO MEDITATE ON QUIETUDE (*ŚAMATHA*)

385 Though familiar in this way with the *Bodhi* mind
And conduct, if I've not realized the True Mode of Being,
Whatever my efforts, I cannot be free from samsara.
Therefore I must endeavour to realize Right View.

386 If my mind is distracted by fading or agitation,

> I cannot perceive the profound Mode of Being, therefore
> To avoid agitation and fading, I must practise
> *Samādhi*, abiding one-pointed on any object.

387 Laziness, not being happy to practise *samādhi*;
Forgetting the object; agitation and fading;
Non-application; and application, are
The five faults in the development of *samādhi*.

388 To avoid them, laziness' antidotes are firm Faith
Perceiving the virtues of the *samādhi* of Quietude;
Induced by this, Desire to strive in *samādhi*;
Impelled by this Desire, painstaking Energy;

389 Fourthly, the fruit of this effort, Tranquillity.
The antidote of forgetting the object is Mindfulness,
That of fading and agitation's Awareness;
That of non-application of the remedies

390 Of fading and agitation is Will to Apply Them.
For applying the remedies when agitation and fading
Are absent, the cure is Unconcern, not applying them.
That's eight remedial actions, avoiding the five faults.

391 I'll adhere to these, and the Six Powers of hearing, thinking,
Mindfulness, 'wareness, energy and acquaintance.
The four Attentions are squeezing, interrupted,
Uninterrupted, and spontaneous.

392 There are placement, continual placement, that with returning,
Close placement, taming, pacification, and thorough
Pacification, making one-pointed, and equipoise.

393 Through these six Powers, four Attentions and nine Mental States,
I must realize the pure *samādhi* of Quietude,
Induced by the bliss of tranquillity of mind and body!
Please inspire me so that I can do this!

MEDITATION 13
HOW TO MEDITATE ON INSIGHT
(VISPAŚYANĀ)

394   If I thus realize *samādhi* of Quietude,
I must cut the root of ignorance and error,
By discriminating analysis of the meaning
Of Selflessness, while I abide in that *samādhi*.

395   So, what is the cause through which I and all sentient beings,
From beginningless time until the present,
Have circled in this state of samsara, afflicted
Uncontrollably by many hundreds of suff'rings?

396   It is this: though this mind's of indifferent nature, first
The thought arises that self and other and so forth
Exist independently and inherently. Through
This appearance that self and other exist inherently,

397   Grow all defilements, such as attachment for self
And hatred for others. Through these one heaps up karma,
And whirls like a firebrand round the realms of the six classes,
Whence comes this disturbance by suff'ring, like ripples on water.

398   Therefore, in the end, the root of samsara
Is that all *dharmas* of samsara and Nirvana
Are not grasped as mere conceptual imputations,
But appear and are grasped as inherently existent.

399   Therefore the object appearing as an I
Existent inherently, not a mere imputation
Of "I" upon the collection of one's body
And mind, is called the object of negation.

400   If that I did exist in accord with that mode of appearance,
That I would have to exist as either one with
Or separate from body-and-mind; for apart from these
There is no third alternative mode of existence.

401 If it exists as one, then as body and mind
     Are two, so the I will be two separate continua;
     Or, just as the I is single, so too
     The body and mind will be a partless unity.

402 And if the body-and-mind are one with the I,
     They must be one without any divisions at all,
     Therefore expressions dividing them separately,
     "My body" and "my mind", are inadmissible.

403 Therefore, since there are many other faults too
     If I and body-and-mind exist as one,
     That self or I does not exist as one
     Entity with the mind-and-body pair.

404 If you say it exists as separate, then
     You would have to be able to say individually
     "This is my mind, this my body, this my I."
     Since this can't be done, it does not exist as separate.

405 Therefore, since that I does not exist
     Either one with or separate from the mind-body pair,
     The I comes from the collection of body and mind,
     And does not exist truly: it is like an illusion.

406 Likewise, the so-called "body" which appears
     To exist inherently, not as a mere imputation
     On this heap of flesh and bones and set of five limbs,
     Is an object of negation, just seeming true.

407 If it did exist in accord with that mode of appearance,
     That body and its parts would have to exist
     Either as one, or else as separate; for
     There is no other way they could exist.

408 If they existed as one, then since that body
     Has many parts, such as the head, it too would be many.
     Or else, since the body is one, its many parts
     Would also be a partless unity.

409 If they existed as separate, then in what was left
     When all separate parts such as arms and legs were

removed,
That body would have to be found. Since it can't be, the body's
A mere imputation upon its collection of parts.

410 For the mind too, the mode of appearance of the object
Negated is that the mind of Mr. Smith
Appears to exist from its own side, not merely imputed
Upon Mr. Smith's mind's past and future parts.

411 If it did so exist, then Mr. Smith's own mind
And the past and future parts of his mind would exist
Either as one, or else as separate, for
There is no other way they could exist.

412 If they existed as one, since the parts, past and future,
Are multiple, it would follow that mind too was multiple.
Or, as the mind is one, so its past and future
Parts would be a partless unity.

413 When they exist as separate, then after the parts,
That mind's past and future moments, are removed,
One would have to be able to show such a mind, "This is it!".
But since one cannot, that so-called "mind" also
Is merely imputed upon its parts, past and future.

414 Just as, when I and body and mind are analysed
With these four points, they lack inherent existence,
So when all *dharmas*, conditioned and unconditioned,
Are analysed thus, they are seen to be like space.

415 In short, ev'ry *dharma* of samsara or Nirvana
Is only a name and conceptual imputation.
There is no *dharma* existing from its own side,
Upon that object itself, not even an atom.

416 Well, if no *dharmas* exist from their own side,
What kind of mode of existence do they have?
They exist in the manner of dreams, illusions, echoes,

Or moons in water, appearing but empty of essence.

417 Yet this does not mean that all *dharmas* do not exist
At all. For example, the echo: it arises
When all its causes assemble; although on analysis
One cannot find it, still it's not non-existent.

418 Just so, when their respective conditions assemble,
Dharmas appear as such and such. When examined
With the logic of ultimate analysis,
They nowhere exist, but they're not non-existent totally.

419 That which is seen, when analysed, not to exist,
Is seen not to exist truly, but is not seen
Not to exist at all. Convention'l existents
Exist, like the echo, but are not truly existent.

420 So, seeing all *dharmas* are space-like when analysed with
The logic that tests the Deep Meaning, and at the same time
Being certain they utterly fit the workings of
Dependent Arising, is the Ultimate View.

421 The post-meditational yoga of Illusion's
Like realizing that, though one sees an illusory horse
Or elephant, that appearance is an illusion,
Because one's sure it does not exist as that.

422 Not denying conventional knowledge, all *dharmas* appear,
But through certainty that they are empty of essence, one sees
Without effort, in post-meditation, the objects' appearance
Is illusive. There's no other way to practice Illusion.

423 I must gain the good Path of Calm and Insight United,
Combining the Space-like yoga of equipoise and
The post-meditational yoga of objects' illusive
Appearance, and perceiving the Profound Meaning.
Please inspire me so that I can do this!

MEDITATION 14
HOW TO ENTER THE ADAMANTINE VEHICLE (*VAJRAYĀNA*)

424   When I have achieved the ordinary Paths
        Of Renunciation, *Bodhicitta*, and View,
        I must please, by means of the three ways of pleasing,
        A Vajra Master with all the qualifications,

425   Take the four empowerments and grow the four
           Kāyas' seeds,
        Strive in the Two-Stage yoga of the Deep Path
        And quickly attain the Stage of Unification!
        Please inspire me so that I can do this!

CONCLUSION

Then say the *Lam rim* dedication prayer, *Der ni ring du* (Appendix 4).

Then one may say:

> Alas! Hitherto, in this samsara
> I've circled like a bucket-wheel,
> Mostly born in the leisureless states,
> Not meeting with this excellent Path.
>
> Now I have gained the opportune rebirth
> And been received by a holy Guru.
> To spend in leisure this chance, having met
> This supreme Path, is idiotic.
>
> Therefore, I'll cast out activities for
> This life, as a snake sheds its skin,
> And striving in the excellent Path
> Day and night, attain the essence.
>
> Through the mass of virtue thus produced,
> Henceforth, in all my lives, may I
> Not separate from this Dharma way,
> And may all beings be freed by this Path!

THE COLOPHON

This essence of the Profound Instructions on the Stages of the Path to Enlightenment, rejecting elaborations such as outlines, and in mnemonic verse, entitled *The Essential Nectar of the Holy Doctrine*, was composed, for his own scanning meditation and in the hope of benefiting others of similar fortune also, by an inferior monk called in the language of fine writing Jñāna-Vīrya, at the Ganden Samten Ling hermitage in Kong-yül.

May the essence of the Doctrine become a never-vanishing banner of victory!

Translated into English verse by Martin Willson, at Tharpa Choeling in Switzerland, March 1981.

Appendices
Glossary
Bibliography
Notes

Appendix 1
The Confession of Downfalls
lTung bshags

Introduction

This is the Bodhisattva's rite of confession to the Thirty-five Buddhas, taught by the Buddha in the *Upāli-paripṛcchā-sūtra*. It appears to be among the earliest Mahāyāna texts; certainly it precedes the second half of the third century, the date of its' first Chinese translation and of Mātṛceta, who composed a hymn to the Thirty-five Buddhas. The rite is still very popular among Tibetan Buddhists who normally recite it while performing full-length prostrations and visualizing the Thirty-five Buddhas.

The Sanskrit, Tibetan and Chinese texts have been published, with a French translation, by Pierre Python (§§23–27 of the *Sūtra* comprise the Confession). In the translation below, words and phrases missing or incorrect in the Sanskrit but found in the Tibetan text of the *Sūtra* are placed in round brackets, while those absent from the *Sūtra* but occurring in the Tibetan text in the Dharamsala prayerbook (*bLa ma'i rnal 'byor dang yi dam khag gi bdag bskyed sogs zhal 'don gces btus*, 1977 edition, pp. 550–559) are placed in square brackets. The omission of titles for most of the Buddhas in the *Sūtra* text could be simply an abbreviation; there is no reason why in recitation all should not be given the same three titles as the first and last – Tathāgata, Arhant, Perfectly Enlightened One (*samyak-saṃbuddha*).

The translation

I, of such-and-such a name, [go for Refuge forever to the Guru.

I] go for Refuge to the Buddha.
(I go for Refuge to the Dharma.)
I go for Refuge to the Sangha.

Homage to [the glorious Conqueror,] Śākyamuni, [the Master, the *Bhagavan*,] the *Tathāgata*, the Arhant, the perfectly Enlightened!
Homage to Vajra-(garbha-)pramardin [Tathāgata]!
Homage to Ratnârcis [Tathāgata]!
Homage to Nāgêśvara-rāja [Tathāgata]!
Homage to Vīra-sena [Tathāgata]!
Homage to Vīra-nandin [Tathāgata]!
Homage to (Ratnâgni) [Tathāgata]!
Homage to Ratna-candra-prabha [Tathāgata]!
Homage to Amogha-darśin [Tathāgata]!
Homage to Ratna-candra [Tathāgata]!
Homage to Nirmala [Tathāgata]!
Homage to Śūra-datta [Tathāgata]!
Homage to Brahmā [Tathāgata]!
Homage to Brahma-datta [Tathāgata]!
Homage to Varuṇa [Tathāgata]!
Homage to Varuṇa-deva [Tathāgata]!
Homage to Bhadra-śrī [Tathāgata]!
Homage to Candana-śrī [Tathāgata]!
Homage to Anantaujas [Tathāgata]!
Homage to Prabhāsa-śrī [Tathāgata]!
Homage to Aśoka-śrī [Tathāgata]!
Homage to Nārāyaṇa [Tathāgata]!
Homage to Kusuma-śrī [Tathāgata]!
Homage to Brahma-jyotir-vikrīḍitâbhijña Tathāgata!
(Homage to Padma-jyotir-vikrīḍitâbhijña Tathāgata!)
Homage to Dhana-śrī [Tathāgata]!

Homage to Smṛiti-śrī [Tathāgata]!
Homage to Suparikīrtita-nāma-dheya-śrī [Tathāgata]!
Homage to Indra-ketu-dhvaja-rāja [Tathāgata]!
Homage to Suvikrānta-śrī [Tathāgata]!
Homage to Vijita-saṃgrāma [Tathāgata]!
Homage to Vikrānta-gāmin [Tathāgata]!
Homage to Samantâvabhāsa-vyūha-śrī [Tathāgata]!
Homage to Ratna-padma-vikrāmin [Tathāgata]!
Homage to Ratna-padma-supratiṣṭhita-śailêndra-rāja, Tathāgata, Arhant, Perfectly Enlightened!

As many *Tathāgatas*, Arhants, perfectly Enlightened Ones [and *Bhagavans*] as are present, remain and live in all the worlds (of the ten directions), beginning with these: may these *Bhagavan* Buddhas pay attention to me!
Whatever evil karma I, wandering through rebirth and transmigration without end or beginning, may in this existence or in other existences have done, caused to be done, or rejoiced in the doing of; whatever wealth of a *stūpa* or of the Sangha I may have taken away, caused to be taken, or rejoiced in the taking of; whatever of the five actions of immediate retribution I may have done, caused to be done, or rejoiced in the doing of; whatever of the ten unwholesome paths of action I may have engaged in the adoption of, caused another to adopt, or rejoiced in engagement in; the karmic obscuration obscured by which I may go to a hell, to an animal state, or to a preta realm, or be born among the border nations or the barbarians, or among the long-lived gods, or obtain an impairment of my faculties, or accept wrong view, or lack pleasure in the arising of a Buddha – all this karmic obscuration I confess before those *Bhagavan* Buddhas, who are Wisdom-knowledge, who are eyes, who are witnesses, who are authorities, knowing and seeing. I reveal it. I do not hide (or conceal) it. Henceforth I take up restraint.

May these *Bhagavan* Buddhas pay attention to me!
Whatever gift I, wandering through rebirth and transmigration without end or beginning, may in this existence or in other existences have given, be it so much as a morsel to an animal, whatever moral discipline I may have kept, whatever root of merit I may have from living in chastity (*brahmacarya*), what-

ever root of merit I may have from ripening sentient beings, whatever root of merit I may have from *Bodhicitta*, and whatever root of merit I may have from supreme Wisdom-knowledge – all this, combined, weighed up (*tulayitvā*) and compressed together, I dedicate to the highest, perfect Enlightenment with higher and higher dedication*, just as past *Bhagavan* Buddhas have dedicated, just as future *Bhagavan* Buddhas will dedicate, and just as the *Bhagavan* Buddhas existing at present in the ten directions dedicate.

(I confess all my sins.)
I rejoice in all merits.
I request all the Buddhas: may the highest Wisdom-knowledge be mine!
The Conquerors, highest of men, who are past, who are to come, and who are present – to all these, of ocean-like virtues and infinite glory, joining my hands in respect I go for Refuge.

*Tib.: "with dedication which is highest, supreme, supreme of the supreme, highest of the high."

Appendix 2
Yon tan gzhir gyur ma
A Lam rim prayer by Je Tsongkhapa

1   Let me see that proper devotion to my kind Master,
    Foundation of all good qualities, is the root
    Of the Path, and devote myself to him with great
    Respect and many efforts – inspire me thus!

2   Let me understand that this excellent, opportune rebirth,
    Found but once, is most rare and of great value,
    And develop the mind that always, day and night,
    Unceasingly grasps its essence – inspire me thus!

3   Mindful of death, when my unstable body and life
    Are quickly destroyed, like bubbles in a stream;
    And firmly convinced that after death, results
    Pursue actions, white or black, as a shadow a body:

4   May I always have watchfulness in the practice
    Of abandoning even the slightest accumulations
    Of wrongful actions, and accomplishing all
    The accumulations of virtues – inspire me thus!

5   Let me understand the faults of samsaric perfection –
    To taste it can't satisfy, it is the door of all suff'ring,

It cannot be trusted! Let striving for the bliss
Of Freedom grow strongly within me – inspire me thus!

6   With the greatest watchfulness, mindfulness and
       awareness
    Induced by this pure motivation, may I
    Practise in its essence the *Prātimokṣa*,
    Which is the root of the Doctrine – inspire me thus!

7   Let me see that just as I have fallen into
    The sea of samsara, so have all mother migrators,
    And train in the supreme *Bodhicitta*, which bears
    The burden of freeing migrators – inspire me thus!

8   Perceiving well that if I produce the mere wish,
    But lack practice in the threefold Morality, I
    Shan't realize Enlightenment, let me train with strong
       effort
    In the Buddha-sons' vows – inspire me thus!

9   By my quelling distraction towards wrong objects, and
    Investigating correctly Reality's Meaning,
    May there quickly be born in my mindstream the Path
       Uniting
    Calm Abiding and Insight – inspire me thus!

10 When, trained in the common Path, I'm a suitable
       vessel,
    Let me enter with ease that noble entrance for
    Fortunate beings, the highest of all Vehicles,
    The Adamantine Vehicle – inspire me thus!

11 Then, let me discover genuine certainty as to
    The Teaching that pure commitments and vows are the
       basis
    On which the two kinds of *siddhis* are accomplished,
    And keep them at risk of my life – inspire me thus!

12 Then understanding correctly the essence of
    The classes of Tantra, and the points of the Two Stages,
    May I not be lazy in striving in four-session yoga,
    But practise the holy Teachings – inspire me thus!

13 Thus, may the Gurus who show the excellent Path
    And helpers of true practitioners all live long!
    May the whole set of hindrances, inner and outer,
    Be pacified – grant such inspiration, I pray!

14 In all my rebirths, not parted from perfect Gurus,
    Let me enjoy abundance of the Dharma!
    Perfecting all qualities of the Stages and Paths,
    May I quickly attain the rank of Vajradhara!

Appendix 3
Je Tsongkhapa on the Six Sufferings and the Three Sufferings
From the Lam rim chen mo[101]

Contemplation of the Six Sufferings

In the commentary to *Suhṛl-lekha* (66–102), seven are taught; but since the last of these (77–102) is the individual disadvantages, here we should contemplate six.

1 THE FAULT OF LACK OF CERTAINTY

As one circles in samsara, one's relatives such as father and mother become enemies in another existence, and enemies become relatives; one's father becomes one's son, and one's son one's father; one's mother becomes one's wife, and one's wife one's mother, and so on. One only dies and transmigrates, in succession. Therefore there is nothing at all one can rely on. This is taught in *Suhṛl-lekha*[102]:

> 66 Fathers become sons, and mothers wives,
> People who were foes become one's friends,
> And vice versa: so, in consequence,
> In samsara there's no certainty.

Even in the same life, enemy and friend can turn into each other, as is taught in the *Subāhu-paripṛcchā*:

> Even a foe in a while becomes a friend,
> A friend also likewise becomes a foe,
> Some equally becoming strangers too,
> And these same strangers turning into foes,
>
> Or, again, close friends. Perceiving this,
> Never will the intelligent be attached.
> Diverting the mental conception that delights
> In friends, he'll easily set [his mind] on virtue.

Meditating in this way, one should cease dividing up enemies and friends and generating attachment and hatred, and feel disgust, beholding the lack of anything one can trust in samsaric *dharmas*.

2 THE FAULT OF DISSATISFACTION

> 67 The mother's milk that each has drunk exceeds
> The oceans four; but beings of samsara
> Who follow still the ordinary beings,
> They will have to drink much more than that.

That is: as much milk as each sentient being has previously drunk from the mother's breast, they will drink again if they still have not trained in the Path of Liberation.

This is just an indication; when one thinks how there is nothing one has not experienced in the excellences and sufferings of samsara, one has to be disgusted. One enjoys pleasure in order to satisfy the mind, but since however much samsaric pleasure one enjoys there is no satisfaction, subsequently craving increases, and by this too one wanders long in samsara. Because of these pleasures, one will experience for a measureless time extremely hard-to-bear sufferings of which one cannot stand even a fraction.

We contemplate as taught in *Suhṛl-lekha* (26):

> Just as a leper who is pained by worms,
> Though he rely on fire for comfort's sake,
> Will find no peace: like that too know to be

Attachment toward pleasures of the senses!

And in the *Pāramitā-samāsa* [of Āryaśūra]:

> If by attaining those desires,
> Relying on them for one day,
> And storing much, one is not sated,
> What greater illness than that is there?

And in the *Śiṣya-lekha*:

> What destiny is there I have not entered a hundred times?
> What pleasure have I not tasted many times before?
> What glory is there, like a beautiful white yak-tail,
> That I have not attained? Yet still attachment grows.
>
> No suffering not tasted many times before;
> No desire in migration that will satisfy;
> No sentient being on whose belly I've not lain.
> How am I still not free of attachment for the samsaric?

If in addition one thinks as taught in the *Śoka-vinodana*, one will be very disgusted:

> The molten copper that I've drunk
> Time and again when in the hells,
> Even the water in the ocean
> Does not have such great volume.
>
> The filthy stuff which I have eaten
> When I've been a dog or pig
> Far exceeds the measure of
> The king of mountains, Sumeru.
>
> For the tear-drops I have shed
> When in samsaric situations
> Owing to total lack of friends,
> The ocean would not serve as vessel.
>
> If my heads which were cut off
> Because of mutual combat
> Were piled up, they would reach even

Je Tsongkhapa on the Six Sufferings and the Three Sufferings

Higher than the Brahmā-world.[103]

> The earth and manure that in hunger
> I have eaten as a worm,
> If the great milk ocean were
> Filled with them, 'twould overflow.

According to the *Gaṇḍa-vyūha[-sūtra]*:

> Recalling those bodies which, in former times,
> You uselessly squandered for the sake of greed,
> And having today the practice of striving for *Bodhi*,
> This time, through practice put an end to greed!
>
> Recall those bodies which, in former times,
> You uselessly squandered for the sake of greed!
> You have not pleased [Buddhas] as many as sands
>   of the Ganges.
> This kind of speech you have not heard from
>   Buddhas.

Remember thus that however much samsaric perfection one experiences, it is deceptive, and having experienced measureless, pointless suffering, one wastes countless bodies as before. If one is still not striving, one should generate disgust in thinking about the manner of transformation in this way.

Chän-nga[104] said, "Master Jowo, however many bodies I have taken since beginningless time, I have never practised the Dharma of the Great Vehicle as at present, so I must make an effort." And Sangp'uwa[105] said, "In this samsara we have to undergo many ups and downs: this is distressing for the mind." One must think [about it] until this kind of state of mind has arisen, and even after it has arisen, one must preserve it continuously.

3 THE FAULT OF GIVING UP THE BODY AGAIN AND AGAIN

> 68 The heap of bones that each has had himself
>   Would surpass a bulk as great as Meru.

The bones of the bodies that each sentient being has taken and discarded would undoubtedly be even greater than Meru.

4 THE FAULT OF TAKING ON A NEW EXISTENCE AGAIN AND AGAIN

> 68c To count one's mothers' limit, in pellets the size
> Of jujube seeds, the earth would not suffice.

The preceding does not mean counting the times that one sentient being has been one's mother; for a Sutra quoted in the commentary says,

> "Monks: suppose some man were to take up pellets from this earth the size of jujube seeds[106], and throw them away saying 'This is my mother; this is the mother of that mother,' then, monks, all the clay in this earth might be used up, yet the succession of the man's mothers would not be."[107] I.e. The Master means the succession of one's own mother, her mother, and so on, in sequence. Also, the text itself says "limit (*thug mtha'*) of mothers".

How this generates disgust is shown in the *Catuḥ-śataka* (VII.10):

> When for even one result
> One cannot see a first cause,
> Then in even one there's vastness.
> Seeing this, how can fear not come?

And one should understand as it is stated in the Commentary:[108]

> Through this, one should feel always disgusted towards the great wilderness of samsara, so hard to roam in because of the great thickets [of ignorance] that continue beyond measure, and meditate on the proper aspects in accordance with this.

5 THE FAULT OF HIGH BECOMING LOW AGAIN AND AGAIN

> 69 Having been Indra, worthy of the world's honour,
> By power of karma, one falls again to earth;
> Though one has been a universal king,

One is a servant even to attendants.

70 When one has long experienced the pleasure
    Of fondling the breasts and waists of heavenly
      maidens,
    Again one partakes in hell of the most
      unbearable
    Touch of machines for grinding, cutting and
      scraping.

71 Having dwelt long on the summit of Mount
      Meru,
    Where the foot's touch finds comfort in its
      softness,
    Think one's again hit by the unbearable
      suff'ring
    Of walking on hot coals and putrefying corpses.

72 When one has been to delightful, beautiful
      groves
    And played, attended by heavenly maidens,
      then
    Again one will find one's feet, hands, ears and
      nose
    Cut off by groves whose leaves resemble
      swords.

73 One's entered Mandākinī[109] River, endowed
      with heavenly
    Maidens with beautiful faces, and golden
      lotuses;
    Then one must enter once more hell's
      Vaitaraṇī
    River, hot water and salt earth, hard to bear.

74 Having won very great pleasure in lands of the
      gods
    Of Desire, or unattached bliss in the Brahma
      realm,
    Again one must partake of the unbroken
      suff'ring
    Of being fuel for the fires of Avīci.

75 One gains the state of the sun or moon, the light
  Of one's own body lighting up the whole
    world;
  Then, when again one's gone into dense
    darkness,
  One cannot even see one's outstretched hand.

The three machines for grinding, [cutting & scraping] are respectively in the Crushing, Black Line and Heating Hells. "Attended by heavenly maidens" means "served by heavenly maidens". "Pleasure in lands of the gods of Desire" means of the gods of the Desire Realm from the heaven of the Thirty-three upwards. The light of the sun and moon is explained according to worldly opinion, not analysing dependent and depended on. If one analyses, it is the light of their celestial chariots.[110]

Thinking about the ways of going from a high plane to a low plane indicated by these [verses], one should be disgusted with samsara, because the end of every samsaric perfection consists of decline.

Also, as taught in the *Vinayâgama*,

  The end of all hoards is exhaustion,
  Exaltation's end is falling,
  Meeting's end is separation,
  And the end of life is death.

6 THE FAULT OF LACK OF COMPANIONS

76 Thus, you will have to pass on; [so,] take up
  The light of the lamp of Merits, of three types!
  Alone, you'll have to set out in an endless
  Darkness, where the sun and moon don't reach.

"You will have to pass on": understand the necessity of death, as taught before,[111] and take up the light of merits. The three merits are either the virtues of the three doors, or the three areas [of meritorious action], that consisting of giving, etc.[112] The endless darkness is the darkness of ignorance.

Setting out without a companion is as taught in *Bodhisattva-caryâvatāra*:[113]

> Though this body arose as one,
> The flesh and bones produced together
> Will, on perishing, be dispersed –
> What need to mention other companions?

> When I am born, I'm born alone;
> And when I die, I die alone.
> Since others can't take a share of the suff'ring,
> What use are obstructive companions?

These six may be collected into three:

(a) The lack of anything in samsara that one can trust.

(b) The lack of final satisfaction, however much one enjoys its pleasures.

(c) Having entered it without beginning.

(a) includes four aspects:

(i) Untrustworthiness of attaining a body: giving up the body again and again.

(ii) Untrustworthiness of helping and harming: lack of certainty.

(iii) Untrustworthiness of attaining perfection: high becoming low.

(iv) Untrustworthiness of company: going without a companion.

(c) is taking on a new existence again and again, no limit to the string of births being apparent.

One should also think about them grouped in this way.

Contemplation of the Three Sufferings

The pleasant feeling of samsaric beings is like the appearance of happiness when cool water is put on a very painful boil or tumour: since in a while it produces suffering, it is *suffering of change*. Not only that feeling, but also the primary mind and other mental factors parallel with it, and the contaminated object based on which [all these] arise, are suffering of change.

One should understand that suffering feelings are like the

great suffering when one tormented by a painful tumour comes into contact with corrosives such as salt water; because they torment the body and mind from the time they arise, they are *suffering of suffering*, like kidney pain. This [suffering] also is not the feeling alone, as before.

The contaminated indifferent feeling is like the painful tumour when not meeting these two contacts. Since it is related to habitual bad tendencies, it is *suffering of conditioning* (*saṃ-skāra-duḥkha*). This too is not the feeling alone, as before. [It is the "pervasive suffering of conditioning", because] it is endowed with habitual bad tendencies that are omnipresent, being governed by previous karma and defilements and related to the seeds which produce subsequent suffering and defilements.[114]

Thus, if happy feeling is born, attachment increases; if suffering is produced, aversion grows; and through such [perverse views] as grasping the impermanent as permanent with respect to the body — these being included in habitual bad tendencies, which are neither happiness nor suffering — delusion increases.

Now, through greed, suffering such as rebirth in the five destinies is generated in later lives; through hatred, sorrow etc. in this life and the sufferings of the realms of woe in later lives are generated; while through delusion, one proceeds without giving up the sufferings generated by both these.

Therefore, when happy feeling is beheld as suffering, attachment is stopped; when in regard to suffering feeling one thinks that since these *skandhas* are a collection of causes of suffering, pain etc. arise from them, then hatred is stopped; when indifferent feeling is beheld as impermanent, exhaustible and ceasing by nature, delusion is stopped. [So] the three feelings are not admitted as causes of the three poisons.

This is explained according to the thought of [Asaṅga's] *Yogācāra-bhūmi* and *Nirṇaya-saṃgraha*.[115]

Just as the bearer of a heavy burden cannot be happy as long as he has to carry it, so one suffers as long as one has to hold the burden of the appropriated aggregates (*upādāna-skandha*). Since in these aggregates the habitual tendencies of defilements are perpetually present, the suffering of conditioning exists in them. There may be occasions when there is no present suffering feeling, but straightaway many sufferings are generated in various ways, so suffering of conditioning pervades all suffering and is the root of the other two sufferings. Therefore meditate a lot on disgust for it!

Besides, present happy feeling, which increases attachment, is the production of a happy mind when ordinary suffering is relieved; but there is no happiness by nature, independent of the removal of suffering. For example, if one is suffering from excessive walking, a happy mind arises through resting. When this gradually stops the great suffering, it appears that happiness is gradually produced, but it is not happiness by nature, because if one rests too long, suffering will again be generated as before. If they were by nature causes of happiness, then just as suffering increases as long as one sticks to a cause of suffering, so happiness would have to increase as long as one stuck to walking, sitting, or lying down, eating or drinking, and sun or shade; but it is apparent that if one does it too long they generate only suffering.

Thus it is taught in the *Garbhâvakrânti*[-*sūtra*]:

> Nanda, each of the postures, walking, sitting, standing and lying down, is to be understood as suffering. If a meditator has understood the nature of these postures, if he spends a day walking, without standing, sitting, or lying down, then he will experience only suffering in that walking. He will experience severity, harshness, unbearableness and unpleasantness, but no recognition of happiness will arise with regard to that walking.

And similarly for the other three postures. Then,

> However, Nanda, because the sufferings of these postures are interrupted, when they change to other, fresh sufferings, the recognition of happiness arises. Nanda, although it arises, only this suffering arises; although it stops, only suffering stops. Although it arises, only *saṃskāras* arise; although it stops, only *saṃskāras* stop.

In the *Catuḥ-śataka* also, it is taught:[116]

Out of increasing happiness,
One observes the opposite;
But from increasing suffering,
There is no opposite in that way.

Appendix 4
Je Tsongkhapa's dedication prayer, at the end of Lam rim chen mo
Der ni ring du

1   By the two accumulations, vast as space,
    Which I have amassed through lengthy effort at this,
    May I become a King of Conqu'rors, a Guide
    For all migrators whose wisdom-eye's blinded by ignorance!

2   In all my lives while I have not attained that, too,
    May Mañjughoṣa lovingly receive me,
    So that I find the best Path, complete in all Stages
    Of the Teaching, and please the Conqu'rors by practice!

3   Through Skill in Means, impelled by strong Compassion –
    The main point of the Path, as I've understood it –
    May I dispel migrators' mental darkness
    And uphold the Conquerors' Doctrine for a long time!

4   In regions where the supreme, precious Doctrine
Has not spread, or although it has spread has declined,
With mind strongly moved by Great Compassion, may I
Make clear that treasure of benefit and bliss!

5   May the Stages of the Path to *Bodhi*, achieved
Through the marv'lous divine acts of Conquerors and Their Sons,
Grant glory to th' minds of those who desire Liberation,
And long preserve the deeds of the Conquerors!

6   May all the people and spirits who set up conditions
That favour the excellent Path's practice, and clear away bad ones,
Never, in all their lifetimes, be parted from
The pure Path, which the Conquerors have praised!

7   When someone makes effort, in the Supreme Vehicle,
To practise properly, with the ten Dharma-conducts,
May the powerful Protectors always assist him!
May oceans of good fortune fill all the directions!

Sarva Maṅgalam!

Appendix 5
Structure of the Text

While the organization of the first part of the text, *The Preparatory Practices*, is straightforward, that of the rest is less so. The charts below present a synoptic view of its structure, with a few additional headings after *Lam rim chen mo* to bring out the relationships between the different Meditations. The scheme is still vastly simpler than that of *Lam rim chen mo*, which boasts around a thousand headings.

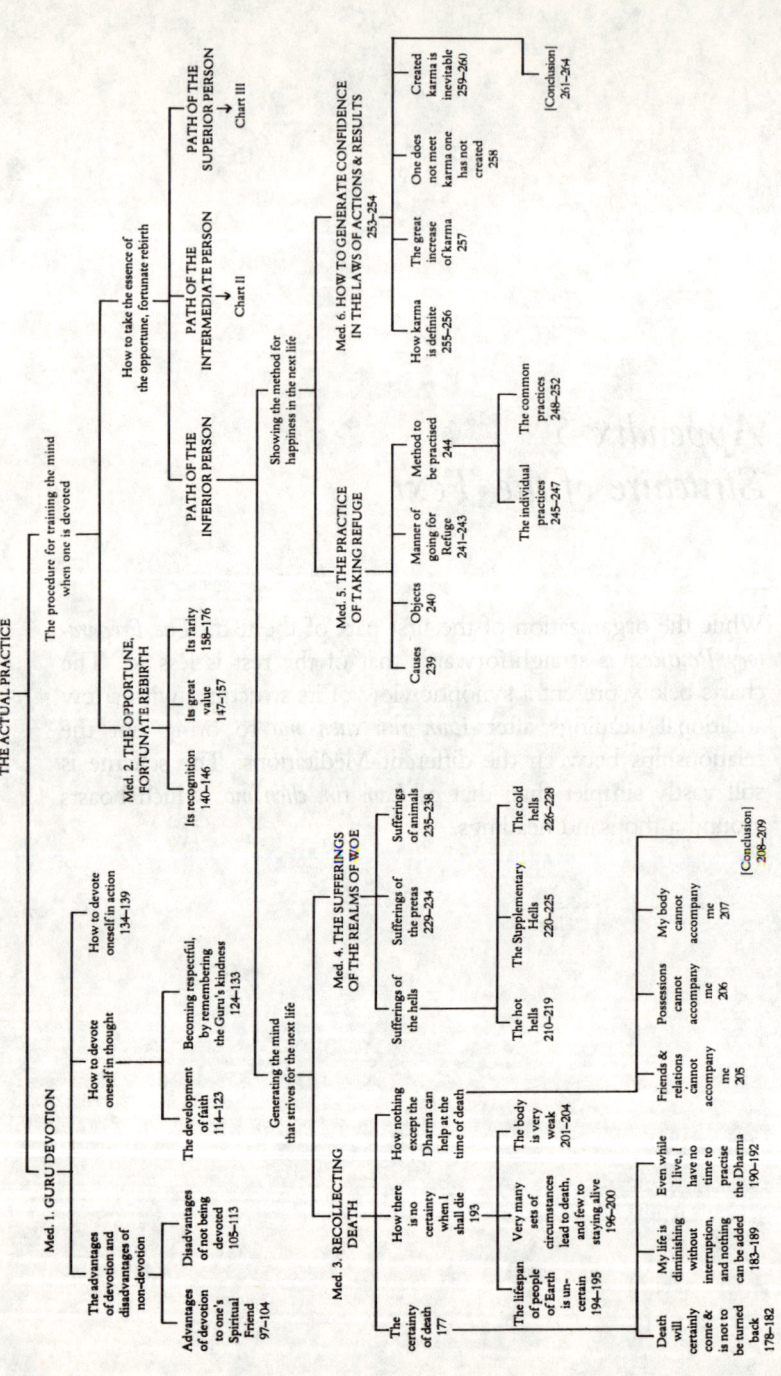

Chart I: The structure of Meditations 1 to 6 (text verses 97 to 264)

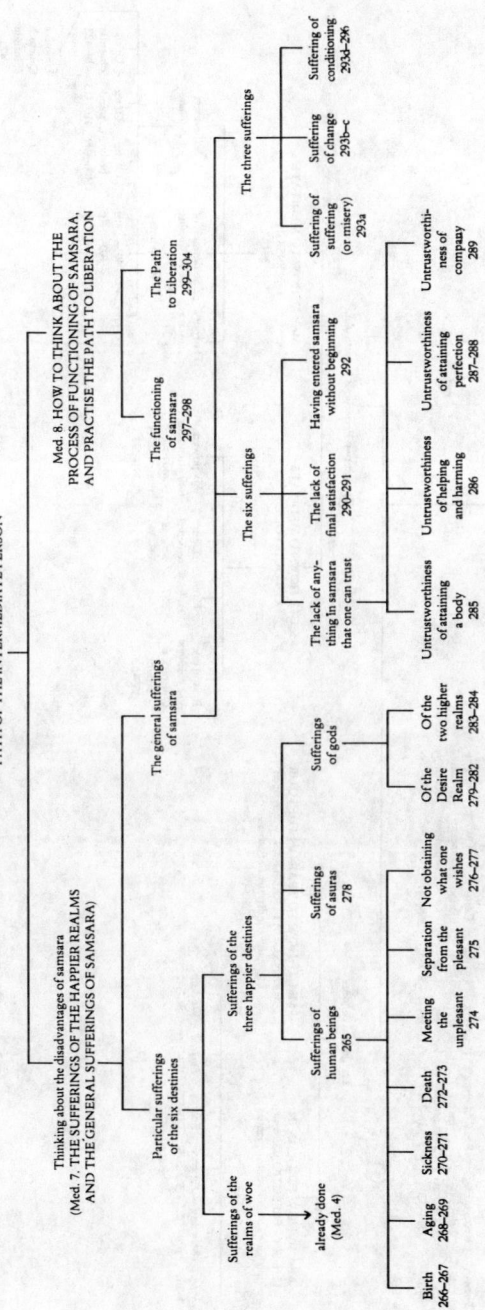

Chart II: The structure of Meditations 7 and 8 (text verses 265 to 304)

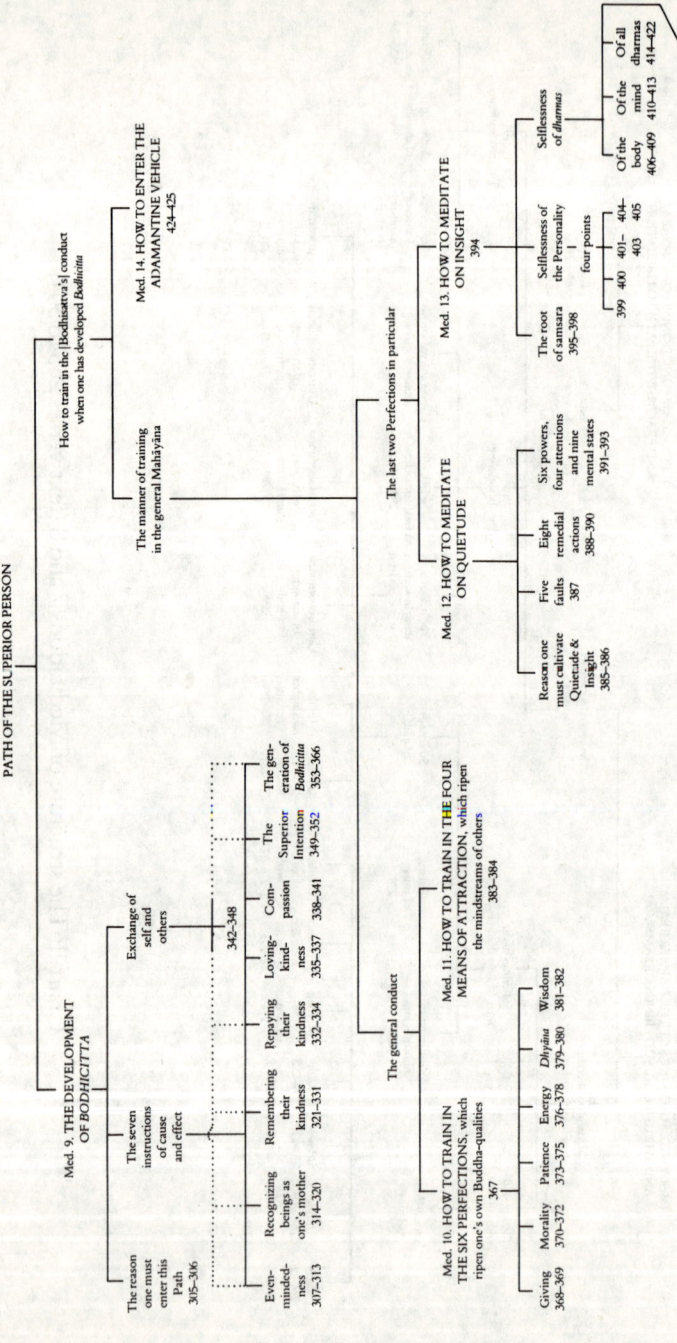

Chart III: The structure of Meditations 9 to 14 (text verses 305 to 425)

Glossary

(S: Sanskrit. T: Tibetan. When both Sanskrit and Tibetan equivalents of a word are given, the Tibetan is first.)

Age of Conflict, Age of Strife (*rtsod dus, kāli-yuga*): the present world-age

Age of Perfection (*rdzogs ldan dus, kṛta-yuga*): time when sentient beings have copious merits, Golden Age

agitation and fading: see "fading and agitation"

All-Good (*kun bzang, Samantabhadra*): name of a Bodhisattva renowned for the extensive offerings he made

amṛita (S) (*bdud rtsi*): nectar, ambrosia – (a) the delicious drink of the samsaric gods; also (b) a transcendental substance emanated by Enlightened deities, which confers such benefits as purification, realizations, long life, etc., according to the type

Arhant (S) (*dgra bcom pa*): one who has realized Nirvāṇa, the goal of any of the Three Vehicles. The three types according to Vehicle are, respectively, Hearer Arhants, *Pratyekabuddha* Arhants, and Buddhas.

Ārya (S) (*'phags pa*): a Noble Being, or Saint – one who has realized the Path of direct Insight into Ultimate Reality, and is thereafter forever superior to "ordinary beings" who have not gained this realization

asura (S) (*lha ma yin*): a demigod or titan, a class of samsaric being who lives within sight of the realm of the gods of Desire awareness (*shes* [*bzhin*], *samprajanya*)

bardo (T) (S: *antara-bhava*): the intermediate state between death and the next rebirth

benefit (*don, artha*): there are two benefits, of oneself and of others

Bodhi (S) (*byang chub*): Enlightenment, Awakening to Buddhahood

Bodhicitta (S) (*byang chub kyi sems*): the "thought of Enlightenment", or determination to attain Enlightenment for the benefit of sentient beings

Bodhicitta vows (*byang sdom, bodhisattva-saṃvara*): 18 root vows and 46 branch vows, which are taken in order to develop *Bodhicitta*

Bodhisattva (S) (*byang* [*chub*] *sems* [*dpa'*]): a being who has realized the generation of *Bodhicitta* and whose sole aim is thus to benefit others

Bodies: see "*Kāya*"

bucket-wheel (*zo chun, araghaṭṭa*): a device for raising water from a well for irrigation, consisting of buckets fixed to an endless rope passing over a wheel, so as to fill themselves at the bottom and empty themselves at the top

Buddha (S) (*sangs rgyas*): Enlightened or Awakened One – a Being Who has completely abandoned all obscurations and perfected every good quality

Buddha-son (*rgyal ba'i sras, jina-putra*): Bodhisattva

childish (*byis rnams, bāla*): ordinary beings, everyone who is not an *Ārya*

concentration (*ting 'dzin, samādhi*)

Conqueror (*rgyal ba, jina*): a title of Buddhas. Their Sons (*rgyal sras*) are the Bodhisattvas

commitments (*dam tshig, samaya*): pledges taken at Tantric initiations

conviction (*mos pa, adhimokṣa*): the mental factor that, once one has recognized the valuable qualities of such an object as the Three Jewels, makes this recognition firm and will not let it be lost

Ḍākinī (S) (*mkha' 'gro*): literally "Sky-goer"

deeds (*las, karman*)

Deep Path (*zab lam*): i.e. Tantra

defilements (*nyon mongs*, *kleśa*): see *kleśa*

Definite Goodness (*nges* [*par*] *legs* [*pa*], *niḥśreyasa*): Liberation, the Ultimate Goal

degenerate times (*snyigs dus*): a time of the five degenerations

delusion (*gti mug*, *moha*): one of the Three Poisons (cf. "greed & hatred")

desire (*'dun pa*, *chanda*): can be either negative, as in verse 282 (*'dod* [*pa la*] *'dun* [*pa*], *kāmacchanda*, "sensual desire"), or positive, as in verse 388 (d. to strive in *samādhi*)

Devadatta (*lhas byin*): literally "Theodore" – Shākyamuni Buddha's evil cousin, who saw Him as full of faults and repeatedly tried to harm Him.

Dharma (S) (*chos*): the (Buddhist) Doctrine; what is right; Truth

dharma (S) (*chos*): an element or ultimate constituent of existence, held by the lower schools of Buddhist philosophy to be truly real; here refers to any constituent of a person, or any phenomenon.

Dhyāna (S) (*bsam gtan*): an advanced form of concentration meditation, which one can practise after passing through the nine Mental States and realizing *Śamatha*, Quietude. Four Form *Dhyānas* and four Formless are distinguished.

dullness (*rmugs*, *styāna*): heaviness and unserviceability of body and mind

eight lucky symbols (*rtags rdzas brgyad*): umbrella, fish, pot of treasure, lotus, conch, knot, banner of victory, wheel

eight properties, with the (*yan lag brgyad ldan*): cool, sweet-tasting, light, soft, clear, clean (not smelly), not harmful to the stomach, and soothing to the throat

eleven ways of helping sentient beings (*sems can don byed rnam pa bcu gcig*): helping those who have suffering, are ignorant of karma, have previously helped you, are in danger, are full of grief, are poor, are homeless, are already on the true Path, or are on a wrong path; helping skilfully, and helping by using any supernormal powers you possess

Emanation (Guru) (*sprul ... bshes*): a Guru who is an Emanation Body of a Buddha

Enjoyment (Guru) (*longs ... bshes*): a Guru who is an Enjoyment Body of a Buddha (see *Kāya*)

eon (*bskal pa, kalpa*): a world-age, an extremely long period of time. The present eon is "fortunate" because a thousand Buddhas appear in it, of whom Shākyamuni was the fourth.

equanimity, unconcern (*btang snyoms, upekṣā*)

exist inherently (*rang gi ngo bos grub pa*), exist from its own side (*rang ngos nas grub pa*), and exist truly (*bden grub nyid du yod pa*) are all synonyms.

extreme views (*rtag chad lta, uccheda-śāśvata-dṛṣṭī*): the views of eternalism and annihilation

fading and agitation (*bying rgod, layauddhatya*): agitation scatters the mind away from the object of meditation through the poison of greed. When this occurs, one should remember impermanence and death, and settle the mind on the object again. Fading is a leaking away of the vividness with which the object of meditation is seen by the mind. Its remedy is to contemplate light, or the qualities of the Buddha.

five degenerations (*snyigs ma lnga, kaṣāya*): degeneration of lifetime, degenerate era, degeneration of beings, degeneration of views, degeneration of defilements

five immediate [sins] (*mtshams med lnga, ānantarya-karma*): killing one's father, one's mother, or an Arhant; drawing blood from a Tathāgata with malicious intent; causing a schism in the Sangha. So-called because on dying, one who has committed any of them is immediately reborn in hell.

five sciences ([*rig pa'i*] *gnas lnga, vidyā-sthāna*): grammar, logic, medicine, arts and crafts, religious philosophy

four continents (*gling bzhi, dvīpa*): according to Buddhist cosmography, a world has four continents inhabitable by humans, surrounding Mount Meru. We live in the southern continent, Jambudvīpa, which is the most favourable for Dharma practice.

four empowerments (*dbang bzhi, abhiṣeka*): in Highest Yoga Tantra, the initiations or empowerments have four parts – the Vase, Secret, Wisdom and Word initiations.

four doors of production of downfalls (*ltung ba 'byung ba'i sgo bzhi*): not knowing right from wrong, recklessness, having strong defilements in one's mind, and lack of respect for the instructions.

four forces (*stobs bzhi*): force of regret, force of the Object (of

Refuge), force of deciding not to repeat the action, force of remedy (repeating Vajrasattva mantras, prostrating, etc.)

Four *Kāyas* (*sku bzhi*): see *Kāya*

four Means of Attraction (*bsdu ba'i dngos po bzhi, saṃgraha-vastu*): Giving, Pleasant Speech, Helping, and Consistency

Freedom (*thar pa, mokṣa*): = Liberation

Friend (*bshes gnyen, mitra*): can imply a Spiritual Friend or Guru

Ganden Kagyü (T): another name for the Gelukpa lineage, founded by Je Tsongkhapa

garuda (*'dab bzang gtso bo*): a large mythical bird

Geshe (T) (*dGe bshes = dGe ba'i bshes gnyen, kalyāna-mitra*): (a) title of certain masters of the Kadam tradition (= "Spiritual Friend"); (b) degree analogous to Doctor of Theology, awarded by the principal monastic colleges of the Gelukpa.

go forth from our homes (*khyim las rab byung*): take up the "homeless" religious life, become ordained as a monk or nun

god (*lha, deva*): samsaric being dwelling for the moment in a heavenly state

good collections (*legs tshogs*): the two accumulations, of merits and Wisdom

Great Secret (*gsang chen*): Tantra

greed and hatred (*chags sdang*): two of the Three Poisons, from which all unwholesome attitudes and actions derive (cf. "delusion")

Guide (*zhing gi 'dren pa*): a Universal Buddha

Guru (S) (T: *bla ma*) (also *bshes gnyen, mitra*): Spiritual Teacher

Guru, King of Sages, Vajradhara (*bla ma thub dbang rdo rje 'chang*): the central figure of the visualization – one's Root Guru, identical with Shākyamuni Buddha, with Vajradhara at his heart

habitual bad tendencies (*gnas ngan len, dauṣṭhulya*)

happy rebirth (*bde 'gro'i rten*): rebirth as a human, asura or god

Hearer (*nyan* [*thos*], *śrāvaka*): a follower of the lowest of the Three Vehicles, especially one who has attained Arhantship through it

heat and moisture, birth from (*drod gsher skyes, saṃsveda-ja*): Buddhist tradition teaches that many small insects etc. are born spontaneously from the effects of heat and moisture. This is one of four ways of birth (verse 317).

heroes (*dpa' bo, śūra*)

high estate (*mngon mtho, abhyudaya*), high rebirth (*mtho ris*): as happy rebirth

Highest Yoga Tantra (*rgyud mal 'byor bla med, Anuttara-yoga-tantra*): the highest of the four classes of Tantra

Hīnayāna (S) (*theg (pa) dman (pa)*): the "Lesser Vehicle" – the Buddhist practices of those who have taken Refuge in the Three Jewels but are not and do not aspire to be Bodhisattvas

hindering demons (*bdud, māra*): see "*māra*"

ill destiny (*ngan 'gro, ngan song; dur-gati*): = realm of woe

Jambudvīpa (S) (*dzam bu gling*): the "Southern Continent", i.e. our own human world

Kadam (T) (*bka' gdam*)

karma (S) (*las*): deed, willed action of body, speech or mind, and the impression or seed this leaves on one's personal continuum, which must eventually ripen and produce a result.

karmic fruition, karmic result (*rnam smin, vipāka*): that result of an action which consists of a particular state of rebirth

karmic fruition with eight virtues (*rnam smin yon tan brgyad ldan*): human rebirth endowed with perfect length of life, complexion, caste or social standing, and wealth, and with credibility of speech, being very influential, being male, and strength (of body and mind). However, in the West, the seventh item of the traditional list is replaced by health and ability.

Kāya (S) (*sku*): "Body" or aspect of a Buddha. The Four *Kāyas* are the Emanation Body (*Nirmāṇa-kāya*), Enjoyment Body (*Saṃbhoga-kāya*), Wisdom Truth Body (*jñāna-dharma-kāya*) and Nature Body (*svabhāvika-kāya*). The Three *Kāyas* are the same with the last two counted as one *Dharma-kāya*.

King of Sages (*thub pa'i dbang po, Munīndra*): an epithet of the Buddha

kleśa (S) (*nyon mongs*): defilement – delusion, greed and hatred and all the unwholesome attitudes derived from them

knowable thing (*shes bya, jñeya*)

kumuda (S) (*ku mud*): a type of white lotus or water lily said to open only in moonlight

Lam rim (T): the Stages of the Path to Enlightenment
lama (T) (*bla ma*): the Tibetan word for *Guru*
leisureless states (*mi khoms gnas*): the eight states of rebirth offering no opportunity to practise Dharma
Liberation (*thar pa, mokṣa*): Release from the bondage of samsara
lung (T) (*rlung*): see note 9 to Introduction
Mahāyāna (S) (*theg (pa) chen (po)*): the "Great Vehicle" – the practices of a Bodhisattva. A Mahāyāna text or school is one in which these practices are taught. Includes both the Vehicle of the Perfections (*Pāramitā-yāna*) and the Vajrayāna, but when contrasted with the latter it refers to the former.
maṇḍala (S) (*maṇḍal*): "circle", in particular the entire world visualized as an offering. When the array of a deity and his or her attendants, or the diagram representing them, is meant, *maṇḍala* is normally translated into Tibetan as *dkyil 'khor*.
Mañjunātha (S) (*'Jam mgon*): Mañjuśrī incarnated in human form, e.g. Je Tsongkhapa
māra (S) (*bdud*): evil one, personified obstruction, "demon"
Marks and Signs (*mtshan dpe, lakṣaṇānuvyañjana*): the 32 major Marks and 80 minor Signs of a Buddha – shining golden skin, blue-black hairs which curl to the right in rings, webbed hands and feet, forty teeth, etc.
Master, The (*ston pa, śāstṛ*): Buddha Shākyamuni
merit (*bsod nams, puṇya*)
Meru, Mount (S) (T: *ri rab, lhun po*): giant mountain at the centre of the world, considerably bigger than this Earth and forming the home of the two lowest classes of gods of the Desire Realm
migrator, migrating being (*'gro ba, jagat*): sentient being, wandering from one samsaric existence to another continually
mindfulness (*dran pa, smṛti*)
mindstream (*rgyud, saṃtāna*): personal continuum
mode of existence (*gnas lugs*): True Nature, i.e. Emptiness
Morality (*tshul khrims, śīla*)
nectar (*bdud rtsi, amṛta*): see *amṛita*
negative (*mi dge, a-kuśala*): unwholesome, non-virtuous
non-virtue (*sdig pa, pāpa*): actions that result in suffering

Nirvāṇa (S) (*mya ngan las 'das pa*)

obscurations (*sgrib pa, āvaraṇa*): two classes of obscurations are generally distinguished, obscurations of *kleśa*, which obstruct one's attainment of Liberation, and obscurations to knowables, which must be removed to gain Omniscience or Buddhahood.

Omniscience (*kun mkhyen, sarvajña[tā]*): Buddhahood

opportune, fortunate basis (*rten dal 'byor*): the perfect human rebirth, complete with eight factors of opportunity (freedom from the eight leisureless states) and ten of good fortune (verses 140–146)

perverse views (*log [pa'i] lta, mithyā-dṛṣṭi*): e.g. disbelief in rebirth and the laws of actions and results

piśāca (S) (*sha za*): class of demons who eat flesh, including human flesh

positive (*dge ba, kuśala*): wholesome, virtuous

post-meditation (*rjes thob, pṛṣṭhalabdha*): the period when a yogin has come out of one-pointed concentration on Emptiness

powerful actions (*spyod pa rlabs po che*): actions of a Bodhisattva

Prātimokṣa (S) (*so sor thar pa*): "the Obligations", the code of precepts for Buddhist monks in the Discipline section of the scriptures

Pratyeka (*rang*): short for *Pratyeka-buddha* (S) (*rang sangs rgyas*), "solitary Realizer" – the higher of the two types of Arhant of the Lesser Vehicle, who attains Nirvana without needing teachings in that lifetime, but lacks the complete realization of a Buddha so cannot benefit limitless beings as a Buddha can.

preta (S) (*yi dvags*): literally "departed" (T: *rab song*), i.e. (the spirit of) a dead person: "hungry ghosts", normally invisible to human beings, one of the six classes of samsaric beings.

Profound Meaning (*zab don, gambhīrārtha*): Emptiness

pūjā (S) (*mchod pa*): offering, worship, veneration

Quick Path (*myur ba'i lam*): the Tantric Path

quick wits (*spobs pa, pratibhāna*)

Quietude (*zhi gnas, śamatha*)

realms of woe (*ngan 'gro, ngan song; dur-gati*): the hells and the realms of pretas and animals

Release (*thar pa*): = Liberation

Renunciation (*nges 'byung, niḥsaraṇa*): the realization of detachment from all of samsara, having understood its faults (verses 265–296)

result like the cause (*rgyu mthun 'bras bu, niṣyanda-phala*): the result of an action that consists of a tendency to experience and create similar actions, e.g. if one has killed, one tends to kill again and to be killed.

Root Guru (*rtsa ba'i bla ma*): the principal Guru from whom one has received teachings in this life

sādhana (S) (*sgrub thabs*): rite of evocation of a deity

samādhi (S) (*ting nge 'dzin*): concentration of the mind on a single object

saṃsāra (S) (*'khor ba, srid pa*): the state of continually having to take rebirth under the control of karma and defilements

Saṅgha (S) (*dge 'dun*): Absolute Sangha, the Object of Refuge, is the Community of Ārya Beings, or Saints. Relative Sangha is the community of ordained monks and nuns.

selflessness (*bdag med pa, nairātmya*): the lack of true, independent, self-existence

self-grasping (*bdag 'dzin, ātma-grāha*): apprehension of the existence of an inherent self of a person or *dharma*

sentient being (*sems can, sattva*; also *'gro ba*): any being who has not yet attained Buddhahood

seven precious things (*rin chen rnam pa bdun, sapta-ratna*): the possessions of a Universal Monarch – the precious Wheel, Elephant, Horse, Jewel, Queen, Minister and General. They symbolize the seven Enlightenment Factors – Mindfulness, Wisdom, Energy, Joy, Tranquillity, Concentration, and Equanimity.

siddhi (S) (*dngos grub*): powerful attainment

sins (*sdig pa, pāpa*): non-virtues, actions that result in suffering

six classes of beings (*rigs drug*): humans, gods, asuras, pretas, animals, and hell beings

Six Perfections (*phyin drug, pāramitā*): Giving, Morality, Patience, Energy, *Dhyāna*, and Wisdom

skandha (S) (*phung po*): heap, aggregate, group. The body-mind organism is made up of innumerable elementary constituents called "*dharmas*", which are grouped into the five *skandhas* of Form, Feeling, Recognition, Volition and Consciousness.

Skill (*thabs mkhas, upāya-kauśalya*): Skill in Means (of benefiting beings)

Sons [of the Conquerors] (*rgyal sras, jina-putra*): Bodhisattvas

Spiritual Friend ([*dge ba'i*] *bshes gnyen,* [*kalyāṇa*]-*mitra*): Guru

Stages and Paths (*sa lam*): the ten Bodhisattva Stages and the five Mahāyāna Paths

stūpa (S) (*mchod rten*): Indian Buddhist *stūpas* were dome-shaped monuments containing relics of the Buddha or His disciples. Their Tibetan successors are usually purely symbolic; of any size and material, they are of carefully-defined shape and proportions and represent the Buddha's Mind.

suffering of being conditioned (*'du byed kyi sdug bsngal, saṃskāra-duḥkhatā*): the suffering that pervades every moment of samsaric existence, and of which we are usually unaware, from the fact of being under the control of karma and defilements.

Sūtra (S) (*mdo*): the Discourses of the Buddha, the scriptural texts and the Teachings they contain

tamable being (*gdul bya, vineya*): sentient being, any being who has not yet attained Buddhahood. Pure tamable beings (verse 111) would be *Ārya* Bodhisattvas of the 8th to 10th Stages, to whom the Enjoyment Bodies of Buddhas appear.

Tantra (S) (*rgyud*): practices involving identification of oneself with a fully Enlightened deity, esoteric practices not taught in the Sūtras. The four classes are Action Tantra, Performance Tantra, Yoga Tantra and Highest Yoga Tantra (*kriyā-, caryā-, yoga-* and *anuttarayoga-tantras*).

Tathāgata (S) (*de bzhin gshegs pa*): a Buddha, Perfectly Realized One

three "baskets" (*sde snod gsum, tri-piṭaka*): the three collections of the Buddhist scriptures – *Vinaya* (Discipline), *Sūtra* (Discourses) & *Abhidharma*

three doors (*sgo gsum, tri-dvāra*): body, speech and mind

Three Jewels (*dkon mchog gsum, tri-ratna*): Buddha, Dharma, Sangha

Three *Kāyas* (*sku gsum, tri-kāya*): Three Bodies of a Buddha, see *Kāya*

three realms (*khams gsum, tri-dhātu*): Desire Realm, Form Realm, Formless Realm

three secrets (*gsang ba gsum*): secrets of the Buddha's Body, Speech and Mind

three sufferings (*sdug bsngal gsum*): suffering of misery, suffering of change, suffering of being conditioned

Three Supreme Ones (*mchog gsum*): = Three Jewels

Three Trainings (*bslab pa gsum, tri-śikṣā*): the Trainings relating to Morality, Concentration and Wisdom

three vows (*sdom gsum, tri-samvara*): *Prātimokṣa, Bodhicitta* and Tantric vows

Tīrthika (S) (*mu stegs pa*): one not following the Middle Way, i.e. a non-Buddhist, especially a Hindu

Tranquillity (*shin sbyangs, praśrabdhi*): the root meaning of this word is tranquillity or quietude, but it also implies suppleness or flexibility of mind and body – a feeling of extreme lightness and well-being, and ability to use the mind in any way desired.

True Nature (*gnas lugs*): Emptiness

Tushita (S) (*dga' ldan*): the Joyous Land, the Bodhisattva Pure Land of the thousand Buddhas of this eon

two accumulations (*tshogs gnyis, sambhāra*): of merits and Wisdom-knowledge

Two-Stage [yoga] (*rim gnyis, dvi-krama*): the Stage of Generation and Stage of Completion, of Highest Yoga Tantra

unconcern: = equanimity, when the sense is not necessarily positive

Unification (*zung 'jug, yuganaddha*): a level of the Completion Stage of Highest Yoga Tantra, shortly preceding Buddhahood

Unity of the two Supreme Bodies (*mchog sku gnyis zung 'jug*): Buddhahood, the Form Body (Emanation & Enjoyment Bodies) and the Truth Body (*Dharma-kāya*)

Universal Law (*chos kyi dbyings, dharma-dhātu*): a name for Ultimate Reality, the Emptiness of true existence of phenomena

utpala (S) (*ut pa la*): blue lotus

vajra (S) (*rdo rje*): a Tantric implement; as an adjective, "adamantine": applied to anything used in Tantric practice to differentiate it from everyday things

vajra position (*rdo rje'i skyil krung, vajra-paryaṅka*): cross-legged sitting posture, the mirror image of the "lotus position" of Hindu yoga.

Vajradhara (*rdo rje 'chang*): aspect of the Buddha which teaches Tantra

Vajrayāna (S) (*rdo rje theg pa*): the "Adamantine Vehicle", i.e. Tantra

Vast and Profound (*zab rgyas*): the two aspects of the Practice–Method or Compassion, and Wisdom

veils (*sgrib*): = obscurations

wanderers (*'gro ba*): = migrators

watchfulness (*bag yod, apramāda*)

Wisdom (*shes rab, prajñā*)

Wisdom-knowledge (*ye shes, jñāna*)

Yidam deities (*yi dam lha, iṣṭa-devatā*): Enlightened deity on whom one's Tantric practice is centred

Yama (S) (*gshin rje*): name of the Lord of Death

yoga (S) (*rnal 'byor*): endeavour, application, practice

yogin (S) (*rnal 'byor pa*): one who engages in yoga

Bibliography

Abbreviations

AdK	*Abhidharma-kośa*, tr. La Vallée Poussin
BCA	*Bodhisattva-caryāvatāra*, verse numbers based on the Tib. as in Batchelor's tr.
Eng.	English translation, see Part 3 below, under translator's name if given, otherwise under author's name
Fr.	French translation, see Part 3 below
ISMEO	Istituto per il Medio ed Estremo Oriente, Rome
Lrcm	*Lam rim chen mo*, Dharamsala edition.
LSPEB	"Linh-Son" – Publication d'Études Bouddhologiques
LTWA	Library of Tibetan Works and Archives, Dharamsala, H.P., India
Mppś	*Mahā-prajñā-pāramitā-śāstra*, tr. Lamotte
Skt	Sanskrit
Tib.	Tibetan
tr.	translation, translated by

1 INDIAN TEXTS (BY TITLE)

Abhidharma-kośa (The Treasury of *Abhidharma*), by Vasubandhu.
  Fr.: La Vallée Poussin (includes author's own commentary).
  Tib. *mDzod*. (Bound with *mNgon rtogs rgyan* & *dbU ma 'jug pa*, Sarnath, Pleasure of Elegant Sayings Printing Press, 1975. Root text only.)

Abhisamayâlaṃkāra (The Ornament of Realization), by Maitreya.
  Eng.: Conze.

Bodhi-patha-pradīpa (Lamp on the Path to Enlightenment), by Atīśa.
  Eng.: (a) Chattopadhyaya; (b) Wayman; (c) Beresford; (d) Sherburne.

Bodhisattva-caryâvatāra (Entering the Bodhisattva's Conduct), by Śāntideva.
  Tib. *Byang chub sems dpa'i spyod pa la 'jug pa zhes bya ba*, Dharamsala, Tib. Cultural Printing Press, 1977.
  Eng. (from Skt.): Matics, (from Tib.): Batchelor.
  Fr. (from Skt.): La Vallée Poussin.

Buddha-carita (The Acts of the Buddha), by Aśvaghoṣa.
  Eng. (condensed): in Conze, *Buddhist Scriptures*, pp.34-66.

Catuḥ-śataka (The Four Hundred), by Āryadeva.
  Tib. *bZhi brgya pa*. In *rTsa ba shes rab/ bzhi brgya pa/ sum bcu pa/ nyi shu pa bcas*, Sarnath,. Pleasure of Elegant Sayings Printing Press, 1974. Quotations were translated using the commentary of rGyal tshab rJe.

Jātaka-mālā (The Garland of Birth-Stories), by Ārya-śūra.
  Eng.: Speyer.

Madhyamakâvatāra (Introduction to the Middle Way), by Candrakīrti.
  Fr.: La Vallée Poussin (first three-quarters of text, with author's own commentary).
  Eng.: Willson (complete, with First Dalai Lama's commentary).

Madhyânta-vibhaṅga (Analysis of Middle and Extremes), by Maitreya.

Tib. *dbUs mtha' rnam 'byed* (no publication details in my photocopy).
Eng.: Stcherbatsky.

Mahāyāna-sūtrâlaṃkāra (The Ornament of the Mahāyāna Sūtras), by Maitreya.
Fr.: Lévi (with Asaṅga's commentary).

Ratna-gotra-vibhāga-Mahāyānôttara-tantra-śāstra, by Maitreya (according to modern scholars, by Sāramati). (Analysis of the Jewel Lineage, a Treatise on the chief essential point of the Great Vehicle).
Tib. *rGyud bla ma*, = *Theg pa chen po rgyud bla ma'i bstan bcos*. Type-set pe-cha, no date. (The main title of the Skt. text is given in the Tib. only in the chapter headings: *dKon mchog gi rigs rnam par dbye ba*).
Eng. (from Tib.): Obermiller, (from Skt.): Takasaki. Verse numbers refer to this version.

Śikṣā-samuccaya (Compendium on the Trainings), compiled by Śāntideva.
Eng.: Bendall & Rouse.

Śiṣya-lekha (Letter to a Disciple), by Candragomin.

Suhṛl-lekha (Friendly Letter), by Nāgārjuna.
Eng. (includes Tib. text)

Sūtra-samuccaya (Compendium of *Sūtra*), compiled by Nāgārjuna.
Eng.: Pāsādika.

Upāli-paripṛcchā-sūtra (The Questioning by Upāli Sūtra). Skt, Tib., Chinese, Fr.: Python.

Vimalakīrti-nirdeśa-sūtra (The Teaching of Vimalakīrti Sūtra).
Fr. (& Eng.): Lamotte.

Viṃśaka-kārikā (The Twenty Verses), by Vasubandhu.
Tib. *Nyi shu pa*. See *Catuḥ-śataka*.
Fr.: Lévi, *Matériaux*.

Visuddhi-magga (Pali) (The Path of Purification), by Buddhaghosa.
Eng.

Yogācāra-bhūmi-śāstra (The Yogācāra Treatise on the Stages), by Asaṅga.
See Conze, *Further Buddhist Studies*, pp.198–204.

2 TIBETAN TEXTS (BY AUTHOR)

rGyal tshab rJe: *bZhi brgya pa'i rnam bshad Legs bshad snying po zhes bya ba* (The Essence of Fine Words, An Explanation of 'The Four Hundred'). Sarnath, Pleasure of Elegant Sayings Printing Press, 1971.

sGam po pa (= Dvags po lha rje): *Dvags po'i thar rgyan*, = *Dam chos yid bzhin nor bu thar pa rin po che'i rgyan ces bya ba*. Recent blockprint, 183 leaves.
Eng.: Guenther, *The Jewel Ornament of Liberation*.

Pha bong kha pa Byams pa bstan 'dzin 'phrin las rgya mtsho: *Collected Works* (*sKyabs rje Pha bong kha pa bde chen snying po'i gsung 'bum*), Vol. 11, New Delhi, 1974.

Tsong kha pa: *dbU ma dgongs pa rab gsal = dbU ma la 'jug pa'i rgya cher bshad pa dgongs pa rab gsal* (The Clarification of the Thought, an Extensive Explanation of 'The Introduction to the Middle Way'). Sarnath, Pleasure of Elegant Sayings Printing Press, 1973.

Tsong kha pa: *Lam rim chen mo = Byang chub kyi lam rim che ba* (The Great Stages of the Path to Enlightenment). Dharamsala blockprint, lithographically reproduced, no date.

Yeshe Tsöndrü = Ye shes brtson 'grus: *Dam chos bdud rtsi'i snying po* (The Essence of the Nectar of the Holy Doctrine), = *Byang chub lam gyi rim pa'i gdams pa zab mo rnams tshigs su bcad pa'i sgo nas nyams su len tshul Dam chos bdud rtsi'i snying po zhes bya ba*. Blockprint, text 25.5 × 6 cm, 44 leaves. Buxa, Thar 'dod gling Dharma Centre, no date.

3 ENGLISH AND FRENCH (BY AUTHOR OR TRANSLATOR)

Bacot, Jacques (tr.): *La Vie de Marpa, le "Traducteur"*. Paris, Geuthner, 1967.

Bareau, André: *Les Sectes Bouddhiques du Petit Véhicule*. Paris, École Française d'Extrême-Orient, 1955 (Publ. E.F.E.O., *XXXVIII*).

Batchelor, Stephen (tr.): *A Guide to the Bodhisattva's Way of Life* (*Bodhisattva-caryāvatāra*), by Śāntideva. Dharamsala, LTWA, 1979.

Bendall, Cecil, and W.H.D. Rouse (tr.): *Śikṣā-samuccaya*.

A Compendium of Buddhist Doctrine, compiled by Śāntideva, chiefly from earlier Mahāyāna Sūtras. London, 1922. Repr. Delhi, Motilal Banarsidass, 1971.

Beresford, Brian C., & Glenn H. Mullin (tr.): *Mahayana Texts on the Graded Path*. Dharamsala, Dharmakaya Pubns., 1978 (pe-cha format).

Berzin, Alexander (tr., ann. & intr.): *Lam rim man ngag. A Standard Intermediate Level Textbook of the Graded Course to Enlightenment: Selected Materials from the Indo-Tibetan Mahāyāna Buddhist Textual and Oral Traditions*. Compiled and explained by dGe bshes Ngag dbang dar rgyas; transcribed & transmitted by Sherpa Tulku & Khamlung Tulku; tr., ann. & intr. by A. Berzin, assisted by Jonathan Landaw. First part: Ph.D. thesis, Univ. Harvard, 1972.

Brahman Net Sutra, The. Tr. from Skt. into Chinese by Kumārajīva, and thence into Eng. anonymously, probably at Gold Mountain Monastery (Typescript, no date). (No resemblance to the famous *Brahma-jāla-sutta* of the Dīgha-nikāya.)

Buddhaghosa, Bhadantācariya: *The Path of Purification (Visuddhimagga)*. Tr. from the Pali by Bhikkhu Ñāṇamoli. Sri Lanka, 1956, 1964; repr. in 2 volumes, Berkeley, Shambhala, 1976.

Burns, Douglas M.: *The Population Crisis in Buddhist Perspective*. Sri Lanka, Buddhist Publn. Soc., 1977 (Bodhi Leaves No. B76).

Chandra, Lokesh: *Tibetan-Sanskrit Dictionary*. New Delhi, Int. Acad. of Indian Culture, 1959–61, 12 vols. (repr. in 2 vols., Kyoto, Rinsen, 1971, and in 1 vol., ib., 1982).

Chattopadhyaya, Alaka: *Atīśa and Tibet*. Life and Works of Dīpaṃkara Śrījñāna in relation to the History and Religion of Tibet. With Tib. sources tr. under Prof. Lama Chimpa. Delhi, Motilal Banarsidass, 1981 (repr.).

Conze, Edward (tr.): *Abhisamayālaṅkāra*. Rome, ISMEO, 1954 (Serie Orientale Roma, *VI*).

Conze, Edward (selected & tr.): *Buddhist Scriptures*. Penguin Books, 1959.

Conze, Edward: *Further Buddhist Studies*. Oxford, Bruno Cassirer, 1975.

Conze, Edward (tr. & ed.): *The Large Sutra on Perfect Wisdom*, with the divisions of the Abhisamayālaṅkāra. Berkeley, Univ. Calif. Press, 1975 (repr. Delhi, Motilal Banarsidass, 1979).

Dagyab, L.S. (bLo ldan shes rab Brag g.yab): *Bod brda'i tshig mdzod* (Tibetan Dictionary). Dharamsala, 1977.

Dhargyey, Geshe Ngawang, & Tr. Bureau of the LTWA: *The Bodhicitta Vows and Lam-rim Puja*. Dharamsala, LTWA, 1974.

Edgerton, Franklin: *Buddhist Hybrid Sanskrit Grammar & Dictionary*. Vol. II: Dictionary, New Haven, Yale Univ. Press, 1953; repr. Delhi, Motilal Banarsidass, 1970.

From Tushita, Nr. 1. Ed. by Michael Hellbach. Dharamsala, no date (ca. 1976).

Goldstein, Melvyn C. (ed.): *Tibetan-English Dictionary of Modern Tibetan*. Kathmandu, Ratna Pustak Bhandar, 1978 (Bibliotheca Himalayica, Ser. II, Vol. 7).

Guenther, H.V. (tr. & ann.): *The Jewel Ornament of Liberation*, by sGam po pa. London, Rider, 1959, 1970; Berkeley, Shambhala, 1971.

Guenther, H.V. (tr. & intr.): *The Life and Teachings of Nāropa*. Oxford Univ. Press, 1963.

Hopkins, Jeffrey: *Meditation on Emptiness*. Ph.D. thesis, Univ. Wis., 1973, available from University Microfilms International. Revised ed.: Wisdom Publ., London, 1983.

Lamotte, Étienne (tr. & ann.): *L'Enseignement de Vimalakīrti (Vimalakīrti-nirdeśa)*. Louvain, Institut Orientaliste, 1962. (Bibl. du Muséon, Vol. 51). (This tr. is also available in an Eng. version: London, Pali Text Soc., 1976.)

Lamotte, Étienne (tr. & ann.): *Le Traité de la Grande Vertu de Sagesse, de Nāgārjuna (Mahāprajñāpāramitā-śāstra)*. 5 tomes. Louvain (-la-Neuve), Institut Orientaliste, 1944-80. (Tome II: Bibl. du Muséon, Vol. *18*, 1944; repr. as Publications de l'Inst. Orientaliste de Louvain, Vol. 26, 1981. Tome III: PIOL *2*, 1970.)

Lati Rinbochay & Jeffrey Hopkins: *Death, Intermediate State and Rebirth in Tibetan Buddhism*. London, Rider, 1979.

La Vallée Poussin, Louis de (tr. & ann.): *Introduction à la Pratique des Futurs Bouddhas (Bodhicaryāvatāra)*. Poème de Śāntideva. Paris, Librairie Bloud, 1907.

La Vallée Poussin, L. de (tr.): *Madhyamakāvatāra. Introduction* au Traité du Milieu, de l'Ācārya Candrakīrti, avec le Commentaire de l'Auteur, traduit d'après la version tibétaine. Le Muséon, 8, 249–317, 1907; 11, 271–358, 1910; 12, 235–328, 1911.

La Vallée Poussin, L. de (tr. & ann.): *L'Abhidharmakośa de Vasubandhu*. 6 tomes, Paris, 1923–31; repr. Brussels, Inst. Belge des Hautes Études Chinoises, 1971, 1980 (Mélanges Chinois et Bouddhiques, Vol. XVI).

Lévi, Sylvain (ed. & tr.): *Asaṅga: Mahāyāna-sūtrālaṃkāra*. Exposé de la Doctrine du Grand Véhicule selon le Système Yogācāra. Tome II: Traduction. Paris, Librairie Honoré Champion, 1911 (Bibl. de l'École des Hautes Études, fasc. 190).

Lévi, S. (tr.): *Matériaux pour l'étude du systeme Vijñaptimātra*. Paris, 1932.

Lhalungpa, Lobsang P.: The Life of Milarepa. (By gTsan smyon He ru ka). New York, E.P. Dutton, 1977; London, Granada Publg., 1979.

Loden, Geshe Thubten: *The Graduated Path to Enlightenment*. Ed. by Tony Duff. Australia, Tib. Buddhist Loden Mahāyāna Friendship Soc., 1980.

Matics, Marion L. (tr.): *Entering the Path of Enlightenment* (*Śāntideva's Bodhicaryāvatāra*). London, Macmillan, 1970.

Nāgārjuna's Letter to King Gautamīputra (*Suhṛllekha*). With Explanatory Notes based on Tibetan Commentaries. Tr. from Tib. by Lozang Jamspal, Ngawang Samten Chophel, & Peter Della Santina. Delhi, Motilal Banarsidass, 1978.

Obermiller, E. (tr.): *The Sublime Science of the Great Vehicle to Salvation*, being a Manual of Buddhist Monism. The Work of Ārya Maitreya with a Commentary by Āryāsaṅga. Tr. from the Tib. with intr. and notes. Acta Orientalia, 9, 81–296, 1931.

Pāsādika, Bhikkhu (tr.): *The Sūtra-samuccaya – Nāgārjuna's Anthology of* (*Quotations from*) *Discourses*. An Eng. tr. from the Tib. version of the Skt. original. In LSPEB, nos. 2 (1977) to 20 (1982).

Python, Pierre (ed. & tr.): *Vinaya-viniścaya-Upāli-paripṛcchā*. Enquête d'Upāli pour une Exégèse de la Discipline. Paris, Adrien-Maisonneuve, 1973 (Collection Jean Przyluski,

Tome V).

Rabten, Geshe: *The Graduated Path to Liberation*. Cambridge, Cambridge Univ. Buddhist Soc., 1972; repr. Kathmandu, Int. Mahayana Coll., 1974; New Delhi, Pubns for Wisdom Culture, 1980; New Delhi, Mahayana Pubns., 1983.

Rabten, Geshe: *The Preliminary Practices*. Oral teaching on a text of Padma Karpo, tr. by Gonsar Tulku & compiled by Georges Driessens. Dharamsala, LTWA, 1974.

Sherburne, Richard (tr.): *A Lamp for the Path and Commentary* of Atīśa. London, George Allen & Unwin, 1983 (Wisdom of Tibet Ser., *5*).

Speyer, J.S. (tr.): *The Jātakamālā, or Garland of Birth-Stories of Āryaśūra*. ca. 1895; repr. Delhi, Motilal Banarsidass, 1971.

Stcherbatsky, Th. (tr.): *Madhyānta-Vibhaṅga, Discourse on Discrimination between Middle and Extremes*, ascribed to Bodhisattva Maitreya and commented by Vasubandhu and Sthiramati. Tr. from the Skt. & Tib. Leningrad, 1936 (Bibliotheca Buddhica, No. *30*).

Takasaki, Jikido (tr.): *A Study on the Ratnagotravibhāga (Uttaratantra)*, Being a Treatise on the Tathāgatagarbha Theory of Mahāyāna Buddhism. Rome, ISMEO, 1966 (Serie Orientale Roma, *XXXIII*).

Tharchin, Geshe Lobsang, with Benjamin & Deborah Alterman (tr.): *The Essence of Nectar*, by Yeshe Tsöndru. Howell, N.J., Rashi Gempil Ling, 1977 (repr. Dharamsala, LTWA, 1979).

Tsong kha pa, rJe: *Lines of Experience:* The Main Aspects of the Practice of the Stages on the Graded Path to Enlightenment. Tr. from the *Lam rim bsdus don*, by Sherpa Tulku, Khamlung Tulku, Alexander Berzin & Jonathan Landaw in accordance with an oral explanation given by Geshe Ngawang Dhargyey. Dharamsala, LTWA, 1973.

Wambach, Helen: *Life before Life*. New York, Bantam Books, 1979.

Wayman, Alex (tr.): *Calming the Mind and Discerning the Real*. Buddhist Meditation and the Middle View. From the *Lam rim chen mo* of Tsoṅ-kha-pa. New York, Columbia Univ. Press, 1978.

Willson, Martin: *Rebirth and the Western Buddhist*. London, Wisdom Archive Publication, 1984.

Willson, Martin (tr.): *Ācārya Candrakīrti's 'Introduction to the Middle Way'* (*Madhyamakâvatāra*), rendered into English verse after the Tib. tr. of Patsab Nyima Drapa; with the commentary of the First Dalai Lama, Gyälwa Gedündrub, entitled "The Mirror of the Clarification of the Thought". To be published.

Zopa Rinpoche, Thubten: *The Wish-fulfilling Golden Sun of the Mahāyāna Thought Training*, Directing in the Short-cut Path to Enlightenment. Kathmandu, Int. Mahayana Inst.; Eudlo (Qld.), Chenrezig Inst., 1975.

Notes

Notes to Preface

1 See the chapter on Christianity in Head & Cranston's *Reincarnation: an east-west anthology* (pp. 32–42, plus Appendix pp. 321–325), presenting with quotations both the views of such fathers as Origen, Justin Martyr, St. Clement of Alexandria, St. Gregory of Nyssa, St. Jerome & St. Augustine, and the curious proceedings of 553 at Constantinople, which led the Church to believe it had condemned this teaching.

2 For a more extensive account, see my review article, *Rebirth and the Western Buddhist*.

Notes to Introduction

3 See *Lam rim chen mo*, 11a6–13b2 (Dharamsala edition).

4 An English translation of this text, with teachings by Geshe Rabten, may be found in Brian Beresford's *Mahayana Texts on the Graded Path* (Dharamsala, Dharmakaya Publications, 1978). Other translations: Alex Wayman, *Calming the Mind and Discerning the Real*, New York, Columbia Univ. Press, 1978: pp. 9–14.

Alaka Chattopadhyaya, *Atīśa and Tibet*, Delhi, Motilal Banarsidass, 1981. pp. 525–535.

5 Not to be confused with his namesake of many centuries earlier, the great logician.

6 *Dvags po'i thar rgyan*, or *Dam chos yid bzhin nor bu thar pa rin po che'i rgyan ces bya ba*. English translation by H.V. Guenther, *The Jewel Ornament of Liberation*.
7 *Kun bzang bla ma'i zhal lung*, or in full, *rDzogs pa chen po klong chen snying thig gi sngon 'gro'i khrid yig Kun bzang bla ma'i zhal lung*.
8 *Lam rim bsdus don*. English translation by the translation bureau of the Library of Tibetan Works and Archives, *Lines of Experience*, Dharamsala, 1973.
9 Tib. *rlung*, literally "air, wind". Here it means a state in which the vital winds (*vāyu, prāṇa*) of the subtle body are imbalanced. According to Tantric theory these winds are the vehicle of consciousness.
10 Tib. *srog rlung*, "life-wind" (*prāṇa*), or a disorder of the life-wind.
11 "Study" for a Tibetan is synonymous with listening to a teacher. In the body of this section we shall have to use the literal translation, "listening", but much the same considerations apply to other forms of study such as reading this book.
12 Quoted in *Lam rim chen mo*, 16a6.
13 *Jātaka-mālā* XXXI. Geshe Rabten's version, much shorter, has here been somewhat revised and amplified, using this source, for the sake of clarity.
14 Quoted in *Lam rim chen mo*, 19a4.
15 Quoted in *Lam rim chen mo*, 15b6.
16 *Adhyāśaya-saṃcodana-sūtra*, quoted *Lam rim chen mo* 19b3 and *Śikṣā-samuccaya* p. 310. "One becomes mindful, intelligent, sensible, steadfast and wise; one realizes transcendent wisdom; one's greed, hatred and delusion become small; Māra finds no opportunity to harm one, the Buddhas think of one, spirits protect one, the gods make one splendid, enemies find no opportunity to harm one, one's friends are constant, one's word is respected, one attains the [Four] Fearlessnesses [of a Buddha], one's mental happiness increases, one is praised by the learned, and one's gift of the Dharma will be worth remembering."

Notes to the Preparatory Practices

17 Tib. *sbyor ba'i chos*.
18 Quoted from *Lam rim chen mo*, 37a6–40a4.
19 *Bodhisattva-caryâvatāra*, VI. 123.
20 Ib., VI. 119. Geshe Rabten may not have quoted these two verses complete.
21 *dbang phyug brgyad*. They are his powers of Body, Speech, Mind, qualities, omnipresence, place, magic, and production of whatever is wanted.
22 See Glossary for examples; E. Conze, *The Large Sutra on Perfect Wisdom*, pp. 657–665, for complete list and explanation.
23 There are many explanations of this word, usually translated as "the Lord," "Blessed One". See, for example, the long discussion in *Visuddhimagga*, VII. 53–64.
24 The traditional order places Equanimity last, after Loving-kindness, Compassion, and Sympathetic Joy. See *Mpps*, pp. 1239–1273, especially 1255–59.
25 Their Tib. names: *'dun pa, smon pa, lhag bsam, gsol ba 'deb*. I have not yet found any mention of this sequence in Indian texts, although several discuss the four Immeasurables at considerable length, e.g. *Abhidharma-kośa* VIII. 29–31 (commentary pp. 196–203), *Mahāyāna-sūtrâlamkāra* XVII. 17–28.
26 Sometimes the visualization of the Objects of Refuge is absorbed and a new visualization of the Field of Merit, almost identical, generated.
27 As in these verses from a hymn to Tārā by the First Dalai Lama:

> Like an outstretched branch of a turquoise, heavenly tree,
> Your right hand tenderly gestures Granting of Boons,
> Inviting the wise to a feast of high realizations
> As if to an entertainment – homage to You!
>
> Your left hand gives Refuge, showing the Three Jewels:
> "You people who see a hundred kinds of fears!
> Do not be frightened, I shall quickly save you,"
> It clearly signifies – homage to You!

> Both hands signal with blue *utpala* flowers,
> "Samsaric beings! Cling not to worldly pleasures,
> Enter the city of the Great Liberation!"
> As if driving with diligent whip – to You I bow!

28 Marpa the Translator, d. 1098, founder of the Kagyü school.
29 cf. J. Bacot (tr.): *La Vie de Marpa, le "Traducteur"*. Paris, Geuthner, 1937. p. 39.
30 cf. H.V. Guenther (tr.): *The Life and Teachings of Nāropa*. Oxford Univ. Press, 1963, p. 107.
31 This rarely-used translation perhaps comes from a folk etymology deriving *maṇḍalaka* (= *maṇḍala*) from *maṇḍa* "essence" + *lak* "obtain". The actual meaning of *maṇḍala* is "circle; round".

Notes to Meditation 1

32 cf. *Vimalakīrti-nirdeśa-sūtra*, V. 20: "Venerable Kāśyapa, the Māras who act as Māra in the countless worlds of the ten directions are all Bodhisattvas established in the inconceivable Liberation, who by skilful means act as Māra in order to ripen sentient beings."
33 H.V. Guenther (tr.): *The Life and Teachings of Nāropa*. Oxford Univ. Press, 1963.
34 gTsan smyon He ru ka: *The Life of Milarepa*. A New Translation from the Tibetan by Lobsang P. Lhalungpa. New York, E.P. Dutton, 1977.

Notes to Meditation 2

35 Geshe Rabten did not mention explicitly all the eighteen factors, and their enumeration is not altogether evident from the root text. They are as follows:
(a) Eight opportune conditions (*dal ba, kṣaṇa*), avoiding the eight inopportune states (*mi khom pa, akṣaṇa*), which are: birth (i) in hell, (ii) as an animal, (iii) as a preta, (iv) among the long-lived gods, or (v) among people of border countries, robbers, barbarians, rapacious and violent, where there are no monks,

nuns or lay-followers . (vi) Being dull-witted, deaf and dumb; (vii) being abnormally opinionated and holding perverse views such as denial of the fruits of good and bad actions, of rebirth, or of Liberation; (viii) no *Tathāgata* having arisen in the world and preached the Dharma. (After the *Ekottarikāgama*, quoted in Nāgārjuna's *Sūtra-samuccaya*. See English translation by Bhikkhu Pāsādika, "Linhson" Publication d'Études Bouddhologiques, 2, 24, 1977.)

(b) Ten good fortunes (*'byor pa, sampad*):
Five involving oneself: (i) being human, (ii) being born in a central country, (iii) having one's faculties intact, (iv) not having created extreme negative karmas, and (v) having faith in the *Tri-piṭaka*, the three "baskets" of the Buddha's Teachings.

Five involving others: (i) a Buddha having arisen; (ii) he or his disciples having taught the Holy Dharma; (iii) the Teaching remaining; (iv) following the Teaching; and (v) the kindness of others, i.e. robes etc. being given by donors or benefactors.
(After *Lam rim chen mo*, 53a–b.)

36 Geshe Rabten: *The Preliminary Practices*. Dharamsala, 1974, p. 58.
37 See Glossary, "karmic fruition with eight virtues".
38 For some, of course, ease and speed are not the only considerations.
39 Eight worldly concerns (*'jig rten gyi chos, loka-dharma*): concern with gain and loss, pleasure and pain, fame and dishonour, praise and blame.
40 The example of the blind turtle in the ocean is from the *Saṃyuktāgama*, quoted in Nāgārjuna's *Sūtra-samuccaya* (English translation, Bhikkhu Pāsādika, loc. cit. note 35, p. 23.)

Notes to Meditation 3

41 See note 39.
42 *Buddhacarita* of Aśvaghoṣha, XXVI.
43 Quoted in *Lam rim chen mo* (henceforth abbreviated to

Lrcm), p. 67a3.
44 Lrcm, 67a4.
45 Each of the three points in this meditation is given three "reasons". Their names have been inserted after Lrcm, which the text follows closely. Comparing this version with Gampopa's *Jewel Ornament of Liberation*, one is surprised to find that Tsongkhapa omitted the second reason, surely the one of the whole nine most strongly emphasized by the Buddha: "Death is certain, because the body is conditioned" (25a1), and kept the symmetrical 3 × 3 structure by adding 3a.3, which stands out as not being a reason for the certainty of death at all.
46 Other lamas, however, teach that these practices can make available in this existence unused life from other existences that were cut short prematurely.
47 Geshe Rabten quoted a verse not unlike this one from the *Caturviparyaya-parihāra-kathā* (Lrcm 70b6):
When one is smashed by falling from
  the summit of a high mountain
To the ground, what pleasure does one
  experience in the air?
Since from birth on, they are always
  rushing towards death,
In what interval will sentient
  beings find pleasure at all?
48 Assassinated three days before this lecture was given.
49 For further discussion of meditation on death, see the very clear article by Geshe Ngawang Dhargyey, "Death and the Way", in *From Tushita*.

Notes to Meditation 4

50 *Bodhisattva-caryâvatāra* (*BCA*), V. 7.
51 *BCA*, V. 8.
52 Some early Buddhist schools – the Sammatīyas, Theravādins, and certain Mahāsaṅghikas – asserted that the hell guardians were sentient beings, while others – the Andhaka group of Mahāsaṅghika schools, the Sarvāstivādins, and the Sautrāntikas – asserted that they were not. (See La Vallée Poussin, *Abhidharma-kośa* (*AdK*), III,

p. 152 n. 3, and Bareau, *Sectes*, pp. 97 and 236.) Thus Vasubandhu teaches in *AdK* (III, p. 153) that the guardians of hell are not real sentient beings, and in his *Viṃśaka-kārikā*, 4, that the whole hell experience is illusory, like a dream.

53 *AdK*, III, p. 148, specifies the depth: Avīci extends from 20 000 to 40 000 leagues and the other seven hot hells are above it.

54 To arrive at the right total, one must count verse 215 as describing two hells, "Howling" and "Loud Howling".

55 Nāgārjuna's *Mahā-prajñā-pāramitā-śāstra* (*Mppś*), p. 958, says it is caused particularly by causing the death of innocent persons through any sort of unvirtuous speech, and by being a corrupt and cruel official. However, the *Udaya-navatsa-rāja-paripṛcchā-sūtra* (quoted in *Sūtra-samuccaya*, LSPEB 8, pp. 22–23) says all eight hot hells and some of the supplementaries are the result of "indefatigably making love to and getting tied up with women, of keeping one's mind on laughter, merry-making, amusements, on songs, dancing, music, etc." (trans. Pāsādika).

56 Nevertheless, according to Nāgārjuna's *Mppś* (p. 959), the animals who still bear a grudge against someone who killed them can come to this hell in their animal form to torment him.

57 See more detailed descriptions in *Śikṣā-samuccaya* (trans. Bendall and Rouse, pp. 77–78), where these tortures are said to be the result of lying and vain speech respectively.

58 The *Mppś* (p. 964) attributes this hell to defiling food to be offered to a field of merit by touching it with unclean hands or putting filth in it, eating before the person who is a field of merit, dumping warm excrement on another's body, and wrong livelihood.

59 Sixteen inches long, according to *AdK* (III, p. 151).

60 According to the *Mppś* (p. 965), she changes into a poisonous snake and attacks you.

61 See *Sad-dharma-smṛtyupasthāna-sūtra*, quoted in *Sūtra-samuccaya* (trans. Pāsādika, LSPEB, 8, p. 24).

62 While the root text describes this river as of molten bronze

(*khro chu*), according to *Suhṛllekha* 73 and *Lrcm* 79b5 it is boiling water, and according to *AdK* III, p. 151, boiling water and burning ash. However, it is well known that the same river appears differently to different beings, according to their karma.

63 The cold hells, according to the *Mppś* (p. 967), result from: robbing people of fuel etc. in winter; causing harm by hailstorms when one is a Nāga; criticizing a Buddha, his disciples, or persons observing morality; or committing grave sins by the four immoralities of speech.

64 In Sanskrit the third to fifth cold hells are called Aṭaṭa, Hahava and Huhuva, after the sounds the beings there make (*Mppś* p. 967, *AdK*, III, p. 154, and *Lrcm* 80a5). In Tibetan, Aṭaṭa is translated *so tham tham pa*, which after Dagyab's and Lokesh Chandra's dictionaries seems to mean "teeth-chattering, snapping of the teeth". But modern lamas interpret it as "teeth locked together", and as in the present text, place it fifth instead of third.

Notes to Meditation 5

65 The section on Refuge in *Lrcm* is extremely complicated, with over ninety headings. Here we give only the major ones, and even of these, the positioning of some is open to debate.

66 Also, just as the sun illuminates the world without deliberate thought, so the Buddha liberates beings without having to think about it. See *Ratna-gotra-vibhāga* (Tib. *rGyud bla ma*), IV, 58–66.

67 Pictures also, such as thangka paintings, must be hung with care. For example, it is disrespectful to put them where one's feet will point towards them when one is in bed.

68 *Lrcm* (96a2): "Avoiding disrespect to Dharma even down to four words – avoiding such disrespect as giving texts as security, treating them as merchandise, putting them on the bare ground or as something to rest on, carrying them next to shoes, or stepping over them – respect it as the Dharma Jewel."

69 *Lrcm*, 96b4.

70 *Lrcm*, 101a3.

Notes to Meditation 6

71 These practices are the four right efforts (*samyak-prahāṇa*), frequently mentioned in the sūtras. See for example *Mpps*, pp. 1123–4 and 1176–7.

Notes to Meditation 7

72 Memories of birth and death experiences recovered under hypnosis support this assertion. See Wambach, *Life Before Life*, Chapter III.
73 Such repression should not be confused with the irreversible amnesia for the few seconds preceding a traumatic head injury, which seems to be due to interruption of the process that normally converts short-term into long-term memory traces.
74 For an account of the process of absorption, see Lati Rinbochay & Hopkins: *Death, Intermediate State and Rebirth in Tibetan Buddhism*. It is misleading to consider the traditional four elements – here translated in terms of their functions – as a primitive version of our ninety-odd chemical elements. A closer analogy would be with the four forces recognized in Physics – strong, electromagnetic, weak and gravitational. Each of these four is generally considered to be "atomic", mediated by the appropriate type of quantum particle – mesons, photons, "weakons", and "gravitons"; and in any macroscopic piece of matter, all four are in general operating, although in particular situations one may be more evident than the others. Likewise the four elements are held to be atomic, and all present in any macroscopic piece of matter, although one may be more conspicuous in a particular case.
75 *The Life of Milarepa*, translated by Lobsang P. Lhalungpa, p. 126. It is not certain whether Geshe Rabten quoted this verse or another from the same song, which is all on the same theme.
76 In *Lrcm*, the general sufferings of samsara are taught in three ways: as the Eight Sufferings, the Six Sufferings,

and the Three Sufferings. The Eight are the seven taught in 7a.1 (a) to (g) as sufferings of human beings, plus "In short, the five appropriated aggregates are suffering." Geshe Rabten discussed the six in general terms and in no particular order, and did not teach on the three. In view of the importance of this topic, I give in Appendix 3 a translation of the sections of *Lrcm* which present the Six and the Three Sufferings. It will be noted that Yeshe Tsöndrü's verses on the Six Sufferings follow the order not of Tsongkhapa's main presentation (derived from the *Suhṛllekha* of Nāgārjuna), but of the alternative arrangement he gives at the end of his discussion:

(a) The lack of anything in samsara that one can trust:
    (i) Untrustworthiness of attaining a body [285].
    (ii) Untrustworthiness of helping and harming [286].
    (iii) Untrustworthiness of attaining perfection [287–8].
    (iv) Untrustworthiness of company [289].
(b) The lack of final satisfaction, however much one enjoys samsara's pleasures [290–1].
(c) Having entered samsara without beginning [292].

77 The Tibetan text of this verse is quoted by A. Berzin, *Lam rim man ngag*, p. 289 (for *'char*, read *'cha'*). According to Berzin, the story comes from Ashvaghoṣha's play, *Śāriputra-prakaraṇa*. His version, leaving out the man altogether, differs markedly from any I have heard from lamas, and is unconvincing. Some say the baby was in its father's lap, which is possible; the verse, devoid of personal pronouns in the Tibetan, allows several interpretations.

Notes to Meditation 8

78 As with the earlier example of Norbu and his carrot, when Geshe Rabten speaks of "thinking 'That is a snake!' ", he cannot mean a conscious thought in words. Here it must mean the bare fact of the triggering of the snake-avoidance reflex. One starts back first, and indulges in conceptual thought and emotional response afterwards,

when if it had been a real snake the outcome of the encounter would already have been settled.

Notes to Meditation 9

78a The Seven Instructions begin with recognizing beings as one's mother; evenmindedness is a necessary preliminary. They are cause and effect in that compassion is the root of the Mahāyāna Path, the first four instructions are the cause of compassion, and Superior Intention and *Bodhicitta* are its result (*Lrcm* 190a5–194a2); or in that the first six are the cause and *Bodhicitta* is the result.

79 Hell-beings, gods, and some other beings (e.g. the courtesan Āmrapālī and Padmasambhava) are born miraculously, and small animals such as insects, whose eggs are generally too small to see with the naked eye, are held to be born "from heat and moisture".

80 Students of the mathematics of infinity will notice that since the number of sentient beings is as infinite as that of one's past births from a womb or an egg, another dose of faith is required at this point in the argument. Logically, ∞/∞ can just as well be 0 (or any positive number) as ∞, and the only reasons offered for assuming the latter are expediency and scriptural authority.

81 BCA VI. 113.

82 BCA VI. 119 (Already quoted above, p. 33).

83 From Tharpa Choeling one sees the town of Vevey spread out below.

84 See the *Jātaka-mālā* of Āryaśūra, translated by J.S. Speyer.

85 BCA III. 13.

86 "Giving and Taking" refers to the practice outlined in verses 347–8. It can be combined with meditation on the breath, as described in detail in Lama Zopa Rinpoche's *Wish-fulfilling Golden Sun*, Meditation 7.

Notes to Meditation 10

87 The list of eighteen root and forty-six branch downfalls appears to have been compiled as late as the tenth century.

More than one version is current. Tsongkhapa does not list the downfalls but refers to *Tshul khrims le'u'i 'grel pa* (= *The Commentary on the Morality Chapter*) (*Lrcm* 232a1). For English versions, see:

 Geshe Thubten Lodan: *The Graduated Path to Enlightenment*, pp. 148–156.

 A. Berzin: *Lam rim man ngag*, pp. 483–514.

 Geshe Ngawang Dhargyey: *The Bodhicitta Vows and Lam-rim Puja*.

 Chinese Buddhists use a quite different scheme of ten major and 48 minor Bodhisattva Precepts. See *The Brahman Net Sutra*.

88 On the suffering sometimes caused by naive attempts to engage in this practice and by its cynical commercial exploitation in Thailand, see D.M. Burns: *The Population Crisis in Buddhist Perspective*.

89 Yeshe Tsöndrü's text, as compared with *Lam rim chen mo*, puts far more emphasis on the more basic practices. Only about 13% of his text is devoted to the advanced practices, from the Six Perfections onwards, as against 58% of *Lrcm*. A detailed and fascinating account of the Six Perfections, with many inspiring stories, can be found in *Mpps*́, Vol. II.

90 "Certain thought" (Tib. *nges (par) sems (pa)*, Skt. *nidhyāna*): "Having found certainty as to the way the object is, one thinks about it again and again, keeping it free of inconsistency" (*Lrcm* 275a3). Tsongkhapa lists eight objects, such as the qualities of the Three Jewels, Suchness, the great strength of Buddhas and Bodhisattvas, Enlightenment and the Path of the Bodhisattva's training, etc. Other translations are "profound reflection, (leading to) comprehension" (Edgerton); "belief, faith" (Goldstein).

91 Such as the Superknowledges (*abhijñā*), the eight Deliverances (*vimokṣa*), the ten All-bases (*kṛtsnāyatana*), and the eight Bases of Mastery (*abhibhvāyatana*) (*Lrcm* 281a5).

92 *Lrcm* 281a6.

Notes to Meditation 12

93 The nine mental stages are taught in *Mahāyāna-sūtrā-laṃkāra*, XIV, 11–14. *Madhyânta-vibhaṅga*, IV, 3–6, gives the five faults and the eight remedial actions, but Tsongkhapa's source for the six powers and the four types of attention is the *Śrāvaka-bhūmi* of Asaṅga (*Lrcm* 345b4, 347a1). For a brief indication of the use of the six powers, see Geshe Rabten's booklet, *The Graduated Path to Liberation*. For extensive explanation of *śamatha* meditation, see Wayman's translation of the relevant section of *Lrcm* in *Calming the Mind and Discerning the Real*.

Notes to Meditation 13

94 Subheadings in this meditation are by the editor.
95 The text applies the four-point analysis called "Freedom from oneness and plurality" (*gCig du bral*). The first point is called in Tib. *dGag bya nges pa'i gnad*.
96 There is no need to stop at visualizing situations. I recall Geshe Thubten Lodan – who recommended spending at least two years on this point before proceeding to the next step – telling of a lama who deliberately frequented busy places where he would be jostled by crowds, so that he could watch the sense of ego arising.
97 Tib. *khyab pa nges pa'i gnad*. Several earlier translators have failed to understand *khyab pa* (Skt. *vyāpti*), which is a technical term from elementary logic. It means "pervasion (of the reason by the predicate)", or in Western terminology, the major premise. Expressed as a Buddhist formal syllogism, the argument of Freedom from Oneness and Plurality is:

> With respect to the personal self:
> it does not exist inherently;
> because it is not inherently one with or separate from
>   the aggregates.

Thus the pervasion, or major premise, is "Whatever is not inherently one with or separate from the aggregates does not exist inherently." However, Yeshe Tsöndrü is using the argument in contraposed form, as a conse-

quence (*prasaṅga*) or *reductio ad absurdum*:
With respect to the personal self:
  it follows it exists either inherently one with or inherently separate from the aggregates;
  because it exists inherently.
Therefore he gives in verse 400 the corresponding, contraposed major premise.

We have at this stage to make thoroughly certain of the validity of this premise, otherwise the disproof of the consequence's conclusion in points 3 and 4 will not have the required effect of demolishing the minor premise, "the personal self exists inherently."

98 Tib. *gCig bral nges pa'i gnad*.
99 Tib. *Du bral nges pa'i gnad*.
100 Several different methods of analysis, besides the one described here, are used. See Hopkins, *Meditation on Emptiness*.

Notes to the Appendices

101 *Lrcm* 143b2 to 149a5.
102 Tsongkhapa does not label the subsequent quotations from *Suhṛl-lekha*, which follow on from this. We shall simply mark them with the verse numbers.
103 Brahmā-world: heaven of the Realm of Form, which is supposed to float in space far above Mount Sumeru.
104 sPyan snga, born 1038, a disciple of Atīśa.
105 gSang phu ba.
106 Skt. *kolāsthi*. As is often the case with plants, the term used to translate "jujube tree" in Tibetan generally refers to a different tree, the juniper; hence "juniper seeds" in verse *292*.
107 In fact, the succession of mothers defined in this way must be finite: eventually one comes to the beginnings of sexual reproduction on Earth. There are organisms that reproduce sometimes sexually and sometimes asexually (by budding, etc.) — if one goes far enough back in the succession of mothers one must at some point reach such a creature. A few tons of clay at the most would suffice for

the counting back to there. According to Buddhist mythology also, the succession would terminate in a mother who was born miraculously and thus did not herself have a mother. This teaching, therefore, cannot be taken literally, but reflects the Indian taste for hyperbole (cf. the discussion on Beginningless mind in my *Rebirth and the Western Buddhist*). Still, even that ton or two of clay pellets is nauseating enough to contemplate.

108 The *Catuḥ-śataka-ṭīkā* of Candrakīrti.
109 "Gently-flowing", name of a river in heaven.
110 *gzhal med khang* = Skt *vimāna*, often "palace", but here plainly to be taken in its original meaning, the self-moving aerial chariot of a god.
111 See Meditation 3.
112 The three areas of meritorious action (*puṇya-kriyā-vastu*) are those consisting of giving (*dāna-maya*), of morality (*śīla-maya*), and of meditation (*bhāvanā-maya*). See *AdK* IV, p. 281f., and *Mpps* 2245–2260.
113 *BCA* VIII. 31–32.
114 Cf. the commentary of Phabongkha Rinpoche: Collected Works, Vol. *11*, pp. 531–2.
115 Part of the *Yogācāra-bhūmi*.
116 *Catuḥ-śataka* II. 12. Gyaltshab Je's commentary:
"It may be objected that if happiness did not exist, its increase would be impossible; but its increase is observed, therefore inherent happiness does exist. This is not so. *Out of increasing happiness, one observes the opposite*, suffering, arising, *but from increasing suffering, there is no opposite in that way* in the end, consisting of happiness alone. When suffering increases, the body and mind become greatly tormented, but the end of the increase of pleasure consists of suffering."

sok-lung p.21